SIT

ZEN TEACHINGS OF
MASTER TAISEN
DESHIMARU

SIT

ZEN TEACHINGS OF
MASTER TAISEN
DESHIMARU

EDITED BY
PHILIPPE COUPEY

HOHM PRESS
PRESCOTT ARIZONA

Copyright © Philippe Coupey

ACKNOWLEDGMENTS: We would like to thank Arnaud Desjardins, Philippe Coupey and Jacques Decriéu for their contributions of the photos contained in this book.

Library of Congress Cataloguing-in-Publication Data:
Deshimaru, Taisen
   Sit : Zen teachings of master Taisen Deshimaru / edited by
Philippe Coupey.   p.   cm.
   Includes index.
   ISBN 0-934252-61-0
   1. Spiritual life—Zen Buddhism. 2. Zen Buddhism—Doctrines.
I. Coupey, Philippe. II. Title.
B09288.D46   1996 294.3'927—dc20   95-51033
                                            CIP

Typesetting, Design and Layout: Kim Johansen, *Black Dog Design*
                    Cover: Kim Johansen

HOHM PRESS
P.O. Box 2501
Prescott, AZ 86302
520-778-9189

I dedicate this book
to the sitting dragon.

WATER FALL

It tumbles over, turbulent like a cloud of rain.
One line becomes two,
And were anyone to ask wherefrom comes its source,
It's the fierce thunder whose roar breaks asunder the high rock.

Daichi, 1290-1366

ACKNOWLEDGMENTS

I wish to thank Lee Lozowick and his editor
Regina Sara Ryan for making this book
available to the American public.

Let thanks also go to Eddy, Charles and Robert.

CONTENTS

⨇IT

Zen Teachings of Master Taisen Deshimaru

contents

SIT

Zen Teachings of Master Taisen Deshimaru

SIT

Zen Teachings of Master Taisen Deshimaru

4TH SESSION, AUG. 23 – AUG. 31   225

SIT

Zen Teachings of Master Taisen Deshimaru

INTRODUCTION

This book represents the oral teachings given by master **Deshimaru*** to his disciples during the summer of 1978 in Val d'Isère, France. The main subjects of these talks are **Soto** and **Rinzai** Zen. In addition to being a comparison of the two, it is a strong critique of both schools of **Zen** today.

IT'S AN EDUCATION

This book is about education. It brings up the fundamental question, what is the purpose of education? It is also, in a sense, a how-to-educate book. Do you just educate the frontal brain, while continuing to ignore the instinctive or central brain (the **hypothalamus** and **thalamus**), the connecting link between the body and the mind?

The idea of education is to develop the full human character, and to do this the entire body and mind, the entire brain, must come to life. Zen is a religion which thinks with both the head and the body.

Concerning this question of education, Doshu Okubo, the well-known professor and foremost specialist on **Dogen,** says: "Academic interpretations or presentations are not suitable for this purpose. First we must clarify what 'Zen' is, and then how

---

* Bold-faced words in the text are found in the Glossary.

it should be applied to education."[1] And that's what master Deshimaru attempts to do in these teachings.

MANY ZEN SCHOOLS

Originally there was one teaching, and each master was pointing to the same truth, the same source. There really wasn't anything which distinguished one from the other, beyond the character of the masters themselves. All the teachings came from the same root; they all had the same twenty-seven Indian patriarchs beginning with the Buddha, as well as the same six Chinese ones, beginning with the 1st Zen Patriarch **Bodhidharma.**

With the passing of time, however, disparity began to separate practitioners into different schools and finally into different teachings. By the time of **Sekito** (d. 790) there were a great many masters, and the disciples began to proclaim their own masters' teaching as the only true teaching.

Some schools were very wide and inclusive (like the Hogen school) and they mixed with the **Nembutsu;** others were exclusive of other practices (like the Soto school) and mixed with none. Some were very wild and rough *(zusan),* and yet others were soft and lenient *(men-mitsu);* some practiced with *koans* and **kensho,** while others practiced only *zazen (shikan-taza).* What's more, Zen had become very polemical. There were lots of discussions between the different schools, and mondos and dharma combats flourished.This is why the ancient master Sekito, forefather to Soto Zen, composed his poem *Sandokai.* In those days, monks and others were much concerned with what teaching was so-to-speak "heretical," and what teaching was "traditional." In other words, what was "the right teaching" and what was not. Sekito in his *Sandokai* answers this question; and being the eternal question that it is, master Deshimaru answers it again, in our own times. At least I think so.

THE ORIGINS OF SOTO AND RINZAI ZEN

During Sekito's time there was another great master by the name of **Baso.** While it was Sekito's temperament to use the gentle *(men-mitsu)* method to awaken his disciples, Baso's way was to use the rough method of teaching *(zusan).* Indeed, Baso was most certainly the first great master to use this technique, that of the shout, the kick and the blow.

Baso (d. 788) set up his *dojo* at Kosei, west of the river Yangtse. At the same time, Sekito set up south of the lake Toung-Ting, and the disciples often travelled between the two. Though there existed little difference between masters Sekito and Baso themselves, the differences could be felt among their respective disciples. So you have the old expression: "West of the river, south of the lake."

Here perhaps is the true origin of Rinzai and Soto Zen— "Rinzai" being the Baso dojo west of the river, and "Soto" being the Sekito dojo south of the lake. Consequently the true forefather of Rinzai Zen is Baso, and the true forefather of Soto is Sekito.

Eno
(the 6th Patriarch)

Seigen	**Nàngaku**
Sekito	Baso
Yakusan	**Hyakujo**
Ungan	Obaku
TOZAN	RINZAI
↓	↓
Soto Zen	Rinzai Zen

RINZAI & SOTO ZEN

Rinzai Zen was founded officially upon the teaching of master Rinzai (d. 867). Much of this teaching can be found in the *Rinzai Roku (Record of Rinzai)*, a small one-volume work that was recorded by Rinzai's disciple Enen. Today this work is counted "among the classical works of Zen Buddhism," writes the prominent Buddhist scholar Heinrich Dumoulin; "indeed, among the classics of world religious literature."[2] Anyway, it is this very text that master Deshimaru continually refers to in the following pages.

Soto Zen, which was founded shortly thereafter as a response to Rinzai Zen during the time of master Tozan (d. 869), is not based on any one book, nor on the teaching of any one master. Of course, there is Dogen and his celebrated work, the **Shobogenzo,** but this came much later, in thirteenth century Japan. So, while the *Rinzai Roku* is at the base of the Rinzai teaching, the *Shobogenzo* is not the base, but rather the confirmation of the so-called Soto Zen teaching (that is, the teaching of Bodhidharma, Eno and **Nyojo,** Dogen's own master).

Education for Dogen is the practice of *being here now.* The real form of Zen is not in theory or in different teaching techniques, says Dogen, but only in the actual practice, the practice entailing not just the mind but the body as well. *Satori* according to Soto (as opposed to Rinzai) is the excellent practice itself, *shikantaza.*

Rinzai Zen follows what they call a "special teaching" *(kyo ge betsuden),* something outside the scriptures and a little separated from the rest of Buddhism. Also, they are concerned with getting satori, and to obtain it they have worked out certain methods, one of them being the use of the koan. A koan is a statement, act or gesture which functions as a tool used to bring about the truth, satori.

The Soto school is not at all like the Rinzai one. In Soto there is no goal, no object: **mushotoku.** One practices for nothing. This is why many people who can't understand this, including certain Rinzai monks and Zen scholars, claim that the Soto practice of sitting "doing nothing" is good only for sleeping. The celebrated Professor D.T. Suzuki claims that if you practice just *skikantaza*, you will "fall into darkness." But zazen is not like this, it's not like sleep. To really sit in zazen you need to be awake to your breathing and attentive to your posture. "Zazen is on the one hand a resolute attitude and a strong posture," said master Deshimaru, "and on the other a delicate, elegant one, like the fragrance of sandalwood or incense."

DESHIMARU

The mind-to-mind teaching

There wasn't anything mysterious or special about Deshimaru's teaching. He held no *dokusan*. In the dojo proper there was no study of koans, and during the practice there was no *sutra* reciting, no breath-counting, visualizations or *mantras;* and there was no quest for satori. Zazen was already satori. "When we do zazen," said the master, "it's like fishing for the moon and tilling the clouds. The mind grows vast, everying becomes calm, and we become intimate with ourselves."

Person-to-person contact counted the most. With words or without. It was a question of character meeting character. And if the master spoke or kept silent, it was the same. Finally, it wasn't so much the *kusens* (oral teachings) in themselves that counted, as it was the *I shin den shin*, the mind-to-mind transmission. *I shin den shin* lit up the zazens and made life around him so fascinating. What Deshimaru gave us was the mind transmission he had received from his own master, Kodo **Sawaki.**

IN HIS DOJO

In Deshimaru's dojo there were no loud Rinzai-like **kwatz**; and no rough-house stuff. Nor were there any zazen initiations, nor any preliminary steps to steps to take. Everyone sat together, the beginner in his jeans and the old-timer in his **kesa,** they did the same practice and listened to the same *kusen*. Of course there was hierarchy, but it wasn't based on any particular Zen knowledge, or any special wisdom, on any Dharma accomplishments or on any *shiho* certificate you might have; rather it was based on how much you helped out: those who helped out the most were on top. Other than this there were no ranks, no first-class monks and no second-class ones, there were no old-hands at the practice and no novices either. Of course during zazen there was the posture, which was of prime importance, as was the attitude of mind and the breathing. The thing is, Deshimaru was a Soto monk in the unamalgamated tradition, and when Rinzai, Tibetan or Theravada monks visited the Deshimaru dojo, like the Tibetan Karmapa and other such religious leaders, they gave no conferences and no special ceremonies were held; they simply sat quietly in zazen with the rest of us.

THE PRACTICE OF ZAZEN

Deshimaru was not a severe man, and he imposed no restrictions on anyone. You could do as you wished. *Comme vous voulez!* he was always saying. However, in the dojo you practiced only zazen and *kinhin*. You sat down in the lotus or the half-lotus, placed your right hand, palm upward, on your left foot, and your left hand, palm upward, on top of your right hand. You sat upright, breathing in and breathing out, and you let your mind think from the bottom of non-thinking *(hishiryo)*.

Mind during zazen

Deshimaru was always telling us to sit without object, without goal. To be beyond thought. His most often repeated story had to do with an exchange that once occurred between Yakusan and a monk. Deshimaru would tell it during zazen:

"One day after zazen a monk asked the great master Yakusan, 'During zazen what is it you are doing which is like the unmoving mountain?'

'I am thinking non-thinking.'

'How do you do that?'

"*Hishiryo!*' replied Yakusan." *(Hi* means beyond, and *shiryo* means thinking.)

"*Hishiryo* includes all things," Deshimaru said on another occasion during zazen. "It includes all existences, the good and the bad, the relative and the absolute, the rational and the irrational. *Hishiryo* is non-egoistic; it is cosmic thinking. It is the secret essence of Zen."

Breathing during zazen

The exhalation is deep and long, the inhalation short and steady. Breathing is the connecting link between the conscious and the subconscious, between body and mind. In fact, the ability to control our body and mind, and to change our lives, our **karma,** depends upon this breathing. One must concentrate on the breathing, or more specifically upon the out-breath. All schools of Buddhism agree that *anapanasati* (mindfulness of our breathing) was the Buddha Shakyamuni's first teaching.

TAISEN DESHIMARU

Born in the Saga prefecture of Kyushu, Japan on November 29, 1914 of an old samurai family, Taisen Deshimaru was raised by his grandfather who was a *yawara* master, and by his mother, a devout follower of the Buddhist Shinshu sect. He graduated from the University of Yokohama, worked as a businessman and practiced Rinzai Zen at Engakuji. However, he left off this practice immediately after his encounter with Kodo Sawaki, who was then functioning as the **shusso,** or second-in-charge, in the temple of Eiheji. When they met, Kodo Sawaki was not officially a master, let alone a *roshi,* but Deshimaru followed him anyway.

When World War II broke out Deshimaru was sent to direct a Japanese-controlled copper mine on the Island of Bangka. The Bangka inhabitants, mostly Chinese, were undergoing methodic torture and mass beheadings at the hands of the invading army, and Deshimaru couldn't stand by and watch. He took up the people's cause and soon found himself undergoing somewhat similar treatment in a Japanese Army prison. Going from prison to prison he ended up in an American prisoner-of-war camp in Singapore.

When the war was over he remained with Kodo Sawaki, traveling with him to the different regions of Japan. After leaving Eiheiji, Kodo Sawaki never set up his own dojo or temple, but taught in the prisons, at the universities and around the countryside, and so his name, "Homeless Kudo." When Sawaki died in 1965, Deshimaru buried the master's skull outside the Temple of Antaiji, then left for Russia and Europe.

He arrived in Paris in 1967, unannounced and unexpected. Not having been sent by any organization, religious or otherwise, he could act as he wished. Furthermore, he had no family (he had left them behind in Japan), and no money, and he knew virtually no one. He was just a Zen monk and he was completely free. Making friends with some macrobiotic people, Deshimaru set down his mat and *zafu* in the basement of the shop. To earn money he gave massages. He also helped in the shop by carrying packages in and out of the basement where he slept. People came to him for massages, and some stayed to sit. Soon a dojo arose, first in Paris, then in the French provinces and in other countries. In 1979 he established himself and his disciples at the Gendronnière, in the Loire Valley, south of Paris.

Deshimaru was not part of the Japanese export stream. He was not a Zen missionary sent over by the Soto heirarchy in Japan. This bureaucratic hierarchy sends its monks and its roshis to the West with officialized lineage transmissions *(shihos)*, and with expenses paid. These lineages, which originally flowed from the Buddha-to-the-master-to-the-disciple, now flow for the most part from the Buddha-to-the-father-to-the-son. Indeed, the Buddha's teaching is presently being disseminated in the West through lineages based on birthright.

Deshimaru had received the essence of the Zen teaching from his master, *I shin den shin*, but it's true he did not have the official Soto *shiho*, and this meant, among other things, that his teaching wasn't recognized in Japan. Much later, of course, when his mission had grown almost to what it is today, he finally did receive official recognition from the authorities in Japan. The late Reirin Yamada Zenji wrote in his preface to *The Voice of the Valley* that, "Kodo Sawaki gave Deshimaru the monk ordination, and with it Zen as transmitted from Buddha to Buddha and from patriarch to patriarch. Kodo Sawaki died abruptly however, and as the representative of the Great Master, as well as Chief of Eiheiji, I, Yamada, officially gave Taisen Deshimaru the *shiho*."[3]

Meanwhile, a **sangha** grew around the master, and within ten years of his arrival in France the number of people sitting with Deshimaru during the summer retreats numbered around fifteen hundred.

"I was very impressed by the story of **Gensha,**"[4] said Deshimaru one day while giving a teaching on this Zen master. "While we only know very little of the history of Zen Buddhism, it's remarkable to see that for the most part, Zen masters and patriarchs who have created the history of Zen don't come from ecclesiastic backgrounds, but from backgrounds that were very difficult to disengage themselves from. Either they came from great aristocratic families or princedoms, or from backgrounds of complete poverty. These monks were beckoned by the idea of an authentic vocation. They were just the opposite to the great number who, because of their birthright, found themselves obliged to assure the responsibility of their position as monks—or by those who became monks out of deception or despair or from misanthropy, or simply by those who sought only personal advantages and profit. The latter I can't respect: they are far removed from the pure faith that has lived in sincere men, who have throughout time accomplished virtually impossible masterpieces. Purity, purity of mind, led these great men like Gensha, Dogen or Kodo Sawaki,[5] men without torment or anxiety, without complications, without prejudice. The cosmic life-force penetrated them unconsciously, naturally, automatically, filling them suddenly with complete determination. It awakened such men to true mind, allowing them to create the greatest masterpieces without the least shadow of a doubt...."

Be this as it may, the growing number of followers did not change Deshimaru very much, his teaching always remained the same. In the old days, when he taught in a small room off the Avenue du Maine in the 14th *arrondissement*, when no one even did the ceremony let alone wore black robes, until today at the temple de la Gendronnière, with the dojo full of disciples in black robes, **rakusus** and *kesas*, the teaching still remained the same. "To understand oneself," explained the master, "is to understand the universe. The microcosm and the macrocosm are one. Evolution always begins with the individual. If a man takes one step forward, he carries the world consciousness one step forward."

ZEN TODAY

Today there exist Rinzai and Soto Zen, and connected to these two main schools are other sub-branches, some whose monks do zazen without the *kesa* and some without any ceremony at all. Then there are some who think of God during zazen, while others work on their koans. Some schools combine koan practice and *shikantaza* (literally, "zazen sitting only"), sometimes doing one, sometimes doing the other. Professor H. Finney of the University of Vermont writes about Zen practice in the States: "A final growth strategy employed by some of the Zen centers is syncretism. To make the practice of Zen more familiar and culturally meaningful, some teachers have sought to blend it with aspects of religion or other spiritual practices already familiar to Americans."[6]

The results from such a syncretism had already been witnessed in Nyojo's time during the Sung dynasty. Zen masters in those days began mixing the philosophy and practice in Zen with that of Taoism and Confucianism. Nyojo, who was Dogen's own master, was a strong critic of this blending: and so he taught only *shikantaza*, only zazen. But it was too late (said Deshimaru). Nyojo was the last of the great Chinese masters; after he died, Soto Zen, which had become so watered down by intellectual discussions and by koan-talk, all but vanished from China. (It's worth noting that Buddhism vanished from the Indian continent in pretty much the same way one thousand years earlier. "Indeed, Buddhism disappeared from India because of inappropriate mixing with Hinduism rather than because of Muslim conquest," writes Sivaraksa, a French Catholic priest in Thailand.[7])

Master Deshimaru was completely hostile to this sort of mixing, the sort of amalgamation that had occurred during Nyojo's time, and the sort that was occurring today. In fact, Deshimaru had on occasion drawn the parallel between himself and Nyojo, and between the time of Nyojo and his own time—our time. Like Sekito, Nyojo and Dogen before him, Deshimaru also wished to "discover which teaching was the 'truest' or the 'deepest.' "

(People tend to think that it's a bad thing to compare. They can mix one teaching with another maybe, but when it comes to saying: "This teaching is better than that one," it's just not done. Particularly in religion. When it comes to religion, we are entreated—to use Christmas Humphreys' words—"to busy ourselves with where we agree, and not with where we differ." Be this as it may, without true criticism, says the master, religion dies. "I must make a profound comparison and not just light criticism," says Deshimaru in this book. "Rinzai Zen is sometimes very accurate. Certain points in the *Rinzai Roku* impressed me very much. But now I understand that Dogen's Zen is much deeper. So this is why I compare them now.")

What was most important to Deshimaru wasn't so much this issue of the purity or impurity of the One Teaching, as it was the *kesa*, the monk's robe you receive during the ordination. "Japanese monks have forgotten the true *kesa*," he said in the closing pages of this book. "Today they wear the *kesa* for ceremony and during funeral services, but in daily life, and during their travels, one does not see many *kesas*... But now this *kesa* is spreading in the West. Those [who wear the *kesa*] are the treasures of this East-West exchange: they are historical treasures. Since two or three thousand years, right up to today, the transmission of the *kesa* has continued. All civilizations change, and so too do the religions: they pass on like water in a stream. Like bubbles on water. But zazen and the true *kesa* have continued until today, from patriarch to patriarch; from China and Japan, and now to Europe. Zazen and the *kesa* have again become fresh."

VAL D'ISÈRE:

The dojo and the kusens

During these five weeks in Val d'Isère we sat in rows, one behind the other, four and five deep. Beyond the large French windows above the heads of those in zazen, some snow-capped mountains could be seen, and the river d'Isère could be heard rushing beneath the dojo. According to the custom, the master was seated to the right of the entrance, and to the left sat the

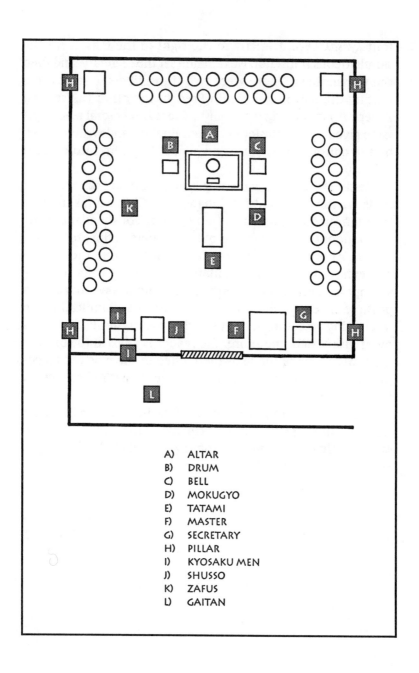

A) ALTAR
B) DRUM
C) BELL
D) MOKUGYO
E) TATAMI
F) MASTER
G) SECRETARY
H) PILLAR
I) KYOSAKU MEN
J) SHUSSO
K) ZAFUS
L) GAITAN

four *kyosakumen*. Directly to the right of the master sat the simultaneous translator. Next in line sat the secretary, and then the transcribers. There were two transcribers, one of them writing the teaching down in French, the other (myself, an American) in the original English. These *kusens* (oral teachings) were given by the master in broken English, and written down by the editor of this book and adapted by him into current English.

Master Deshimaru, in quoting from the *Rinzai Roku* and other texts written originally in Japanese or Chinese (as he does throughout this sesshin), often spontaneously adapted the translations to suit the needs of his listeners in the present situation. At other times he translated directly from these original texts, also rendering spontaneously. In this edition, every attempt has been made to verify sources, but this was not always possible. The editing process was somewhat handicapped in not having access to all the texts that the master used. Unless otherwise stated, therefore, the reader is advised to consider the translations of the texts mentioned in the master's teaching to be his own adaptations, not the verbatim versions of translators.

This book is not the work of a Zen writer nor of a Buddhist scholar, but rather that of a disciple: an ordained monk, who sat regularly with the master from 1972 until his death on April 30, 1982.

Philippe Coupey
Paris 19/9/95

THE ZEN TRANSMISSION IN CHINA

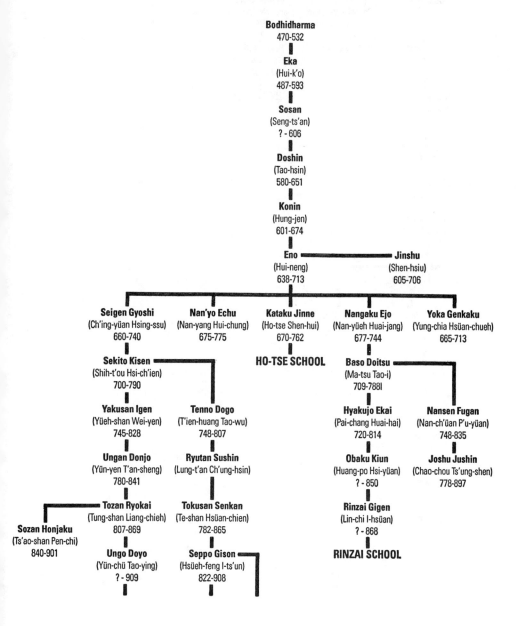

Bodhidharma
470-532

Eka
(Hui-k'o)
487-593

Sosan
(Seng-ts'an)
? - 606

Doshin
(Tao-hsin)
580-651

Konin
(Hung-jen)
601-674

Eno ━━━━━━━━━━━━━━━━━━━━━━━ **Jinshu**
(Hui-neng)   (Shen-hsiu)
638-713   605-706

Seigen Gyoshi   **Nan'yo Echu**   **Kataku Jinne**   **Nangaku Ejo**   **Yoka Genkaku**
(Ch'ing-yüan Hsing-ssu)   (Nan-yang Hui-chung)   (Ho-tse Shen-hui)   (Nan-yüeh Huai-jang)   (Yung-chia Hsüan-chueh)
660-740   675-775   670-762   677-744   665-713

Sekito Kisen   **HO-TSE SCHOOL**   **Baso Doitsu**
(Shih-t'ou Hsi-ch'ien)   (Ma-tsu Tao-i)
700-790   709-788l

Yakusan Igen   **Tenno Dogo**   **Hyakujo Ekai**   **Nansen Fugan**
(Yüeh-shan Wei-yen)   (T'ien-huang Tao-wu)   (Pai-chang Huai-hai)   (Nan-ch'üan P'u-yüan)
745-828   748-807   720-814   748-835

Ungan Donjo   **Ryutan Sushin**   **Obaku Kiun**   **Joshu Jushin**
(Yün-yen T'an-sheng)   (Lung-t'an Ch'ung-hsin)   (Huang-po Hsi-yüan)   (Chao-chou Ts'ung-shen)
780-841   ? - 850   778-897

Tozan Ryokai   **Tokusan Senkan**   **Rinzai Gigen**
(Tung-shan Liang-chieh)   (Te-shan Hsüan-chien)   (Lin-chi I-hsüan)
807-869   782-865   ? - 868

Sozan Honjaku
(Ts'ao-shan Pen-chi)
840-901

Ungo Doyo   **Seppo Gison**   **RINZAI SCHOOL**
(Yün-chü Tao-ying)   (Hsüeh-feng I-ts'un)
? - 909   822-908

SIT

Zen Teachings of Master Taisen Deshimaru

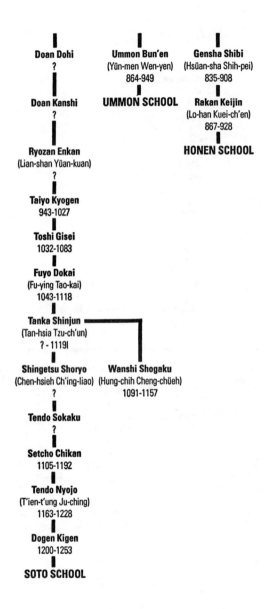

Doan Dohi
?

Ummon Bun'en
(Yün-men Wen-yen)
864-949

Gensha Shibi
(Hsüan-sha Shih-pei)
835-908

Doan Kanshi
?

UMMON SCHOOL

Rakan Keijin
(Lo-han Kuei-ch'en)
867-928

Ryozan Enkan
(Lian-shan Yüan-kuan)
?

HONEN SCHOOL

Taiyo Kyogen
943-1027

Toshi Gisei
1032-1083

Fuyo Dokai
(Fu-ying Tao-kai)
1043-1118

Tanka Shinjun
(Tan-hsia Tzu-ch'un)
? - 1119l

Shingetsu Shoryo
(Chen-hsieh Ch'ing-liao)
?

Wanshi Shogaku
(Hung-chih Cheng-chüeh)
1091-1157

Tendo Sokaku
?

Setcho Chikan
1105-1192

Tendo Nyojo
(T'ien-t'ung Ju-ching)
1163-1228

Dogen Kigen
1200-1253

SOTO SCHOOL

THE TRANSMISSION
OF SOTO ZEN IN JAPAN

Dogen Kigen (1200-1253)
Koun Ejo (1198-1280)
Tettsu Gikai (1219-1309)
Keizan Jokin (1268-1325)
Meiho Sotetsu (1277-1350)
Shugan Dochin (-1387)
Tessan Shikaku (- 1376)
Kegan Eisho (-1412)
Chuzan Ryoun (- 1432)
Gizan Tonin (- 1462)
Shogaku Kenryu (- 1485)
Kinen Horyu (- 1506)
Teishitsu Chisen (- 1536)
Kokei Shojun (- 1555)
Sekiso Juho (- 1574)
Kaiten Genju (- 1632)
Shuzan Shunsho (-1647)
Chozan Giketsu (1581-1672)
Fukushu Kochi (-1664)
Myodo Yuton (-1668)
Hakuho Genteki (1594-1670)
Gesshu Soko (1618-1696)
Tokuho Ryoko (1648-1709)
Mokushi Soen (1673-1746)
Gankyoku Gankei (1683-1767)
Kokoku Soryu
Rosetsu Ryuko
Ungai Kyozan
Shoryu Koho
Shokoku Zenko
Somon Kodo Sawaki (1880-1965)
Mokudo Taisen Deshimaru (1914-1982)

SIT

Zen Teachings of Master Taisen Deshimaru

1st session

JULY 21 – JULY 29

JULY 21ST / 10 A.M.

NO STEPS TO CLIMB

Don't move!

Not to move; this is the most important principle in zazen.

Stretch the backbone. Don't drop the thumbs. During zazen to concentrate means to concentrate on your posture.

Only *shikantaza.* Do not disturb others, do not become aggressive. It is not good and it is not profitable to try to distinguish oneself. *Mushotoku:* no object.

This is very important. Just shikantaza. Follow the cosmic order. Not for one's own ego, not for individual ego. But to become close—to touch—true mind.

This is the meaning of *sesshin.*

In daily life, we are always following egoistic mind. In sesshin, we must abandon egoistic mind and follow the cosmic order. We must become the mountain, we must follow the sound of the valley. It is a fine sound, the river d'Isère flowing below the dojo window.

■

When we do zazen alone, it is not the same as when we do it with others. To do it alone the result is not so deep. And to continue doing it alone is difficult. But to do zazen with many others is the same as many logs burning.

As of today, there are more than two hundred people practicing zazen here in this dojo. They come from all over Europe, from America, from Japan, and from all over the world. This is completely an international sesshin. Those who practice here today will become eternal spiritual friends. One's family is only a family and lasts one lifetime; but you who are here practicing together, you are creating links through eternity.

■

What is satori? Satori means zazen. Zazen itself is satori. Satori means to return to the normal condition of mind and of body. In modern civilization most people are in an abnormal condition in both mind and body.

Zazen is the best method for returning to the normal condition, quickly. There are no steps to climb.

9 P. M.

TWO BRAINS:

The great crisis

Now, how do we think during zazen?

Some meditations teach us not to think. Other meditations, such as the Christian one, teach us to imagine God or Christ and to communicate with him. This is a form of thinking. Both methods are bad.

How do we think during zazen? Think about non-thinking. Don't think about thinking.

How do we think about non-thinking? How do we think about thinking? *Hishiryo*.

Hishiryo is the secret of zazen. It is the secret method of Zen.

Hi means absolute, it means beyond. *Shiryo* means thinking. So we must be beyond thinking.

■

Here and now, concentrate.
This is the meaning of sesshin.
How do we think from the bottom of thinking? How do we not-think from the bottom, from the state, of non-thinking? *Hishiryo-tei.* (*Tei* means bottom or state.)

■

How do we solve the contradictions existing between the frontal brain—the intelligence which is always counting profit—and the central brain, the thalamus?

It is more difficult for human beings to function through the thalamus than for animals. The intellectual prefers to use his frontal brain, his mental abilities, than to use his instinctive brain, which is based on practice.

A great imbalance has arisen between these two brains, and this imbalance is the cause of the most dangerous crisis existing in the history of modern civilization. Modern psychology has confirmed this. All religions, all moral doctrines, must in the end deal with this problem.

Our system of education is based on developing the frontal brain and filling it up like an encyclopedia.

Still, we have the impulse to follow the original instincts and desires of mankind: to act, to eat, to make love; to go to the Santa Lucia (the local bar) and to move about and to dance; to love and to feel passion. This is instinct coming from the central brain. These are actions arising from the thalamus.

How do we solve this contradiction, this dualism? How do we solve the problem existing between the material and the spiritual? Between natural medicine and chemical pharmaceutical medicine? Between the real and the ideal? Between the evolutionist and the traditionalist? Between the artificial and the natural? Between the negative and the affirmative? Between the individual and the community? Between the civilized and the wild? Between the philosophic and the methodologic? Between movement and non-movement? Between the objective and the subjective?

How do we solve these dualistic contradictions of the human condition? This is the problem of mankind; almost all people answer them on one side or on the other. But this is not possible, and so we have the great crisis of modern civilization.

In modern times many "isms" have arisen. And so we have created the comparative. Yet there is only one summit to the mountain.

Chukai!

JULY 22 / 7.30 A.M.

SOFT EDUCATION OR HARD?

(The master arrives right after the beginning of zazen. A nun, ringing a small bell, walks in front of him. The master does *gassho* and takes his seat. After about forty minutes of silence, the master addresses the assembly:)

Zazen is the best posture of the human being. Zazen is satori; it is God; it is Buddha.

When I enter the dojo at the beginning of zazen, I do *gassho* not only for the posture of the Buddha, but for your posture as well. For your living Buddha posture. For what you are now.

■

Scientific education, university and school education—these are mostly intellectual methods developed in Europe during the Renaissance. This education is based primarily on the accumulation of knowledge. And it develops only the frontal brain of man.

In modern times education is too soft. You here all receive soft educations. You have all received educations which make your minds become like encyclopedias.

■

Which is better, soft education or hard? Is the Spartan education correct? (In the past in England and still today at Gordonstoun school[1] they educate very strongly, like the army.) Is this the correct way?

Which is better, the Zen developed in China, or the Buddhism of India?... Indian Buddhism, like modern Hindu meditation, has become imaginative—they both think with the brain.

So, how educate mankind? In this sesshin we hope to resolve this problem.

Now I wish to compare the Rinzai and Soto methods of education.

■

Bodhidharma visited China in the 500s. He passed the transmission to Eka, and from Eka it went on through Sosan, Doshin, Konin, and to Eno the 6th Patriarch. At this point two disciples, Seigen and Nangaku, separated the line into what came to be known as the Soto and the Rinzai lines.

From Nangaku came Baso and this soon came to be the Rinzai line. Baso had a large forehead—he was always doing *sampai* (prostration with forehead touching the ground) on a stone. Doing *sampai* on a stone, Baso's mind completely woke

7

up. The ideogram *Baso* means horse's ancestor. He had a face like a horse. He was a very strong master.

Baso's disciple Hyakujo is famous in zen history for implimenting *samu*. He organized the Zen dojo and he wrote his *Hyakujo Shingi (The Rules of Hyakujo)*. And so Chinese Zen became active. Hyakujo wrote that if a disciple does not work for one day, he does not eat for one day.

9 P. M.

A HERO OF CHINESE ZEN:
Rinzai, disciple of Obaku

Zazen is to become intimate with oneself, with one's ego. In daily life we forget our true ego. We are always being influenced by our surroundings. But in zazen we are completely alone, and in solitude. So we can look at ourselves, at our minds, objectively.

It is not necessary to seek the truth, to seek satori. We must obtain enlightenment but enlightenment is a mistake. It is not necessary to cut our *bonnos* (illusions).

We must not run after something, nor must we escape it. With the habit of zazen you will not run after, nor escape from anything. Most of us run after something, and not after just one thing, but after many things. It is the same too with running away from things. Zazen means to stop running after and to stop running away.

■

Kyosaku!
(This said, four monks take up the *kyosaku*—a flat stick—and begin administering it to those who ask.)

Kyosakumen must examine the postures. They must correct. They must not just stand still like trees.

■

Concentrate on your exhalation. The exhalation must be long, long, with expansion under the navel. This is followed by the inhalation which is short. Under the navel we have what is called the *ki kai tanden*. *Kikai* means the ocean of energy and activity, *tanden* means the field of essence.

■

Now I continue the *kusen* (oral teaching) from this morning.

Obaku, the founder of the *Obaku sect,* was the successor of Hyakujo; and Rinzai was the disciple of Obaku. Since the time of Seigen and Nangaku, Zen began to spread. From Nangaku came the Rinzai and the Igyo sects. And from Seigen and his disciple Sekito came the Soto sect. The third generation of Zen began with Nyojo and went on to Dogen. With Dogen began Japanese Zen.

When Dogen returned from China, he admired Rinzai and wrote that Rinzai is a great hero of Chinese Zen, a great master and a true disciple of Obaku.

Rinzai followed Obaku's teaching for three years, with total purity and practice. But he never asked his master any questions—he never held even one *mondo* with him. He just followed Obaku consistently for three years.

So one day Chin Son Shuku, the chief of the dojo, said to Rinzai: "You must go visit the master. Have you no question to ask him?"

"No," Rinzai replied. "What should I ask him?"

Three years with the Master and not one question to ask! Maybe Rinzai already had satori.

"If you have no question," said the other, "then ask him what is the essence of Buddhism."

So Rinzai went to Obaku's room. "What is the essence of Buddhism?" he asked.

Obaku did not reply. Instead he gave Rinzai the **rensaku** (a series of blows given with the *kyosaku)*. Obaku was big and strong, like his own master Baso, and when he hit Rinzai, Rinzai quickly escaped.

"You back so soon?" the chief asked.

"Yes," answered the disciple, "because I only got the stick from him."

"You must be patient. Return and ask the question again."

Rinzai returned. He did *sampai,* and Obaku again gave him the *rensaku:* the *kyosaku* twenty times. Rinzai escaped once more.

The chief was waiting for him: "What? You back again?"

"I have had enough!"

"Ah, you must return, go back."

"I am not a football!" replied Rinzai, but he went back anyway.

This time Rinzai got the stick even before he finished his question....

Rinzai told the chief he was tired and that he wanted to go traveling. The chief, who was very considerate, told him that he could go. "But you must pay a visit to the great master Taigu." (Taigu in Chinese means Great Fool.) "Taigu is truly a great master. His dojo is far from here but you must go visit him."

Rinzai left and a week later he arrived at Taigu's dojo.

The master addressed him: "Why do you come to me?"

"I have been with master Obaku for three years now," said Rinzai, and he told Taigu all that had happened between him and Obaku. "And when I asked Obaku what was the essence of Buddhism, he gave me a total of sixty blows. So please tell me, what is the essence of Buddhism?"

"Obaku gave you the exact answer to your question," answered Taigu. "You're foolish and your head is thick."

Rinzai's mouth fell completely open. He got satori at that moment.

"But now you must return to Obaku," said Taigu. "He is a great master, and anyhow your karma is to be his football."

So Rinzai returned and went straight to Obaku's room.

"How are you?" said Obaku to him. "Do you understand the essence of Buddhism now?"

"Oh yes, I understand completely." Rinzai got to his feet and punched Obaku and said: "This is the essence of Buddhism."

Rinzai punched him hard and Obaku was not so happy. "You must return to the dojo," he said, "and next time you be careful not to touch the tiger's whiskers."

But Rinzai had understood. He had satori.[2]

Master **Tokusan** was considered stronger than Obaku, He was always giving the *kyosaku* to everyone's questions and so he was known as Kyosaku-Tokusan.

But he could not outdo Rinzai. Rinzai became the most eminent of the distinguished masters. And soon he became a hero of Chinese Zen. Like Tokusan who had become famous for his strong *kyosaku*, Rinzai became famous for his loud cry, *kwat!*

The story of Rinzai is interesting. It is exciting reading, exciting study. And Dogen admired this account, at first. He admired Rinzai.

But Dogen did not much care for the *kyosaku* technique of Tokusan. Nor did he for the Rinzai *kwat*-cry. In the latter part of *Shobogenzo* Master Dogen gently, softly criticizes Rinzai.[3]

JULY 23 / 7.30 A. M.

SHIKAN SAMU

Planting pines and drying mushrooms

When Rinzai was living at Obaku's dojo, he dug the earth and planted pine trees with some of the other disciples. So one day while Rinzai was busy planting trees, a *mondo* took place between Obaku and Rinzai.

"Why do you plant these pines in the deep mountain?" asked Obaku.

"First to make the mountain temple more beautiful," replied Rinzai, "and secondly as a symbol of vocation for future generations, and for successors of the transmission."

Dogen later questioned this reply of Rinzai's. *Samu* is only *samu*. There is no need to have an object in what you do. It should be *shikan-samu*. (i.e., Only concentration on the work itself.)

So Obaku, pointing with his stick, said: "Right. You are not so foolish. But you know, you received sixty blows of the stick from me. You ate my sixty blows earlier in my room."

Rinzai replied by exhaling deeply three times. This has a

deep meaning. Then Rinzai knocked on the ground with his hoe, three times. That is all. A koan.

Obaku admired Rinzai. He said to him: "Surely you will spread our Zen in the future and develop our seat."

Samu is very important and Dogen understood this. Dogen was very intelligent, a philosopher. And very delicate. But he understood the importance of *samu*.

During his stay in China, Dogen was about to leave for Japan on his boat when an old monk came to buy some mushrooms on board. Dogen watched him dry the mushrooms in the hot sun, and he said to the old monk: "Why do you do such hard work, and in the hot sun too? You are very old. Instead you could be doing zazen. Or reading books and sutras in your temple. You are certainly a great roshi, I can see that."

"You don't know true zen," replied the monk. "To study true zen, to study the true way, is not only found in books or in zazen. To concentrate on the true way is to find it in daily life. I am the *tenzo* (chief cook), and so this is what I must do: be *tenzo*. This is my responsibility. Others cannot do my work; they are not me and so they cannot do my work."

Through *samu* we can equilibrate the brain; the hypothalamus and the frontal brain find their proper balance.

Dogen wrote in 1243 in *Shobogenzo Katto* that Rinzai Zen is too severe, too barbarian, and not delicate enough for educational purposes. **Joshu,** though (who was a Rinzai master around the time of Rinzai—he became a monk at the age of 80 and he died at 120) was greatly admired by Dogen. Joshu's teaching was much more delicate than was Rinzai's or Tokusan's, and Dogen admired him.

8.30 P. M.

THE GENTLE JOSHU

Those who ate too much spaghetti at dinner are sleeping during zazen. You must not eat too much. Those who are sleepy, please put your mind inside, behind the eyelids. And concentrate on posture. Concentrate on the position of your fingers... Sleepiness is called *kontin:* the mind drops down, down and becomes dark and drowsy. *Sanran* is the opposite state of mind; here the mind is agitated, dispersed and unconcentrated. *Hishiryo*-consciousness means no *kontin*, no *sanran;* it is between *kontin* and *sanran*. It is beyond consciousness.

Master Dogen wrote in *Fukanzazengi* that zazen is not a mortification. True Zen has no steps. It is not like Yoga. In true Zen, the door to the *Dharma*, there are no steps. Understand this and you understand the essence of *hishiryo*. Through *hishiryo*-mind find true liberty. This is like the dragon entering the water, like the tiger entering the mountain.

If you become *hishiryo*-conscious, *kontin* and *sanran* will vanish.

Kyosakuman! Those who ate too much spaghetti, give them the *kyosaku*. This way they will digest it quickly.

◾

(The bell for *kinhin* has been struck and everyone doing zazen stands up. *Kinhin*, which is zazen in motion, is practiced in a line, one behind the other.)

I always say that *kinhin* is the basic posture at the root of all the martial arts. It is the posture of a king. It is the royal posture.

One must learn dignity in one's walk.

Concentrate on exhalation, below the navel.

(The bell ending *kinhin* has been struck and everyone returns to his place.)

Some women sit on their *zafus* (cushions) as they would on a toilet—lifting up their skirts from behind and completely showing themselves. The *zafu* must not be covered by a kimono or by a skirt. Only the large *kesa* (monk' s robe) can cover the *zafu*. But nothing else.

Behavior and manner are very important. In our time people do not much care for formalism. But good behavior and comportment is not formalism. If we continue to repeat good comportment and good behavior, it becomes habit. And so it influences the brain and the consciousness. When we do *sampai*, when we perform the ceremony, this too influences the brain and the unconsciousness and it becomes good karma.

Dogen regarded Joshu as a great Rinzai master. Joshu is the moon while Rinzai and Tokusan are the stars. So when Joshu's moon shines, the light is so strong, like that of the full moon, that one cannot see the stars because of the brightness of the moon.

In *Shobogenzo Katto* there is an account of Joshu's famous koan mu. This is the finest koan in the *Mumonkan* (a collection of koans compiled by Master Mumon in the thirteenth century).

A monk asked Joshu: "Does a dog have Buddha nature?"

"*Mu*," replied Joshu. This *mu* is not a negation. In the Rinzai sect this koan presents a very important problem.

The gentle and kind Joshu received the monk's ordination while in his eighties and he died at the age of 120, and so he had much experience in many things.

But why did Dogen admire Joshu so much?

A disciple entered Joshu's room for a *mondo,* and he asked the master: "What is the essence of Zen?" (This is the same as Rinzai's question: "What is the essence of Buddhism?")

Monk: "What is the essence of Zen? Please, master, teach me."

Joshu: "Did you finish your breakfast?"

Monk: "Of course, I finished it."

Joshu: "And did you clean your bowl correctly?"

This *mondo* has become historical. Joshu is teaching that which is most important. *Ici-et-maintenant* (Here and now). Action, work. One's behavior, one's manner after eating. This is not idealism. The way exists under our feet. On entering the dojo, how you arrange your shoes is most important. Do it correctly and mind becomes clean. Mind becomes clean unconsciously and automatically.

Zen is a physical education. It is not a gymnastic, nor is it a martial art. Action of the body influences mind and consciousness.

So Joshu answered the monk directly, accurately and simply. This *mondo* has become historic in all Zen schools.

Though in the end Dogen criticized Rinzai's **katsu** method, he admired Joshu's soft education and all his methods completely. His method is very soft, but it is shouting exactly.

JULY 24 / 7.30 A. M.

ANSWERING BY THE STICK AND THE KATSU

To practice zazen automatically, unconsciously and naturally is to look at oneself.

Do not look at those sitting beside you during zazen. Some people here cannot fix their eyes, so they look about at the others and sometimes they even wink. This way certainly they understand other peoples' postures. ("Oh, his posture is not so good, not at all straight. Hmmm, she has big hips!") But to look at their own posture is another matter. This is very difficult to do. Please, shoulders down. Press the sky with the head, press the earth with the knees.

The teaching of Rinzai is written in *Rinzai Roku*. It is said in this text that the governor of the province where Rinzai taught had one day invited the master to come and sit on the conference seat. The governor also happened to be the chief of police and so Rinzai paid him a visit, while saying to himself: "I do not want to visit him but as it is difficult for me to avoid it, I will go."

So at the conference given by the governor, Rinzai said: "I could not refuse your demand to come and talk. According to the tradition of the patriarchs, I should not even open my mouth to treat this important subject. But you will not find any foothold anywhere. Being invited today by the governor, how could I conceal the principles of my line and hide from you the important points of the dharma? So, I will tell you everything. Please open your ears and hear me and prepare yourselves for an exchange. I will certify truthfully that which is true and that which is not."[4]

So a monk stepped forward and asked Rinzai: "Master, what is the essence of Buddhism?" (This was the same question Rinzai himself had once asked Obaku.)

"*Kwat!*" Rinzai quickly shouted.

The monk did *sampai*. He understood, and so Rinzai thought that this monk was certainly capable of having an exchange with him.

At this moment the monk said softly: "From where comes this music that you sing? What style, what school is it?"

(Clearly the monk knew that Rinzai came from the Obaku line.) So Rinzai replied: "When I was in the Obaku dojo, I asked three times the same question of Obaku, and three times I got the stick from him."

Just then the monk showed a moment's hesitation and Rinzai cried quickly: "*Kwat!*" and just as suddenly hit the monk with the *kyosaku*. "This is like driving a nail into the sky," said Rinzai.

■

Rinzai's second koan recorded in *Rinzai Roku* begins as follows: "The teacher of the scriptures asked if the three vehicles and the twelve divisions ascertain the nature of Buddha." (This text I am reading has many errors.)

"Rinzai replied: 'Your bad grass has not been torn up.'

Scripture master: 'How could the Buddha deceive people?'

Rinzai: 'Where is he, the Buddha?'

The scripture master was speechless.

Rinzai: 'Here in front of the governor you would take the old monk for a ride! Get out! Don't disturb others and prevent them from asking questions.' "[5]

This *mondo* represents a big problem. Master Dogen criticized this exchange.

In Rinzai they always speak of *kensho*, which means to look for the Buddha inside one's own mind. So in Rinzai this *kensho* is very important; it means whether one has obtained satori. Find the Buddha-nature inside your own mind and the master will give you the *shiho* (the transmission).

What is Buddha-nature?

Master Dogen writes that Rinzai mondos are always this way. This question is often asked, but never does the Rinzai master give an answer except through a *katsu* or by the *kyosaku*. A common question in all Zen schools, but in the Rinzai school the question always remains a koan, and so it is never resolved.

The result is that Rinzai monks are always thinking: "What is the Buddha-nature? What is the essence of Buddhism? Of religion?" The monks think of these koans while they eat, while they are on the toilet. This is Rinzai Zen.

But the Rinzai master Joshu was different. I explained the Joshu koan on the true actualization of satori: "Did you finish your breakfast? Then you must wash your bowl."

This method of teaching is very natural. Dogen liked it. I too ask you sometimes: "How are you? *Ca va, madame?*"

Dogen does not deny the nature of Buddha. It is simply that we cannot find it. All existences in the cosmos are the nature of Buddha. In *Shobogenzo Bussho* Dogen explains in detail what is the nature of Buddha.

Every chapter in *Shobogenzo* is a commentary on deep and real koans. All Shobogenzo and even the title itself, is a koan.[6] Whereas *Rinzai Roku* are only the words of Rinzai, and nothing is resolved. *Rinzai Roku* consists mainly of questions. Only questions. Nothing is resolved.

In the chapters entitled *"Bussho"* and *"Bukkyo"* of *Shobogenzo*, Dogen gives many commentaries and many explanations of the nature of Buddha. What is the nature of Buddha? Dogen explains gently, delicately and profoundly.

The Zen of Rinzai is active; it is fascinating. The Soto Zen of Dogen is delicate, tranquil, thoughtful.

To this question of the scripture master ("What is the nature of Buddha?"), Dogen explains that the three vehicles and the twelve divisions are **Hinayana** teaching and represent the five thousand sutras of *Bukkyo* (the Buddhist Teaching). Dogen explains that all the sutras of the Buddha, all teachings of the Buddha are the mind of Buddha. To understand the Buddha's mind is to understand the Buddha's sutras.

Outside the Buddha's teaching—say the Rinzai school—there exists another transmitted mind.

At the big conference once held by Shakyamuni Buddha, no one understood it except **Mahakasyapa.** When Buddha twisted the flower in his fingers, Mahakasyapa understood. So at that moment Buddha transmitted this special mind on to his disciple, Mahakasyapa.

Dogen does not agree with this. No special mind was ever transmitted.

Mahakasyapa knew all the teachings of Buddha and when Buddha died, he gathered them all together. And Dogen says that the mind of Buddha is his teaching, his sutras. We must respect all Buddha's sutras: they are the one-mind and they are the cosmic order.

In Dogen's poem *San Sho Doei*, it is written:

> The color of the mountain,
> The sound of the valley
> Everything together
> Is of our Shakyamuni Buddha
> His holy posture and his voice!

What are sutras? They are all the phenomena, all the cosmic order. The river in the mountains, the sound in the valley, always repeat the sutras of the Buddha.

■

Master Rinzai was always giving the stick and the *katsu*, and so everyone continued to ask the same question: "What is the nature of Buddha?" And in the end one obtained the Rinzai *kensho*.

Dogen, on his return from China, did not give koans to his disciples. And at the temple of Koshoji in Uji near Kyoto Dogen explained the meaning of **genjo koan** (*genjo* is the immediate manifestation of things as they are), of *Maka Hannya Haramitsu (Great Sutra of the Profound Essential Wisdom and Beyond)*, and in *Bendowa (Study on the Importance of the Practice)* he explained Buddha's teaching. What is it? It is like this. Dogen explains all this exactly.

This is Dogen's taste, it is his style, it is his Zen.

Dogen's commentaries in *Bussho (Buddha Nature)* are very long.... Everyone has Buddha nature. It is always here and never changes. All existence is the realization of the nature of Buddha.

Dogen makes commentaries in many directions. Dogen was gentle and delicate, and he never gave strange koans. He explains in detail, minutely, carefully, and this is *Shobogenzo*.

JULY 27 / 7 A. M.

(The morning zazen begins, the master is at his place and the dojo is completely quiet. Then, suddenly, there is the sound of voices coming from the far end of the dojo, by the river, and then a woman shouting. She is quickly escorted to the door. After a while the master says:)

To become mad means to become attached to something; rest fixed on something and the mind becomes sick.[7]

JULY 27 / 10 A. M.

FIVE THOUSAND SUTRAS
Furniture of the great way

What is *Bussho*, what is Buddha nature? In Rinzai this question always becomes a koan, and it is never really explained.

So the disciple thinks about it during zazen. What is Buddha nature? He thinks of this everywhere—on the toilet, in bed, and finally even in his dreams; and in the end he becomes like a crazy man.

"Why must I eat?" This is what the crazy girl (who caused the commotion earlier) asked me this morning during *genmai* (rice soup).

To stay on one thought is very dangerous.

■

In Rinzai they say one should not heed the teachings of the patriarchs, one should not read the sutras. "Do not use the sutras. During zazen only koans. Make your body and mind as dry trees, as dead ashes. Be like a tub without a bottom."

"After this fashion," writes Master Dogen, "Rinzai followers are completely in heresy and in devilry. They use that which they should not use. And so the true Buddha Dharma becomes a mad dharma, a devil's dharma. This is a pity."

Dogen admired the sutras.

I understand Rinzai's method. But he criticizes too much the sutras.

There exist more than five thousand sutras and very few people have ever read them. Rinzai people haven't read the sutras, and yet they criticize them.

Rinzai went himself to the high seat, called himself a true master and opened a dojo. He is not a true master, and so Rinzai followers are more and more in error and in obscurity and in darkness. This is a great pity.

If someone asks a question all he receives is a *kwat!* Or a display of the thumb.... Certainly this technique is all right sometimes, if you can understand it.

Dogen always says that there is only *shikantaza*. That you must concentrate only on zazen. But reading sutras is also important. A balance is necessary.

Rinzai himself understood. But his disciples and his school only imitate Rinzai, and imitation is not so good. These masters do not at all understand. Just *kwat!*, the showing of the thumb, the waving of a fly swatter, the hit of the stick.

Soto Master Tozan's *Goi* method (or Five Stages method) of education was not so accurate either. Because Tozan's disciple **Sozan** over developed it. Sozan was too attached to this method.... Balance is important.[8]

You must not criticize the sutras. In the sutras you can find the true **Bodhisattva,** you can find the true Buddha teaching. The sutras are the furniture of the great way.

When we protect the sutras and when we read them deeply, then we are true Buddhists.

Dogen studied Rinzai carefully, and in the end he called Rinzai's way the "crazy way."

Now we will have a *mondo.*

MONDO

(Everyone turns around to assist in the *mondo*—questions and answers—between the master and the disciples.)

Tobacco, not so good not so bad

QUESTION: Many people here smoke. Is tobacco good or bad?

Master: Not so good, not so bad. Tobacco calms you. And for those who think too much tobacco is good. Whisky too is not so bad. But too much of anything is not good. Balance is important.

But with drugs I don't agree. With drugs the brain becomes sick: and then afterward it is difficult to come back to the normal condition.

Many who first came to the Paris dojo were on drugs. So I educated them slowly, slowly.... Stéphane was completely crazy when he first came to the dojo. He is still crazy but less so. Now he has become clever.... Before he took all kinds of drugs, so I told him to change to whisky: whisky is better. So he changed to whisky and he drank and drank, and he forgot drugs. Then I told him to drink less, and he followed my education and he drank very little. A good education. Now he drinks not at all.

He is a good monk now—no sex, no whisky, no drugs. A great monk unconsciously, automatically and naturally.

Understand? About tobacco?

A dojo is a holy place, not a hospital

QUESTION: In reference to what happened this morning concerning the sick woman...

Master: Yes, madame?

Madame (excitedly): She was asking for help! She was asking for love! Yet she was quickly removed from the dojo. Does the Zen community here reject such people?

Master: If one person disturbs two hundred others, necessary out. She must go to the hospital.

(There is a sudden turmoil in the dojo and several people are standing and they are all trying to ask questions at the same time.)

Madame: I understand! It is the manner, I mean, the manner!

Master (taps his temple): You are a bit like her, too.

Second person (standing and interrupting): Why didn't the nuns remove her then, and not the monks?

Master (taps his temple): You too, madame, are a bit crazy. The nuns would not have been strong enough.

Third person (interrupting): She needed love and kindness!

Madame: You did nothing for her!

Master: We consulted her father. We consulted her doctor. We consulted the hospital. I must deal first with my normal disciples. Not with mad people. A dojo is a holy place, not a hospital....

When Madame's son (the master points to his disciple Stéphane, then to the mother who has asked the question in the first place)—when Stéphane first came to the Paris dojo, the mother would always come to shout at me and to criticize. But then she became impressed with her son and how he has changed, and now she has come here, too. Finally, even she was impressed; but not completely. When she saw the mad woman she became influenced by her, and now she too is a little mad.

I could have helped the crazy girl. As I did at the other camp in Lodève in southern France. This time in Lodève I told her to look at my face. "Look at my face." But she wouldn't. She looked everywhere but at my face.

I could help her, of course, but it would take a long time, and if I spend a long time on her, then I cannot teach you. Today I could not give you the *kusen!* There was no *kusen* this morning! Why?

Bon appétît! (says the master closing the *mondo* and rising to his feet.)

JULY 27 / 4 P. M.

THE QUACKING DUCK THEATER

During zazen if you cannot concentrate completely on your posture, concentrate on your breathing, on your exhalation. It should be long. Push down under your navel, and the *kikai tanden* will expand. Then inhale, and concentrate again on your exhalation. There should be no sound to your breathing.

Master Rinzai said from the high seat: "Upon the lump of red flesh there is a true man of no status"—this is very famous in Rinzai—"who ceaselessly goes out and in through the gates of your face. Those who have not yet recognized him, look! look!" A monk came forward and asked: "What is the true man of no status?" The master came down from his high seat, grabbed the monk and said: "Speak! Speak!" The monk hesitated. The master let him go and said: "What a shitstick this true man of no status is!" Then he withdrew to his quarters.

Very funny.

"Upon the lump of red flesh" means our body, or the five aggregates.[9] *Mui shin jin:* the man of no status—this means the man of no class, of no grade, of non-status, the true man.

This *mondo* of Rinzai's is very interesting. But Master Dogen criticized it. In the *Shobogenzo Sesshin Sessho* (The Exposition of Mind, of Nature), Dogen wrote that Rinzai only knew *mui shin jin*. Why didn't Rinzai also study *wui shin jin*, wrote Dogen. (*Wui* is the affirmation of grade while *mui* is the negation of grade.) Why? Because Rinzai does not know the man of status. He only knows the man of no status.[10]

Rinzai would not have understood Dogen's *Genjo Koan*, and in the end he does not arrive to the deep bottom. He goes only halfway down.

■

When Master Tozan was traveling with master Shinzan Somitsu, Tozan pointed to a hermitage near the road and said: "In this hermitage someone lives. And this 'someone' expounds on mind and on nature."

Master Somistu: "Who is he?"

Master Tozan: "You asked, so he died" (because of the question).

"Who is he?" Somitsu asked again. "Who expounds on mind, on nature? Who expounds?"

Tozan: "He is dead, but he can live in death."[11]

This is a difficult *mondo*. It cannot be understood by logic, by common sense. But Dogen, using this mondo, explains on mind, on nature. It is the great source of the way of Buddha; Dogen explains this very deeply for his mind is very deep. It is a wonderful conference.

Without explaining mind, without explaining nature, there would be no wonderful conference, there would be no decision to become a monk, to practice zazen, and there would be no Buddha's satori. This is how Dogen explains it, more and more deeply.

Rinzai could not get to the very bottom. By the true man of no status he cannot get satori. This is only half. By the man of status he must get satori too.

■

While on the high seat a monk approached the master and did *gassho*. Rinzai pronounced a *katsu*. The monk, surprised, said: "Old Venerable, it would be better not to test me."

Rinzai: "Then you say it—where did it fall, the *kwat?*"

In the end the monk too gave a *kwat!*

Dogen makes an interesting point on this *mondo:* Why at this moment, didn't Master Rinzai give the stick to the monk?

Even the famous Japanese Rinzai monk, Daito Kokushi, wrote in his commentaries of this *mondo:* "At this moment Rinzai should have given the *kyosaku* to the monk, but he forgot."

■

(Reading from *Rinzai Roku:*)[12]

Another monk asked: "What is the essence of Buddhism?" Rinzai replied with a *katsu*. The monk replied with a *gassho*.

Rinzai: "Was that a good *kwat?*"

Monk: "The highway robber had a big defeat."

Rinzai: "Who, then, is at fault?"
Monk: "It is not permitted to do it a second time."
Rinzai gave a *katsu*.

■

Rinzai Roku: "The chief monks met each other and both did *katsu* together."
Interesting theater. Dogen's *Shobogenzo* is not like this.

■

A monk asked: "What is the essence of Buddhism?"
Rinzai raised his **hossu** (fly whisk). The monk went *kwat!* The master hit him.
Very interesting.

■

Another monk: "What is the nature of Buddha?"
Rinzai raised his *hossu*. The monk *katsus,* Rinzai *katsus*. Like dogs, like ducks. To understand this by common sense is impossible.
The monk hesitated and Rinzai hit him.

In *Rinzai Roku* the *katsu* is always repeated. And later Rinzai masters simply imitated Rinzai, like ducks quacking.
In *Shobogenzo* Dogen writes that his own master Nyojo always laughed and made good fun of these Rinzai methods, as well as of the stick of Unmon.

■

This is not the real, the true way to study the Buddha. The way which has been transmitted from Buddha to the patriarchs, says Dogen, is not like this.
Understand deeply by body and mind. If we want to understand deeply there is no theater. True, we must create our own

method. But it is not necessary to have discussions and *mondos*. Continue *shikantaza* and we can understand; continue theater and we cannot understand.

■

We must not make this mistake. In a true mondo we must question our true mind. There's no time to understand others; think of others and you forget about yourself. No need to think about mad people. You, here in this dojo, are studying your own true mind. You are studying yourselves. The way of Buddha means to understand oneself; to continue zazen. Know yourself, said Socrates. No need to think of mad people, or of your family, or of other people here during *sesshin*.

To study ourselves is to forget ourselves. In the end you must forget yourself. Zazen is true *shikantaza*. But people like to think of others and so they completely forget their own minds.

Now we will have a *mondo. Mondo* for idiots. *Mondo* for fools. *Messieurs, mesdames, tournez-vous.*

MONDO

Sex and the zen monk

QUESTION: What is your opinion about sex?

Master (surprised): Sex?... Necessary. People need it. Especially the young. But balance is also necessary. Too much sex is not good. Always changing partners, always thinking of sex. Balance is necessary, but if you cannot be balanced, then it is better that you stop.

During *sesshin* it is not necessary to think of sex. Do you have a husband?

Answer: Yes. (ponders question) Yes, several.

Master: Ah, so you change men a lot?

Everyone is different. Some have strong karma for sex and some have no need for it. For each person sex and love is different.

QUESTION: And what about sex for Zen monks?

Master: It is not necessary for you to think of the monks.

Answer: No, no. All I want is to compare Zen monks with Christian priests.

Master: In the past Zen monks did not marry. In modern times everyone marries. My master, however, was not married. Better not to be married. But if you are and you have peace and quiet and continue to progress in your zazen, then that is fine. Not an important problem. What is important is to do zazen; what is important is to become a true Zen monk. Zen is not a mortification, nor is it asceticism.

If, in the monastery, you are always thinking about sex, then it becomes a problem. Alone, without a woman and always thinking of sex and always masturbating is not good.

When I visited the Trappists the first thing the Christian monks there asked me was how I handled the sex problem: "How do you solve sex for the young that are with you?"

"Oh, no problem," I said. In the Trappist monastery sex was forbidden. Masturbation too.

The Trappists told me that their religion is very strict on this account. So I replied that it is natural that all their monks escape…. It is a delicate problem and it cannot be cut or solved.

Anyway, sex is not an important problem. Time resolves it.

The ceremony

QUESTION: What is the use of the ceremony?

Master: A little ceremony is necessary.

QUESTION: Every day?

Master: Yes, every day. It must become a habit. Good manners, good behavior. Repeat it every day and your manner becomes beautiful.

Ceremony is very good for the concentration. When you sing the *Sutra of the Hannya Shingyo* you can concentrate on the exhalation. It is difficult to always concentrate on the exhalation during zazen, but when you do it during the chant, it becomes unconscious, automatic and natural. Same with the *mokugyo* (the wooden fish which is beat during the chanting), the same with *sampai.*

You must repeat. This is very important. Repeat the good things and your karma can become better. Repeat sex and you just become tired. Sex is neither good nor bad, but repeat the good things and your karma can change. Your face can change. Repeat the bad things and your face changes, too.

When we sing the *Bussho Kapila* before we eat, we are saying that the first spoonful means that we practice the good. The second means we cut the bad. The third is to help all beings.

What does it mean to help others? It is not what Stéphane's mother thinks. If we do good things and if we cut bad things, then we can truly help others. If we do zazen we can help people—by influencing them unconsciously. To help others does not mean to forget oneself.

Repeat the ceremony—this is very important. And very simple. Only *sampai.* It is better to repeat the ceremony than only to look. Those who practice do better than those who only observe. It is not the same as when you are at the theater.[13]

Ceremony is not the theater. Another question? No? So it is time to stop.

◼

QUESTION: I have a question.

Master: Tomorrow, tomorrow, Madame.

Madame: It is only a little question.

Master: Ah? A little question? Alright, a little question.

Madame: When the *kyosakumen* gives the *kyosaku* does he give it as strongly to big people as he does to little people?

Master: No, not the same. The *kyosakumen* have been taught to give it differently to weak people like you.

Madame: Well, one of the *kyosakumen* hit me very hard. But before they didn't hit me hard.

Master: So? Never mind. It is better that way. You should say to the *kyosakuman:* Thank you very much.... Certainly it is because your posture seen from behind looks very strong. In the beginning surely you were weak. But now you are stronger. That is why you now receive a stronger *kyosaku*. A strong *kyosaku* is better; it is not a massage, the *kyosaku*. A soft *kyosaku* is not at all effective. If I give you the *kyosaku*, I give it strongly, and you can get satori.

JULY 27 / 8.30 P. M.

EXACT CRITICISM, THE WORDS OF BUDDHA

When we criticize people, it is best that we criticize exactly. In modern civilization mothers are too soft with their children and so we have the modern crisis. Mothers are too soft, they do not give correct criticism, and the children make mistakes. The more intelligent children expect criticism from their parents. But the parents are more stupid than their children, and when the criticism does not come, the children are not happy and soon they leave their families.

One must criticize exactly. But egoistic criticism is not good. Politicians in modern times criticize others for their own advantage. But real criticism is necessary and it can help the future development of civilization. It is so written in **Shodoka**. The words of criticism, if given exactly, are the nectarean words of Buddha Shakyamuni.

Most people do not like criticism. But they should. They should say thank you.

Yet, most criticism is wrong.

Most people who are crazy—it is because of their mothers. The mother has two lovers in the same house, and the child becomes complicated.... Those who commit suicide, those who are neurotic—the mental hospitals are full of them. Why? Because of the education of the mothers.

The feminine movement is not necessary. Here, during this *sesshin*, there is one woman who is doing propaganda for the woman's movement. Do it outside, but not during *sesshin*. There is no point in coming to *sesshin* to do that.... There is another woman here who has been with us for many years, and now she too helps the woman's movement. She is a "golden" disciple.[14] I don't understand. She is heading in the direction of a small disciple.

■

Dogen's criticism of Rinzai in *Shobogenzo* is exact. *Shobogenzo* is not a dramatic work, nor is it theatrical; yet for me it is very interesting.

My disciple, Monsieur Brosse, published a criticism of Professor D.T. Suzuki's Zen. His criticism was exact.

Someone (I don't want to give the name—he's the Vice-President of Zen d'Europe) said that one must not criticize the Professor Suzuki. This Vice-President is not at all intelligent.[15]

■

In religion it is necessary to criticize. Without enough criticism religion falls. As with Christianity. Christ himself understood this, and he criticized. He made criticisms and he was condemned to death for them, and he still continued to criticize. Christ was big and now he lives for eternity.

■

Rinzai had been a disciple of Obaku. And he received sixty blows from the *kyosaku*. Finally he went to visit Master Taigu, the Great Fool.... Then Rinzai returned to Obaku, and the story became famous. And from here on, Rinzai became the number one disciple of Obaku. And Rinzai transmitted the true Zen of Obaku.

Most people believe that Rinzai's Zen is greater than Obaku's Zen. But Rinzai Zen is foolish.

■

For three years he did not ask one question of his master, Obaku. He was scared to go to Obaku's room, and all he did was zazen. So the *shusso* insisted he go see the master.

"You have no question to ask?"

"No," said Rinzai.

(Then why become a monk? To become a monk one must have an important question to ask at some time.)

Obaku gave Rinzai the *rensaku* and Rinzai escaped. "Why did you leave the master's room so quickly?" the *shusso* asked. "Very painful," replied Rinzai. "The master's *kyosaku* is very strong and I was afraid."

At this time Rinzai was too weak, too timid—like the woman in the mondo today.

Dogen's cricitisms are deep, strong and exact. If you become a monk, you must concentrate on your own proper problem. It is not necessary to think about the mad woman.

Until today Rinzai hasn't created one real, true phrase. All he did was to imitate other masters. That he hit Obaku, good. Good theater. But in doing this, all Rinzai did was to imitate Master Taigu.[16] Taigu educated him, and all Rinzai did after that was to imitate him. Only imitation. To be a great master, you must create.

Goethe wrote *Faust;* I was impressed by Goethe. But I am not impressed by this kind of acting. Only playing. Only imitating. The successors of Rinzai are only actors. While Goethe, when he wrote *Faust,* he created it. This is Zen.

One must create from the bottom of mind. This way others are influenced. Actors, when they create from their own experiences, then their acting also influences others. This is art. This is creation. The error of democracy is that people imitate others and do not create anything. They have forgotten to create. To create is very important. During zazen the power of creation arises automatically, unconsciously, naturally. Certainly if you continue zazen your power of creation will become great. I certify this…. So please, continue zazen…. There is only one day and a half left.

Chukai!

JULY 28 / 7 A. M.

THE FOUR PRINCIPLES OF RINZAI

I will now explain the Rinzai *Shi Ryoken. Shi* means four. So the *Shi Ryoken* are the four principles of the Rinzai sect.

According to the tenth chapter of *Rinzai Roku*, Rinzai explains the Four Principles as follows: "Sometimes I snatch away the man but not the environment (surroundings, objects); sometimes I snatch away the environment but not the man. Sometimes I snatch away both the man and the environment; (and, fourthly,) sometimes I snatch away neither man nor environment."

This statement has become famous and it is the principles of Rinzai.

Rinzai Roku Chapter Ten continues:

"A monk asked the master: 'How do you snatch away the man but not the environment?'

Rinzai replied: 'The warm sunshine covers the earth in a rug of brocade. The hair of the child is white like a silk thread.'

The monk asked: 'How do you snatch away the environment but not the man?'

Rinzai: 'When the king commands, his orders extend up to the generals on the frontier, and the fighting ceases.'

Monk: 'How do you snatch away both man and environment?'

Rinzai: 'The provinces of Hei and of Fu are cut off entirely, each alone in its own place.'

Monk: 'How do you not snatch away man or environment?'

Rinzai: 'When the king enters his precious palace, the peasants in the field burst into song.' "[17]

These are analytic methods of thinking based on four categories.

■

In European philosophy there exists the material dialectics of the Communists, of Marxism and of Leninism, with their system of the three theses: the thesis, the anti-thesis, the synthesis. There also exists Einstein's theory of relativity.

In the Orient it is more complex; western relativity is dualistic. For occidental science this theory, this affirmation and negation, this thesis, anti-thesis and synthesis, is enough. It is a more intellectual method, a more dualistic method, and so it is less complex than in the Orient.

Western political movements, the masculine-feminine movement—they like the *monsieur-madame* dualism.... Women criticizing men.... (Even during *sesshin*.) Always this dualism. So it is not possible to harmonize.... This works for a while. But then comes the divorce.

There is no way to harmonize these opposing dualities. And so we have the fatality which exists in occidental philosophy.

Even here the women militate for the woman's movement. Even between man-and-man dualism arises: the man becomes a woman. A homosexual. This shows the sickness of the civilization.

Zen is beyond this: there is no man, no woman. During zazen, no female, no male. No masculine, no feminine. The sexual organs are not at all important. Women in zazen are better off—they don't have testicles which get in their way.

Dualism is not good, not convenient…. It is difficult for me in French to distinguish the masculine from the feminine. Some rivers are masculine, others feminine. La Seine, le Rhin. Same with the mountains.

■

In Indian logic there exist four elements. Rinzai imitated this. The Principles of Rinzai are not at all principles created by Rinzai.

In the *Hannya Shingyo* we have **shiki soku ze ku, ku soku ze shiki** (form is emptiness, emptiness is form). *Shiki* is the first principle (i.e., sometimes I snatch away the man, but not the environment).

So, the first principle is to throw away the man but not the environment. Man is the subjective—while environment, the object, is the objective. So the first principle is the negation of the subjective, and the affirmation of the objective. (To say it differently:) *Shiki* is the objective, the phenomenon, while *ku* is the subjective—it is not shiki but the void. (*Shiki* means phenomenon and *ku* means emptiness.)

The second principle: sometimes I snatch away the environment, but not the man. The environment is the objective. So we have negation of the object and affirmation of the subject.

So we only have *shiki*, and not *ku*.

The third principle: sometimes I throw away both man and environment. This is the negation of both. Here the subject and the object are both denied.

The fourth principle: neither are snatched away. It is the affirmation of both.

So the first is the object, not the subject. The second is the subject, not the object. The third is the negation of both. The fourth is the affirmation of both.

In *Rinzai Roku* Rinzai explains that he does not reject either. Like this, like that. And Rinzai disciples say that their method of education, that these Four Principles, are very deep philosophy.

But their method of education is not at all creative, not at all fresh, and only imitation taken from ancient Indian logic.

■

In occidental science you have the synthesis of the three degrees, and for them this is enough.

The world is limited. Secondly, the world is infinite. Thirdly, it is limited but unlimited: man or woman. This is the negation. In this case nothing can be decided, discovered, resolved: this is skepticism. The world is not limited, nor is it infinite.... And fourthly, the world is both limited and unlimited: this is the compromise.

These four categories are necessary.

■

In dialectics there is no doubt, no skepticism. Only thesis, anti-thesis and synthesis. But in our daily lives it is not like this.... I love you. You love me? No. Sometimes love, sometimes not.... So with this, the double personality appears. Much more appears too: doubt, skepticism.... The body loves but the mind does not. From this point of view many complications arise. The thalamus and the frontal brain find themselves in contradiction. We speak nicely, sweetly, but what we say is not what we feel. In daily life we become complicated.

How can we solve this problem in our daily lives? This is not a problem simply of relativity.

The *Four Rinzai Ryoken* (the four kinds of judgment) is more developed than Einstein's theory of relativity. The four factors are deeper than what we have here in the West. Nevertheless, they are still only an imitation.

In Soto we have the **Five Go-i**, the Five Degrees. One step, one principle, has been added (to the four of Rinzai). I have explained the *go-i* many times. *Sho* is the subject, *hen* is the object. So you have *Sho chu he*— which became very well known in the time of Tozan and **Sozan.** The object in the subject and the subject in the object. *Sho chu rai* is only the subject. *Hen chu sho* is only the object. *Ken chu to* is both.

But for master Dogen, not only the *Four Rinzai Ryoken*, but also the *Five Soto Goi* are childish methods. Rinzai's method is very practical for koan discussion. But this method, and the Soto method, are only a question of philosophy and they activate nothing but the frontal brain.

The way of Buddha is beyond rich or poor, abundance or scarcity, writes Dogen in *Genjo Koan*, however there is birth and death, illusion and satori, sentient beings and Buddha. But even if this is so, even if we love the flower, it will die. Even if we hate the weed, and even if we abandon this hate of the weed, it will grow.

Dogen's philosophy is very deep, very deep.

What I have been saying is very complicated and many here are sleeping. But this is an important point, nonetheless. What is the Zen of Dogen? And that of Rinzai? And physics? And metaphysics?

Most religions are metaphysical, and philosophies have always been intrigued by metaphysics: does this exist or does it not exist? Such a method—such questions as these, are of no use in our daily lives.

What is important? What is the use of the actualization of satori? The here and now. How we act, here and now. It is the phenomenon which is important.

Philosophies and metaphysics are topics of discussion in most religions, but they are not important. How do we act? How can we experience? How do we practice? It is this which is important. The problem of here and now.

This is Soto Zen. The now is important. Not the past or the future. Now, here. How do we do.

But many think of others and forget themselves. Even during zazen. Even during zazen they think of other things, and they forget to look at themselves.

JULY 28 / 10 A. M.

BEYOND THE FOUR PRINCIPLES

Many people have not come for zazen today. The *kyosaku-men* must verify in the rooms and take names, and find out why these people did not come to zazen. Why? Sick? Fifteen people sick?

This is only the second day of the first sesshin.

(Thirty minutes later the master says:)

Kyosaku! (No *kyosakumen* appear.)

There are no *kyosakumen!?*

They haven't returned yet.

Now it is they who are resting.

Zazen is effective. And if you are tired and if you continue your zazen, then it is even more effective.

Magic power means will power. When you are in difficulty, force yourself and you can obtain magic power.

(Addressing the *kyosakumen,* who have since returned:) For the older people, and for those who are in difficulty, the *kyosakumen* must massage their waists and their shoulders.

■

Dogen's *Genjo Koan* does not discuss metaphysics. It solves practical problems: how we must function in our daily lives. It discusses how we solve the contradictions existing in our lives. The contradiction which exists between our consciousness and our subconsciousness.

■

Most people who are influenced by complicated matters develop a double personality. Their thinking, their words, their actions: none of them are the same.

All people have desires which cannot be realized. But this civilization stimulates these desires, desires such as unrealized love, and so people become more complicated. These unsatisfied desires become what is known as the collective unconsciousness.

In the brain there exist many contradictions. In zazen these contradictions can be resolved.

After a *sesshin* our eyes become clear, our face pure.

The *sesshin* is short, but if you concentrate, it can be very effective.

■

How must we do to be here now? We must be beyond, beyond logical formulas. In philosophy you have thesis, antithesis, and synthesis. Only logic. All else is negated. This is dualism.

43

However, in the stream of history contradictions arise, changes occur. So it is not possible to decide against something.

In historical social movements, the condition of anti-(of opposition) is not unique or fixed. One cannot decide logically. Logic is low dimension. *Genjo Koan*, different from dialectics, from Einstein's theory of relativity, from master *Rinzai's Four Principles*, and from master Sozan's Five Degrees, is beyond the constructions of logic.[18]

■

Reality must become the ideal. But again this is a contradiction. The world of Buddha, of God, and our daily lives are not the same. Between illusion and satori the difference is great. The world of the son and the world of the mother are far apart. We always feel the contradiction between the ideal and the real. So how do we harmonize? This is the problem, the koan.

During zazen man becomes Buddha. Reality and ideality become unity.

In *Hokyo Zan Mai* (**Samadhi** *of the Precious Mirror,* by Master Tozan) it is said that to run after, or to escape—both are mistaken. Touch the flame and we get burned; escape the flame and we get cold.

We must be beyond both, beyond *shiki* and beyond *ku*, existence and non-existence. Neither are true. One must also be beyond Rinzai's Four Principles.

Don't think of after or of before. This is the secret of kendo. Only of here and now. During a combat, don't think of defeat, nor of victory, but be in the freedom of here and now.

■

If we obtain one thing, we loose another. One thing is everything. Everything is one thing.

What is satori? My master Kodo Sawaki always asked this. Satori is to undergo a loss. It is nonprofit. *Mushotoku.*

If we look from the coffin, we can see the highest dimension.

Even if we love flowers, they die. Even if we reject weeds, they grow. A flower is a flower. It does not think. Even if people love the flower, even if they hate the weed, they grow old and die.

■

At the dead person's house the disciple Zangen pointed out the coffin to his master Dogo. "Is this dead or alive?"

Dogo: "I won't say."

"Dead or alive?" the disciple repeated angrily.

This is a big koan. How can it be resolved?

MONDO

Compassion, not love

QUESTION: In Buddhism we speak of compassion. What exactly is it?

Master: Universal love. Universal love and egoistic love are not the same. In the former you must have sympathy. If one becomes sad, you become sad. Same mind. It is not for one's self, not for egoistic reasons.

True Buddha's compassion is to go to the source. Love is important, but compassion is deeper. We must solve this deeply. To have compassion is to have the same mind as the other. Understand? (The questioner looks bewildered.)

QUESTION: I want to know if compassion is charity, pity.

Master: I said it is to become same mind. It is not dualism.

In love there is always duality. There is always opposition between the two partners. But in compassion the man becomes the woman's mind. Usually when there are two people there is opposition, and so love becomes relative.

Without wisdom love is blind, and blind love is not true love.

In modern times most parents love, love, love their children. Attachment. Egoistic love. So the children escape.... A mother whose daughter was always doing zazen came to me to complain. This mother was not at all happy. She wanted to keep her daughter to herself and to protect her. The daughter was twenty-four or twenty-five and she wanted to escape. So the mother gave her a beautiful house, but the daughter broke down the walls. There was too much attachment. This is not real education, not real compassion.

The Obaku sect: Noisy in the mind

QUESTION: How was the transmission of the Obaku sect?

Master: It still exists today. Obaku's disciples have continued the transmission. But the sect is finished now in China. In Japan it continues, at Uji, at Obakusan. There is an Obaku temple in almost all the prefectures in Japan. Not so many.

The Rinzai line also exists today; but it was the *shusso* of Obaku who was the one who actually created the Obaku line (and not Obaku's disciple Rinzai).

Ingen, a Chinese monk, brought the Obaku line to Japan. Around 1650.

The architecture of the Obaku temples is completely Chinese. Like the Obakusan temple in Uji near Kyoto. Many of my disciples have visited Obakusan. Very beautiful, and the food is good too. Murase Roshi is the chief educator of Obakusan. He is a big drinker of sake, and he is a good friend of mine. He has visited the Paris dojo, and whenever I return to Japan he always invites me to Obakusan. Last year I did a *sesshin* at Obakusan with one hundred of my disciples.

After the time of Obaku (d. 850) his sect began to mix Zen and Nembutsu. During zazen they recite the *nembutsu*. A bit noisy in the mind. In the Chinese temples on the mainland, which I visited before the Second World War, there too it is completely mixed. In China there was no Tendai, no Shingon, no Tibetan, but only Nembutsu and Zen. And the Obaku sect mixed the two.

In Japan the Rinzai, Soto and Obaku sects are very separate. In Japan the Rinzai temples are beautiful, like Dai Nan Myoshinji in Kyoto and Kenchoji Engakuji in Kamakura. But these temples are completely separate, one from the other. In the Rinzai sect there exists no general chief, for each temple has its own chief (and he is autonomous). While in Soto there is only one chief (Eiheiji); it has been so since the time of its founder, Dogen.

Bowl and kesa: Symbols

QUESTION: Concerning the bowl and *kesa* transmitted by Bodhidharma to Eka, are these the true bowl and *kesa* of Shakyamuni Buddha, or imitations?

Master: I don't know. No one knows. Had someone put the *kesa* in a vacuum fifteen hundred years ago, it might be possible to know.

Once I looked at the *kesa* of Fuyo Dokai (who taught around the year 1000). It was in the treasure room at Eiheiji. Master Nyojo had given it to Dogen, who brought it with him from China, about eight hundred years ago. I opened its box and looked inside. There was almost nothing, only dust, and bits of material. It did not have the form of a *kesa*.

But the Buddha's bowl was of iron, so it is possible that this has lasted. No it's not possible. The symbol is enough. Symbol.

The *kesa* of Shakyamuni is the same as Bodhidharma's.

What is important is not the reality, but the symbol. Another question?

Without object, this is better

QUESTION: Yesterday you said that to help someone it is enough to do zazen. And today you say that you helped the girl in question (the crazy girl) by concentrating on her. So, is it possible to concentrate on someone without thinking?

Master: Both are best. You always want to make categories, so it is very difficult for you. There are many methods for helping her. There is not only the here and now.

What is to help? (No answer.)

Wisdom is necessary.

Answer: Yes, but how do you help her—concretely?

Master: If you do not forget her, you will forget another. If you concentrate on her, you cannot concentrate on another. So, without object is better. If you think I must do zazen now, so that I can help her, then this is not such a good zazen.

Mushotoku zazen is the most important. It is beyond object. This is the highest zazen.

"I must do zazen so that I can influence another," it is not necessary to think this way.

Shikantaza means without purpose. Do zazen unconsciously, automatically and naturally, and it will have an infinite influence. Then everything is possible. But if your object is limited, then this object is not so large, it is not infinite. Dogen wrote that if one person does zazen only for one hour, it will influence all people, all the world. This is true for everyone's zazen.

The important thing is to be beyond. If you want to make categories you become narrow, narrow. *Hishiryo* consciousness is infinite. It is difficult to solve this by using only one method.

Commentary on metaphysics

QUESTION: A Tibetan monk once said, "The world exists but the world is not real."

Master: Maybe this monk wished to explain the principle of *ku*. In Tibetan Buddhism, which is **Mahayana**, it is the same as in Zen. There is no **noumenon**. The world exists but noumenon does not exist. There is no substance.

I exist, but what does this mean? (The master holds his head.) Ah, but no, this is only my head. This is skin.... Today, tomorrow: the body changes. The cells change. In seven years all the cells will have renewed themselves. The skin, the intestines. In seven years it is no longer me. It is the same with the world.

QUESTION: Yes, but what is real?

Master: The world exists: this is a physical problem. The world does not exist: this is a metaphysical problem. Reality is a physical problem, it is physical. And to compare these two (i.e., the physical and the metaphysical) is difficult.

Religions sometimes make mistakes on this point and then confusion arises.

But in true Zen there is no comment on metaphysics. In Buddhism too. In Mahayana, in **Nagarjuna's** philosophy, in the Buddha's sutras, there are no commentaries on metaphysics.

It is impossible to decide on metaphysical problems, on death, on after-death, on before birth. Metaphysical problems cannot be resolved by conception, by science.

It is foolish to think about life-after-death. These are the preoccupations of egotistical people. It is only through the imagination that one can think about such matters. This is egoistic religion. "If I give a big *fuse* (gift), surely I will go to heaven." This is religious merchantilism. It cannot be solved through metaphysics, and only through the imagination can anything be done with it.

When one dies another world exists. Each person has his own cosmos, and when he dies his cosmos finishes; but this karma continues, continues. When we die our body returns to the elements of the earth, and so we never finish. Mind and body are unity.... But metaphysical problems cannot be certified. This is imagination. And not a religious problem. In a true religion they do not touch on this problem, and they do not make commentaries on it. Only egoistic people think of living for eternity.

The metaphysics of reincarnation

QUESTION: So you don't believe in reincarnation?

Master: Iwazu! Iwazu! I won't say.

Reincarnation is not at all important. That it exists, or doesn't exist, it is not at all necessary to believe in it. Reincarnation is a subjective problem. I'm not negative on the subject, but I don't say, "I must believe in reincarnation." I don't have any attachment to it.

Reincarnation is practical—for conferences. So sometimes I use it: reincarnation, transmigration. Here, last year, in Val d'Isère, I talked for forty days on this problem. I wrote a book about it. So buy my book, *The Voice Of The Valley*.[19] I explain deeply on karma, and it is very interesting. I don't want to waste time repeating myself now.

Reincarnation? No one has ever come back, no one has ever seen it. This subject is very imaginative, and in primitive religions there were many ideas on this matter.

But one cannot completely decide, one way or the other. Sometimes believe, sometimes not. Dogen has written on metaphysical problems, and I, myself, have had many metaphysical experiences. I believe in the metaphysical world, but one must not make something small out of it: the cosmos is infinite.

People write on metaphysical matters, but they write on only one small point; yet the metaphysical world is infinite. Categories make things small.

So please, do not have too much attachment for reincarnation.

Transmission of the highest posture

QUESTION: Why sit in the lotus posture? What is its advantage?

Master: Always why? Why? Why? For physical reasons? For health reasons? For mental reasons? Which do you mean?
Answer: For everything.
Master: From the medical point of view it is very effective. The pressure of the foot on the thigh: this is a meridianal line for acupuncture. Press on both sides here (the master points out where the heels press against the thighs) and it is an auto-massage.

In the lotus you can sit for a long time without fatigue. But sit on your knees, Japanese style, and you are not stable. You swing back and forth, you quickly get tired, and right away your knees begin to hurt.

The lotus posture is very exact. (The master takes up the full lotus.) See? Now the posture is fixed.

This is the highest posture. It is the posture transmitted by Buddha. And my master transmitted it on to me. Kodo Sawaki said that it was the best posture. It is a question of faith, not logic. I believe, I have faith in zazen. If science were to prove that zazen was very bad, I would still have faith in it. I've done it for too long now, for more than forty years, and I cannot stop.

Anyhow, modern science has proved that physiologically the zazen posture is excellent for the health. Please believe it.

JULY 28 / 4 P. M.

BEYOND THINKING, BEYOND NON-THINKING

It is hot in here. Everyone is sweating. It is good to sweat. *Shojin:* one must make an effort. When your practice becomes difficult, and you make more of an effort, this is the best.

▪

Zazen is not asceticism. It is the door to the Dharma. It is the teaching of peace and enjoyment.

If you want to obtain magic powers, then asceticism is necessary. In Hinduism, in Tibetan Buddhism, in traditional Yoga, the adepts of these religions seek for magic power. So they practice asceticism.

If you wish to deepen your metaphysical understanding, if you wish to enter the metaphysical world, then the practice of asceticism is necessary. Continue your practice for one, two, three weeks, without eating, and your brain will become more clear and your imagination will spread. Your brain will change and your metaphysical understanding will expand.

▪

"In this coffin, master, is there life or death?"
"*Iwazu, Iwazu.* I won't say."
"Please, Master, teach me! Living or dead?"
But Dogo would not tell him. To tell him was impossible.
On their return to the temple, the disciple Zangen said again: "Please, tell me!"
"*Iwazu.*"
The disciple hit the master, and it was a hard blow. In the past the disciples were very strong. But so was Dogo. (Dogo

was in the line of Seigen and Yakusan.)

Had Rinzai been Rinzai in Dogo's place, certainly he would have answered Zangen with a *kwat!*

Anyway, even after being hit by his disciple, Dogo still would not say anything more.

After Dogo died, Zangen went to visit master Sekiso, and he asked the same question.

"Alive I won't say," replied Sekiso, "and dead I won't say."

"Why do you not give me an answer?"

"I won't say," replied Sekiso.

Then one day Sekiso came across Zangen while he was digging the ground with a hoe, and he asked him: "Why do you dig the ground?"

"I am searching for the spiritual bones of the master," said Zangen. "And even if I can't find them, my power will become strong."

Zangen now has respect for the master, though dead. Before he doubted and he hit his master. Now he digs, without doubt.

◾

What is *Iwazu?*... A Tibetan monk once said that the world exists, but that it is not real. This problem is both physical and metaphysical. Put these two factors together and four possible answers appear. These answers are explained through a method found in ancient Indian logic, and later in Rinzai's Four Principles.

One: life, non-death. Two: death, non-life. Three: non-death, non-life. And four: life, death.[20]

By establishing such categories as one, two, three, four, it becomes complicated.

Iwazu, iwazu: this answer is beyond categories and it is much deeper.

Does the earth exist, or not? The Tibetan monk gave only one answer: it exists but it does not exist. It exists therefore it is nonexistent.

Masters Dogen and Dogo do not answer. Why? It is beyond logic. Dogen expresses this in his *Genjo Koan*—by not answering. This is deeper.

Yet today during the *mondo* I answered the woman's question (about the world existing or not existing). A good *mondo*. Better than most.

In these *mondos,* there are too many questions. So I too would like to go *kwat!* like Rinzai. But I am a Soto monk and I don't *kwat....* Some questions are so stupid.

The world exists but does not exist, this is an answer. And Dogo's *"Iwazu, Iwazu!"* is also an answer. But *hishiryo* is beyond all this. No answer. Silence is sometimes the best answer.

While master Rinzai used the method of the Four Principles, Dogen used infinite thinking.

Dogen always repeated that the method of zazen, that *shikantaza,* is the deepest. Still, he thought very profoundly on the subject (at hand). He thought *hishiryo.* Absolute thinking. He did not create conceptions or categories. His thinking was beyond. It goes into infinity.

In Rinzai's text I do not find even once the mention of zazen. In *Shobogenzo* it is mentioned time and again.

The solutions to these koans are found in Dogen's work, but they are found in a form beyond that of Soto master Sozan's Five Degrees, beyond master Rinzai's Four Principles, beyond professor Einstein's theory of relativity.

My disciples have told me that we should go out into the mountains for the next *mondo.* So we will go outside. I am not a strong master. Sometimes I follow my disciples....

MONDO

(Two hundred people, most of them dressed in black robes and *kesas*, walk with the master into the valley. They cross the bridge which spans the river Isère, and settle down on the grass not far from the dojo. They are surrounded by mountains on all sides. These are the French Alps. Their peaks, covered in snow, rise into a cloudless blue sky.)

QUESTION (Stéphane): Sometimes, when I have a big problem I sit in zazen, and it passes. Like when I have a headache—it passes when I sit in zazen....

Master: Is your problem solved?
Stéphane: Yes.
Master: Good. But zazen is not a method for curing headaches. If you do zazen for this reason, then I cannot give you the *shiho* (transmission).
Stéphane: Is the *shiho* good for headaches?
Master (laughing): You are crazy like your mother. You are just one step ahead of the crazy girl.... Stéphane is very honest and pure, and he has lots of humor—but not much wisdom. Another question?

The merits of zazen: None

QUESTION: I am from the Strasbourg dojo, and sometimes when people come to the dojo they ask me why should one do zazen. What must I answer new people?

Master: No object. I only do zazen. Because I have faith in it. Zazen is good but I cannot explain its merits. It is infinite and I cannot explain this!

For each one of us it is different. The first time I asked my

master what was the merit of zazen, he replied: "Nothing....".
This impressed me very much, I became very interested. But
my friend who was with me left when he heard this answer....

If you do zazen I will give you a piece of chocolate—this is
food for children.

The object of zazen is *mushotoku* (no object). If you want to
receive the *shiho* you must understand *mushotoku*-zazen.

But as each person is different, you must look at his face
before you answer. Even though the merits of zazen are infinite, you must still use a means. Another question?

Giving the transmission

QUESTION: What is the *shiho*?

Master: Shiho is the authentic certificate given to the disciple
by which he can become a master. Not only a master, but a
true master, a successor.

My successor, completely. If I die, then you represent me....
It is not necessary to give the *shiho* only to one disciple. I want
to give it to one hundred of my disciples. But until today—and
during these ten years—I have given it to no one. No one has
received it. I am very sorry. I want to give it, but there is no
one to give it to. Stéphane: good. He has continued with me
for a long time. He lives in the dojo in Paris and he does zazen
from morning till night. He is number one. Still he does not
understand the essence.

If I want I can give the *shiho* to everyone. To receive the *shiho*
means that you understand my Zen. Dogen wrote very exten-
sively on the giving of the *shiho*. Three papers are necessary.
The *shiho* is given, alone with the master, at midnight. Two can-
dles. The document. The master and the disciple cut their fingers and mix the blood. Then there are the signatures and the
stamp. After this follows the secret teaching.

In modern times giving the *shiho* is not so difficult. But to get it from me, you must first receive the monk's ordination. Then, three years after the ordination, you can get the *shiho*.

This year I have been thinking of whom to give it to. The *shiho* is not at all difficult; but I must send the documents to the Central headquarters in Japan (Eiheiji). This is formalism. If I give the *shiho*, and if it is not truly official, it is still the true *shiho*. With it you can become a true, great master. An international master.

■

QUESTION (in German): Creativity is art. So, is Zen art too?

Master: Art? You must not make categories. German people are always making categories. Zen and art are not the same. Zen is infinite, and so it can of course include art. Zen is art, fine. Zen includes art. Sometimes art, sometimes religion. It includes everything.

Understand? No. He does not understand because he has a narrow mind. You wish to create your own personal logic, so it is very difficult for you. Zen is also logical. Dogen's Zen is very logical. Understand? No.

Kwat!

Fifteen thousand Soto masters

QUESTION: How many Soto Zen masters exist in the world?

Master: Mainly in Japan now. There are none left in China, or very few—and one in Hong-Kong. And very few too in America.

In Japan there are more than fifteen thousand Soto temples, and there should be a master in each one of them. The rule is that to become chief of a temple you must receive the *shiho*.[21] In France there is the temple at Avalon and the Paris temple.

So if I give the *shiho*, each one of you will nominally become the chief of these temples for one or three months. I make it very easy.

Anyway, I think there are about fifteen thousand Soto masters.

True ego: Your original self

QUESTION: You once said that we must be ego and we must be beyond ego. What does this mean?

Master: Contradiction. But you must have both. To have a strong ego and to have an egoistic ego are not the same. You must have confidence in yourself. You must find your true ego—and at the same time abandon it. Yet, you must not forget yourself.

Continue zazen and your true ego will become strong, and you will find your original self.

You are not interchangeable with someone else. You are only you. A man is not just hair and organs. You have a speciality, an originality of your own. But if you wish to find it, you must abandon ego. Abandon all, and only true ego remains. Everyone has karma, everything has it—dust, mud. But clean your karma and you can find your true originality. To abandon your ego, you abandon your karma. Abandon egoistic ego and you become true ego. This ego here is very important. Socrates said, "Know yourself." You are not another. You must find your true self.

QUESTION: These *mondos* seem to consist of special answers, and people on the outside, in the social world, cannot understand them. People on the outside cannot understand your answers.

Master: I answer for you.

There are people here who understand. My answers are clear. Only foolish people cannot understand.

True criticism is necessary

Master: Yes, Madame, you have a question?
Madame: Yes, my question concerns the woman who caused the disturbance in the dojo yesterday (the crazy woman). Until now I had thought Buddhism to be a very tolerant and compassionate religion. I simply do not understand this criticism of her.
Master: Discussion is necessary in order to progress. Personal criticism is not so good, and for religious people this sort of criticism is even forbidden. But discussion on different schools, on doctrine, on philosophy, discussion on what is true, is necessary, True criticism is important. I want to receive true criticism. Dogen's criticism of Rinzai Zen is true criticism. If you want to seek true Zen, then criticism is necessary.

An historical comparison: Rinzai and Soto

QUESTION: If Dogen criticizes Rinzai, then he is also criticizing Obaku, who gave the *shiho* to Rinzai. Yet, Obaku, you say, was a greater master...?

Master: Some say Rinzai is greater than Obaku, but Dogen doesn't agree with this. For Dogen Obaku is greater.

Rinzai Zen spread widely during Dogen's time (in the 1200s), and many many Rinzai monks from the mainland visited Japan. So Dogen felt that he too must spread Soto Zen, and he studied more and more deeply Rinzai.

Before, I too, like Dogen, admired Rinzai Zen.[22] But now as

I must certify Soto Zen, it is necessary to compare the two. I must make a profound comparison, and not just light criticism. Rinzai Zen is sometimes very accurate. Certain points in *Rinzai Roku* impressed me very much. But now I understand that Dogen's Zen is much deeper. So this is why I compare them now. Nobody until today has compared them like this. I am making a true, deep comparison.

Certainly I want to find out where Rinzai Zen is deeper than Dogen Zen, but....

Surely I will be able to find some point, somewhere. I want to find this. It is necessary.

JULY 28 / 8.30 P.M.

NO DIFFERENT THAN THE PATRIARCHS

This *sesshin* of ten days is almost over.

During these ten days I have been very happy. Everyone has continued zazen. Your postures are very good. The new people are very sincere, and my Paris disciples have completely developed. Now it is they who must educate the new disciples.

■

I have said that there is no object in zazen: *mushotoku*. Some question this.

During zazen we must not hold to an object; not to becoming strong or healthy, not to (obtaining) *kensho*, not to satori.

We must not have a goal. But we must have hope, an ideal.

I think that the reason why you have all assembled here to do zazen is because you are seeking the true way. If you were here just for your own health, then you could have gone to the beach, to Cannes or Nice.... Why have you come here? For the mountains and the fresh air? I do not think so. I see this in your back when you are in the posture.

In the end we are completely alone. Our life is a solitary trip. We go alone, we walk alone. But for those who seek the Way, for those who have found it, then it is possible to play, and to play together. Zazen is play.

Zazen is the true gate of the Dharma, the gate to true peace, to true freedom, for eternity. Zazen is the highest play, and I am very pleased to have played here together with you.

I have said that to do zazen alone is good—I have experienced it alone for many years—but to do zazen with others is more impressive, more powerful.

You, united here, form a spiritual family which extends into eternity. Your intimacy here is greater than any other; greater than the intimacy of family, of parent, of brother or sister. The family is only for one lifetime, but for those who enter the dojo, and sit beside one another, and practice together this ten-day *sesshin*, an eternal family has been formed.

Only half-an-hour left. Please be concentrated and calm.

Only during zazen can you become truly deep. Here you can find your true ego, and your karma can vanish—even if you are in pain, even if *bonnos* arise.

"Without muddiness in the water of the mind," says Dogen in *Sansho Doei*, "clear is the moon. Even the waves break upon it and are changed into light."[23]

Our lives are all complicated and difficult, even when in the best situations, in a happy family life, in a good husband and wife relationship. Life is not always smooth. Sometimes there is serious trouble: in the family, in the social world, in business. Big waves, huge storms arise. But do zazen and all the waves, little ones and big ones, and the storms too—everything—will break, on the moonlight of zazen.

A woman in the *mondo* today asked me when my faith first developed. It was a deep question for me. Sometimes I forget this, and madame's question woke it up in me again. My faith became fresh once more.

My faith in zazen has continued until today: ever since I met my master Kodo Sawaki in my youth.

I hope you too have faith in zazen.

I certify exactly that zazen will help you throughout all your life.

When we die we enter alone into the coffin. In the end our voyage is completely alone.

But through zazen, we are already alone: we become intimate with ourselves, with our ego, and so when we die we have no need of fear and we die naturally.

I have long experienced solitude and now my mind and face are fixed.... Along the way, in my youth and for fifty years, many waves came, many troubles and difficulties, and it was not always easy. Zazen alone helped to support my mind, and so I could still become strong. My disciple, Stéphane, said that whenever he has troubles (and even headaches), he does zazen and they go away. I told him that he was foolish, but this is not true. At such times zazen supports our lives.

◼

Kodo Sawaki became, right from the first, my object of faith. He was always saying to me that you must not have faith in me, but in zazen. And sometimes he would become angry with me and he would criticize me. But his anger and his criticism were full of compassion. He would say to everyone: *"Baka! Baka!* Complete fools!" But this *"baka"* was completely compassionate. "Silence! *Baka!...."*

My master educated diplomatically. But not always. If he had been always diplomatic he would not have been able to make great men. When someone makes a big mistake, true anger is necessary for a true education.

For some people, to cut their bad karma, criticism is necessary. A great teacher cuts the karma of his disciples (for you cannot cut karma by yourself).... So Dogen criticized Rinzai Zen.... Dogen's *ketsumyaku*[24] includes both the Rinzai and Soto lines. Nonetheless, it is necessary to decide, to realize, which is best, which is the most accurate.[25] This is the role of a true educator. There is no need to be diplomatic.

◼

Dogen was at first completely impressed with Rinzai Zen. But when he changed temples, when he moved from Uji temple to Eiheiji ten years later, Dogen's religious spirit developed and deepened, and so his mind changed.

At that time in Japan many Chinese Rinzai monks were arriving from China. They had been invited by the governor of Kamakura, and also by the emperor himself. But the emperor made mistakes concerning Rinzai Zen.

If mistakes are being made on Zen, if the direction is wrong, then it is the work of the truly religious person to criticize. And so Dogen began to criticize Rinzai.

Almost all Rinzai monks admire Dogen's *Shobogenzo,* then

and today. And Rinzai masters, even today, use *Shobogenzo* as a text.

Yes, what I am doing now is comparing *Shobogenzo* and *Rinzai Roku*.

■

Shobogenzo is complete. It includes many contradictions, but these contradictions are *hishiryo*. Read it carefully and you will see that these contradictions are not contradictions. Dogen wrote in many directions and this is why it is so deep.

Eighty percent of *Rinzai Roku* is like Soto. Rinzai was a close brother to Soto. He had experienced zazen...yet he never wrote about it and so people make mistakes on this account.

■

Rinzai said: *"Doru"* (followers of the way; Rinzai is here addressing everyone in the mondo, *messieurs, mesdames*, followers of the way), *"Doru*, do not let yourself be deluded by anyone—this is all I teach. If you want to make use of it" (of a genuine interior spirit) "then use it now, without delay or doubt. But disciples of today do not succeed because they suffer from lack of self-confidence. Because of this lack, they run here and there and are driven around by circumstances, and kept whirling by the ten thousand things. You cannot find deliverance this way, but if you can stop your heart from running after whisps of the will, you will not be different from the Buddha and the patriarchs. Do you wish to know the Buddha? No one else than the-who-here-in-your-presence is now listening to the Dharma. Just because you lack confidence in yourself you turn to the outside and run after seeking. Even if you find something there, it is only words and letters and nothing of the spirit of Buddha or the patriarchs." (Rinzai did not like books and sutras.) "Venerable Zen students, if you do not meet him at this very moment, you will be reborn in the wombs of asses and cows. Followers of the way, you are not different than Shaka."[26] (If you follow the six senses then you are no different than Shakyamuni Buddha.)

I said today that you and Shakyamuni are the same. I have sat for thirty years in the posture of Shakyamuni Buddha. It is the same as the boddhisattva posture. It is the same as Dogen's. If the posture is the same, the mind is the same. The flow of the six senses never ceases.

What master Rinzai says here is completely true. Dogen, though, who was more humble and more respectful, says that we must "approach" Shakyamuni Buddha. He says that he wants to "become like" Shakyamuni Buddha. Rinzai, whose words are stronger, says that you are the same as the Buddha, and "no different" than the patriarchs. But then this statement of Rinzai's becomes a koan.

Chukai!

JULY 29 / 7 A. M.

THE ANCIENT FEUD:

The practice was forgotten

In China during the time of Soto master **Wanshi** and Rinzai master Daie, in the twelveth century, a strong opposition developed between the two. Followers of the Rinzai school called followers of the Soto school *mokusho-zen*. (*Moku* means silence and *sho* means to shine.) Silence, only silence, but at the same time shining—shining on others, on other existences; the posture of zazen, its mind, shining but not only oneself shining, not only one's ego shining, but shining for others too.

At the same time Soto people called the Rinzai followers *kanna-zen*. *Kanna-Zen*, which was established by master Daie, means to observe the spoken word. This was a talking Zen, discussion and debate Zen. It always ended with a *katsu*.

The opposition started when Rinzai Zen began spreading rapidly with the koan system as its spearhead.

"Does a dog have Buddha nature?"

"*Mu!*"

What is *Mu?*[27]

Many interesting discussions developed around the koan, and the practice of zazen was almost forgotten. And it was only the Soto monks who continued the practice: no discussions, nothing, only zazen facing a wall.

In discussion and debate Soto monks were not clever.

So Rinzai Zen spread in China while Soto did not. Because Soto was only *mokusho*, silence. Shining on others in silence. Shining by oneself.

Discussion has nothing to do with Zen. Not all Rinzai disciples are like this.

In Soto too they are not always so good.

Monks who sleep during zazen, who only eat and sleep and never think, these monks are the worst.

Nyojo and Dogen completely respected master Wanshi (1091-1157). And **Fuyo Dokai** (1043-1118) too. Fuyo Dokai was another great master of the Soto line. But he ran into problems with the emperor.

The emperor presented Fuyo Dokai with the highest violet
kolomo[28] and also invited him to teach in the capital. But Fuyo
Dokai refused (both the gift and the invitation) and so the
Emperor became angry and put him in prison. When he got
out, he went off to the mountains where he built a dojo. Very
soon his dojo became full of people. Many from the capital and
from the imperial palace joined him there. They came and
received ordinations, and even some princesses became nuns.
Fuyo Dokai began to worry: the emperor might get angry again.
So Fuyo Dokai created severe rules in his dojo. He wanted to
discourage them, he wanted them to return to the capital. So
he finally decided to decrease the food.

Asceticism and mortification are good methods for testing
people. Another method is to forbid sex for the young. Difficult,
but possible—in a prison. But to reduce the food, this is even
more difficult to bear.

In a Zen dojo one eats only twice a day, breakfast and lunch.
There is no dinner. So, depending upon the number of people
arriving regularly at his dojo, Fuyo Dokai would decrease the
rice by increasing the water in the morning *genmai* soup. More
people more water.

Sometimes, at the Paris dojo, I imitate this method.

So, Fuyo Dokai watered down the morning *genmai*. And
sometimes he cut out lunch. Even so, no one left.

It was at this time that Soto began to flourish.

Then came Soto master Wanshi and Rinzai master Daie. And
in the dispute between the two schools, the two methods developed (*mokusho* and *kanna*).

Anyway, in the end Daie respected Wanshi and they ended
up good friends. When Wanshi died, Daie organized a big ceremony for the dead Soto master.

SIT

Zen Teachings of Master Taisen Deshimaru

JULY 29 / 10 A. M.

ZAZEN, SUMMIT OF THE MOUTAIN

This is the last zazen of the first *sesshin*. The permanent disciples, however, will continue to do zazen throughout the month of August.

Soto Zen: silence. *Iwazu, Iwazu.* Beyond all discussions. *Mokusho* **Zen:** silence is shining. But with wisdom.

Master Dogen wrote in *Fukanzazengi* that there is no selection in zazen. Do not select the clever, do not select the fool. Zazen is for everyone. Anyone can get satori.

In Buddhism wisdom is the perfect and highest dimension. It is not cleverness, it is not simply intelligence.

■

Dogen concentrated on the education of his disciples. And especially after establishing himself at Eiheiji. He concentrated on his disciples in order to make true educators out of them. To make masters.

If you do zazen you can understand yourself profoundly, and you can become a great educator, a great master. For all people. For all people in the social world. In this modern civilization there are few true educators. There are many professors, many doctors—there are enough of them for this civilization. But as for true educators, there are not enough. And so we have the crisis of modern times.

The first spoonful, it is said in the sutra *Bussho Kapila*, is to cut the bad. The second is to practice the good, and the third is to help, to educate, all mankind. This does not mean to educate with knowledge, or to educate through science.

You must give to everyone: *Hannya Haramitsu. Paramita* in Sanskrit. A *fuse* (gift) does not consist only in giving money, not only in material things. But to give good words, good knowledge, good wisdom, good education—to give this to others is also a gift. Giving the *kyosaku* too can be a gift. So too with anger, if it is to educate.

■

The *kai,* or the *sila* in Sanskrit, are the **precepts,** the morals, the rules. In Mahayana Buddhism the kai are of a very high dimension.

In Buddha's time there were no rules, but when you do zazen together with others in a dojo, rules are necessary. Don't disturb others.... So in collective life rules must be created.

In Buddhism it is the **six paramitas** which are most important. The first is *fuse*—gift without purpose. The second is morality, harmony. The third is patience. The fourth paramita is *shojin,* effort. The fifth is *samadhi,* concentration, and the sixth is wisdom.

It is the same as in ancient times: Don't move! Don't move! In zazen patience, in the end, is the most important, the most effective.

Complete these six paramitas and you can become a great master.

But zazen is of the greatest importance.

It is the *shikantaza* of *samadhi.*

It is very difficult to have a perfect, normal personality. Even I have not yet been able to become a perfect, complete personality.

But I concentrate on zazen and zazen draws everything along with it. Have faith only in zazen, unconsciously, automatically and naturally, and we can climb to the summit of the mountain, we climb without steps, we go by cable car.

SIT

Zen Teachings of Master Taisen Deshimaru

■

(The bell for *kinhin* has rung and everyone rises.)

Stretch the neck.
Stretch the knees.
This is your last chance to stretch them.

(The Master walks up and down the lines of two hundred people practicing *kinhin*. He examines the postures.)

Everyone here has a good posture now. Don't forget this posture when you return to your homes. Come back again for another *sesshin*. Come back and practice again.

Everyone's face has changed since the beginning. Everyone has completely changed. Dignity.

(The bell is rung and everyone returns to his place, and after a silence, the master continues the teaching.)

The third mouthful is to influence others, to educate them profoundly, through zazen.

Sometimes one must jump into the muddy waters of social life. In Mahayana Buddhism one is to become pure, not just for oneself but for others too.

"Even if I, (who am) too foolish, do not become Buddha," writes Dogen in *San Sho Doei*. (Dogen is here talking of himself; he says that he is too foolish to become Buddha but, *tant pis*, it doesn't matter.)... "Even if I, too foolish, do not become Buddha, I hope to become the body of the true monk, causing all sentient beings to pass." It is *hannya haramita:* to let others pass. Sometimes one must sacrifice his own personality. This is the true Bodhisattva.

Some men say that they must help others, so what they do is they help women. They pass through one after another. So too with women: they pass on from gigolo to gigolo.

One must not forget the *kai*, the moral precepts, for they too are important.

In Mahayana Buddhism, in the end, if you want to break the *kai*, even this is not possible. Why?

Because, finally, all is the same. No increase, no decrease.

Take the thief: objects change place, and looked at from a high dimension, there is no crime, anywhere.

But don't forget morals: they are important. Don't kill, don't steal, don't practice sexual perversity, don't lie or harm with words. It is like this.

In Buddha's time drinking alcohol was not allowed. Transposed into contemporary times this means don't become drunk, don't become foolish.

In modern times: don't take drugs.

Patience, effort. In modern education, in schools, the students do not make enough of an effort.

To educate others, to influence them, effort is necessary.

Through patience your power of effort will increase; it will increase automatically. To educate, these factors are of great importance.

Patience. This is the last zazen, the last *kyosaku*, the last *fuse*. Receive the *kyosaku* and it will become a *fuse*.

Diminish desire, become calm, don't have illusions, don't have foolish discussions.

Silence is beyond discussion. These are the last words of Dogen's testament: zazen is complete silence.

When you return to your homes I hope that you will not forget your postures as they are now. And your pure mind. I truly hope you will remember.

Chukai!

SIT

Zen Teachings of Master Taisen Deshimaru

2nd session

AUGUST 1 – AUGUST 9

AUG. 1ST / 10 A.M.

SESSHIN:

To touch true mind

(The sound of the **inkin** (the small bell) can be heard tinkling in the distance. The master is coming. Before taking his seat, the master quickly passes behind the two hundred fifty people sitting in zazen, examining their postures. His tour completed, the master takes his seat and the dojo falls quiet. After a silence of thirty or so minutes, he addresses the assembly:)

Beginning people must understand what is *sesshin*.[1] *Sesshin* is the practice of zazen, but not only zazen. From morning to night one must concentrate on all one's actions, on one's behavior, and one's manner in daily life. On how we eat. On how we make sounds. How we go to the toilet, how we wash our faces, brush our teeth. Master Dogen talks of this in *Shobogenzo*.

Sesshin means to touch true mind. You must find your own true mind.

Zazen is to find the true ego, zazen is to become intimate with oneself. So, during zazen you must follow the rules of the dojo. How we do zazen in the dojo. How we walk in the dojo, how we stand.

If you follow exactly this *sesshin*, you can change your body and your mind.

Dogen's Zen is very severe on posture: the zazen posture, the *kinhin* posture, on your behavior.

If your posture is exact, then your body and mind will return to the normal condition.

■

There are many Germans here for this *sesshin*.

Rinzai Zen has spread throughout Germany first because of Professor Suzuki, and now because of Professor Durkheim and the Christian father Lassalle.

Various Indian types of meditation and different kinds of esoteric and mystical practices have also begun to spread in Germany. Dogen's Zen is not like any of these.

■

I just received a Japanese newspaper expressing with admiration that Dogen's Zen is today taking root and spreading in Europe.

Rinzai followers in Kyoto and in Kamakura and elsewhere in Japan today are also following Dogen's Zen expressed in *Shobogenzo*. This is true also for the Obaku sect in Japan. My friend Murase, at the Obaku temple in Uji, teaches Dogen's Zen.

Soto Zen and Rinzai Zen are not the same. Professor Suzuki spread Rinzai Zen, but only through books. Not through practice. He did not practice zazen. This is a great pity.[2]

I have brought Dogen's Zen to Europe, and now it is here for the first time. So I hope that those who have come to this *sesshin*, I hope that all people will become educators and masters of Soto Zen.

It is difficult to become a master after only one *sesshin*. But if you continue for one, two, three, five years, it is possible.

Anyhow, you can understand what is the true posture, what is the essence of Soto Zen, you can understand this exactly, even after one *sesshin*.

If in Germany and elsewhere people ask you what is Soto Zen, I hope that you will be able to explain it and to teach it exactly.[3]

■

RINZAI EDUCATION:

Severe but not strong

Soto is not so severe as Rinzai. There are no *katsus*, no hard *kyosakus*. Rinzai Zen is severe but its education is not strong. They educate through *mondos*, through animated discussions, between disciples and the master. They use loud *katsus* and heavy blows with the *kyosaku*. The Rinzai *kyosaku* is very big and very long and it is used during *sesshins*, during zazen, and in the garden. It is used everywhere.

Rinzai *sesshins* are very strong, and for powerful people it is not so bad. I experienced *sesshins* in a Rinzai temple when I was young. I escaped. Rinzai Zen is tougher than the army.[4]

Professor Suzuki never underwent this experience.

HITTING TO EDUCATE

Those who wish to receive the *kyosaku*, please ask for it. When you are in *kontin* or in *sanran*, then you must ask for it. When your knees are in pain and you can no longer be patient, then it is good to receive the *kyosaku*. To receive the *kyosaku* is not like receiving a punishment.

Dogen himself seldom used the *kyosaku*. Nonetheless Dogen had been deeply impressed by Master Nyojo's way of educating: sometimes by using the *kyosaku* and even sometimes by using his sandals. When Nyojo got angry, he hit only out of a profound compassion. "I do not want to hit," Nyojo said to Dogen, "but when I do, I do it only to educate more profoundly. Sometimes I hit because it cannot be avoided."

In Soto, hitting is used as a means to truly deepen one's education. It is not for formalism.

Receive the *kyosaku* during a *sesshin* and your brain becomes clear. It is given on acupuncture points above the shoulders.

77

So when you receive the *kyosaku*, your nervousness, your tensions finish. Also the mind becomes strong. It changes. Exactly, it changes.

ADMINISTERING THE RENSAKU

During the day off yesterday some of the permanents entered the kitchen without permission. This is forbidden. To enter the kitchen during the day off, and to eat the food during *sesshin*, this is forbidden! And it has been this way since the beginning.

In Soto Zen the *tenzo* (chief cook) is very important. Like that of the chief of the dojo. If the *tenzo* makes even the smallest mistake during *sesshin*, he is removed as *tenzo*. The atmosphere of *sesshin* depends also on the *tenzo*, and so the teachings to the *tenzo* are very important. Dogen wrote this in *Tenzo Kyokun*.

I do not want to order the *rensaku* (a series of blows given by the *kyosaku*) for these people, but yesterday they made a serious mistake. So it is unavoidable.

I do not want to mention their names. They are two strong boys, however they must receive it.

They ate food in the kitchen. They stole food that even the dog didn't steal. Worse than dogs.

They must be given the *rensaku* ten times on each shoulder.

(The *shusso* administers the *rensaku*. The sound resounds through the dojo.)

This morning we will perform a mortuary ceremony for the death of a disciple, a Bodhisattva who was very faithful and who was with us for many years. He died suddenly yesterday, in Paris, from a heart operation.

I want to do him a heartful ceremony! Please, sing *Hannya Shingyo*!! *Kan ji Zai Bo Satsu* (Bodhisattva of true liberty). Please, sing in a big voice! Surely he will arrive in heaven.

AUG. 1ST / 8.30 P.M.

Zazen is like water in a glass. Leave the water to sit quietly and soon the dirt will sink down, down, and the water will become pure.

When we do zazen our dirtiness drops down and our mind becomes quiet and tranquil. This is true during *kinhin*.

Continue zazen for the next ten days and you will become completely calm.... But then one must also follow the rules of the dojo, and not go to the Santa Lucia and become dirty and abnormal.[5]

MIND MOVING

Our life is similar to traveling on an auto route. If we only look out at the landscape, then this is a mistake; we think that the landscape is moving and we forget that it is the car which is moving.

But if we return into ourselves, if we look exactly at ourselves, if we look at the car itself, we see that it is the car and not the landscape which moves. It is the same when traveling by boat. Dogen describes this in *Genjo Koan*. We look out from the boat and soon we have the impression that it is the river bank which is moving. But look down at the boat[6] and we see that it is not the riverbank but the boat which is moving.

Zazen is exactly like this. In our daily lives, we are always looking towards the outside. Ah, the big mountain, the Mont Blanc! The big city, the big beautiful forest! It is like this, and we never have any understanding of ourselves.

It is not the landscape which moves, it is us, we are moving.

So, satori means to return to the normal condition, to the original condition. Satori is not a special condition. A special language is not necessary.

79

The condition of satori is not at all difficult to obtain. Satori progresses, changes, deepens.

But do zazen even once and you get satori: because satori is to come back to the normal condition.

But then, after zazen, after the drum (announcing the end of zazen), after the ceremony, everyone runs into the town (of Val d'Isère) and starts dancing again—especially the permanents here—and the dirt returns.

To look outside is easy. To look inside is difficult, and not very interesting. To become intimate with oneself is not so easy (and many people are scared to become intimate with themselves, to look inside themselves); but, still, if you do look inside, you can return to the normal condition.

It's like looking at the car we are in. Oh, it is the car that's moving!... Moving towards the coffin.

At this moment the true religious mind arises. But most people do not understand this. They think that it is the landscape moving. Especially the child. For the child everything is beautiful, everything moves. The landscape is beautiful. So is Tibetan Buddhism. So is Yoga.

During the first *sesshin*, a woman gave me a book by Castaneda.[7] It is in English and I read a little. Interesting landscape. The sounds too: Don Juan. The woman told me she has been studying this teaching for ten years now. But now, she says, she understands that Zen is of a much higher dimension. "At exactly the moment I looked at myself, I understood."

Our car is moving. It is moving toward an objective place, which really exists.

Once people understand that they are moving towards the coffin, they try to slow down, they let up on the accelerator.... However, others in our modern civilization seem only to want to go faster and faster. At one hundred kilometers an hour. At two hundred kilometers. Dangerous.

In any case, we must arrive at the coffin.

For those who have a pure, clear, tranquil mind, in the end their karma becomes good and they become happy.

It is mind which moves, not the exterior. Most people though, do not understand this, and they sleep in their coffins.

AUG. 2ND / 7.30 A.M.

Pas bouger! Don't move!

There is one person here who is always moving. Patience is important. One person moves and it influences the others.

MASTER NYOJO:

He was like raw iron

When Dogen first visited China, he was following the practice of Rinzai under master **Myozen.** Myozen had been a disciple of master **Eisai,** and master Eisai had been the founder of Rinzai Zen in Japan.

So Dogen studied Rinzai Zen, and he thought that master Rinzai was the greatest of all the Zen masters.

Why, then, did he later come to criticize Rinzai's methods?

At first Dogen observed the landscape and it was Rinzai Zen which was moving. But later his mind deepened and he began to look at himself, and when he finally met great Soto master Nyojo, Dogen understood, and at that time he had received a big satori.

The Rinzai Zen which Dogen practiced was like all Rinzai

Zen: the *katsu*, the *kyosaku*, raising the *hossu*,[8] holding up the thumb, and conducting clever discussions. Then he met master Nyojo.

Nyojo had a strong, gentle face, and he was always doing zazen. Without *katsus*, without discussions, and with little *kyosaku*. Nyojo did not much use the *kyosaku*, but he was not always gentle and sweet. Sometimes he would get angry, like thunder.

"Nyojo is like a hard diamond. He is like raw iron," wrote Dogen. Nyojo's words were like a heavenly dome; they were fresh, exactly like raw iron…. Nyojo's personality held everything. And when he became angry, he would flare up in a rage—he would become truly angry. It was impossible to bite him (to bite the essence, the substance of his personality), he was like a diamond, like iron.

It was better to look at him from the outside. This is how Dogen saw him, from the outside.

Master Nyojo was simple; he was sincere and completely honest.

■

At the age of thirteen, Dogen left his family and went to the Tendai monastery on Mount Hiei. It was there that he received the monk's ordination. He studied Tendai for one year, but at fourteen he escaped Tendai to follow master Eisai.

So, Dogen became a disciple of the Rinzai master Eisai, the most prominent Zen master of the time. And it was then that he also became close friends with Eisai's *shusso*, the disciple Myozen.

Eisai had introduced Rinzai Zen to Japan; his Zen was not so pure as his disciple Myozen's. While Eisai was a Rinzai monk, he was also a Tendai monk, a Shingon monk and a *kito* monk.

In ancient times in Japan, monks had also to be *kito* monks, otherwise they were of no use to the governors and to the emperor. This is why monks who did not practice *kito* could not become famous; nor could they eat.[9]

So Eisai was at times a Tendai monk, a Shingon monk, a Rinzai monk, and a *kito* monk.

There are many monks like Eisai in Europe and America: sometimes Zen, sometimes Hinayana, sometimes Tibetan, sometimes Christian.

When master Eisai died, Dogen followed Eisai's *shusso*, Myozen, to China.

Until now all the masters Dogen had met had told him that he must distinguish himself, that he must become famous, that he must become useful to his country, and that he must obtain the greatest honors in Japan and in the entire world.

When I was young and a disciple of Kodo Sawaki's, my brother disciple Kosho, and others too, were always telling me the same thing: that I must distinguish myself and become famous serving my country and that I must get the greatest honors. Everyone was telling me this, except Kodo Sawaki and Narita....[10] But I did not want to become famous. I wanted only to come back to the normal condition.

And so with Dogen. I understand Dogen.

Dogen had read the autobiographies of the great monks of the past—of Kukai and of Denkyo, the (respective) founders of Shingon and Tendai in Japan—and they were not like Eisai.[11] So Dogen read Chinese history. He wanted to find a true Rinzai master there. This is why after Eisai's death, Dogen went with Myozen to China.[12]

During zazen some people become sleepy. *Kontin.* They are too calm, too tired, so they sleep.... Others are too nervous, too active, they think too much. *Sanran.* Both states are bad. Between these two states is *hishiryo*.[13]

This morning a doctor, a disciple of the Marseille dojo, visited my room. I told him that I had a little pain in my shoulder. My own doctor Evelyne, who is very good at acupuncture and who has often cured me of different things, was not here, so the Marseille doctor told me that he could cure me. So very quickly he stuck fifty needles in me. Needles sticking in me from the top of my head to the tips of my toes. On my behind too. I couldn't move and I was very surprised. I was just like a porcupine. He told me to stay quiet for one hour. To stay like this, with needles all over me, for one hour! (With Evelyne, it only lasts five minutes.) It was not possible. I wanted the needles to be taken out, but the doctor had quickly left, for lunch, and I could not take them out alone. (General laughter.) Very funny. I was in complete activity. Before the doctor had run out, he had said: "Now you can sleep." But not at all. I was completely in *sanran* and it was impossible to sleep.

I called my secretary: "Anne-Marie, I want to smoke!"

"No, **Sensei**, you must sleep."

But I couldn't sleep. One hour.... When the doctor returned he explained that tomorrow my shoulder would be better.

Anyway, my shoulder is still not well. Worse, even.

But right now I am completely in *sanran*. I feel my activity here, now, in zazen.

When you are in *sanran*, you must drop your mind, down, onto your fingers.... Right now there is too much activity rising in me and I want to cough. When you are in *sanran*, this is what happens: you want to let out your breath. So, at this time you must push down with your breath, you must exhale deeply and so push down on your intestines, and at the same time you must place your mind on your fingers between the thumbs.

When in *kontin*, though, you must place your mind between your eyelids. With these methods you can find your balance, your equilibrium. This is how it always is in daily life—sometimes sleepy, sometimes active.

■

After zazen you go dancing. A good gymnastic. Good for the body. But not so good for spiritual training. Better to become quiet. Like water in a glass. The water settles and so it becomes clear. But shake it up and the water only becomes troubled. Zazen is to return to the normal condition. To become pure and clean; like dirty water clearing in a glass. Down, down, down. And so it returns to its normal condition.

A MASTER NOT CONCERNED
WITH GREATNESS

To understand the ego is to understand that it is not the car which is moving, not the boat, but it is ourselves moving.

People want to make a lot of money, they want a beautiful house, the best food, and they also want success, honor and fame.

When I first met my master Kodo Sawaki, he spoke one simple phrase which has influenced my life ever since: "I am always making a great effort," he said, "not to succeed." When I first heard this, I was surprised. Maybe he was getting too old and didn't know what he was talking about. "I make a big effort not to succeed." But I was impressed. Completely.

When I was a child, my father was always telling me that I should go to the best university, that I should become a successful businessman, make lots of money, accrue profits and become famous. My mother was the opposite: she was always telling me that it was not necessary to be a big success or to make a lot of money. Instead, her idea was that I become an educator, a monk.... So my parents were always arguing over this, and I suffered.

It was then that I met Kodo Sawaki. "I make great effort not to succeed. And the best method for this is zazen." What a waste of time, I thought.

■

When I arrived in Europe ten years ago, no one was doing zazen. But now it has spread.

I don't want success. But only to concentrate on those who wish to practice zazen. Those who understand zazen, this is enough. To have a few precious stones is better than to have many pebbles. If everyone became a precious stone, then the stones would lose their value.

SEARCHING IN OLD CHINA FOR A MASTER

So Dogen did not want to become great. And yet his name is even more historic that Eisai's, the founder of Rinzai in Japan.

Eisai kept telling Dogen: "You must become a great master. You, alone, must become the National Master, the master to the emperor." But Dogen did not understand this. Instead he thought that he should sail to China. Perhaps in China he could find a truly great master, a master not concerned with greatness.

So in 1223 he went to China. He was then twenty-three years old…. After visiting all the Rinzai masters he could find in China, he gave up and returned to his ship. There were no rooms available, no hotels, so he stayed on the ship, waiting for the day when it would pull anchor and return to Japan. The ship was anchored just off the coast of Shanghai.

It was then that an old monk came out to the ship to buy some *shitake* (a special sort of Japanese mushroom), and an important staple in this monk's temple…. Well, (it so happened that) this old monk was the chief *tenzo* of the Soto temple Keitokuji.

So, Dogen and this *tenzo* had a *mondo*. Not a strong *mondo*. Just a conversation. But which later became famous in Buddhist history.

This *tenzo* was very strong and he had a big and very deep face. But now it was in the middle of summer and very hot—

too hot to work—and this monk was old; he was in his late sixties. Dogen and the *tenzo* had a conversation, and the exchange completely impressed Dogen. Dogen did not get satori, and yet he remembered this conversation until he died. It was this conversation he had with the *tenzo*, with this *tenzo* who worked like a common laborer, which changed him and opened his doubt.

Chukai!

AUG. 3 / 7.30 A.M.

Yesterday, as you know, an abnormal woman disturbed others in the dojo.[14]

Last night I could not sleep and this morning I am in *kontin*. Even for a master, it is not always easy to do zazen. At 2 A.M. this morning a mad woman came to visit me. I opened the door and she embraced me. There was no way to escape; she is big like a hippopotamus, and she held me in a rugby hold. My secretary came running up, but she couldn't break the big woman's hold on me. My secretary is too small and too thin, and all she could do was to look at us. Then Madame Monnot arrived. Then the doctor, and also Evelyne. And finally Cassan came. Cassan is a strong monk and he helped me (free myself from the woman's embrace). It was completely comic theater.

Then, early this morning, around five or six, I heard the banging of the *han* (the wood). Stéphane, who wakes us up with the wood in the morning, must have made a mistake, I thought. Too early. I opened the door and again the woman threw herself on me. (She had been knocking at my door, imitating exactly the sound of the *han*.) So Stéphane came and others too. Most of my disciples who sleep near me did not sleep last night. And me, I only slept two hours. *Kontin*.

THE PRETTY YOUNG MONK
AND THE OLD TENZO

So Dogen offered the old monk some good Japanese tea, and then he said: "What do you want these Japanese mushrooms for?"

"I must prepare them for the many monks in my temple. We are in *sesshin* now and these mushrooms are necessary. They are very good. So I have come here."

"When do you return to your temple?"

"I will leave after lunch. But first I must go shopping."

"How far is it to your temple?"

"Thirty-five kilometers."

"Oh," said Dogen, "you have very far to go. And even if you leave right now, you won't arrive at your temple before dark. So perhaps, if you will, you can stay with me here in my state-room. I want to speak to you. Please, you must teach me true Zen."

"No, I cannot stay," replied the *tenzo*. "If I do not return now, then tomorrow morning I will not have enough time to prepare the food."

"But there must be many monks in your temple, and other cooks too. So I cannot see that there would be any problem if you were absent for just one night. Please, stay here."

"No, no, no. A *tenzo's* work is of great importance. It is a work which has been transmitted from Buddha to Buddha and from patriarch to patriarch, so it is not at all possible to let someone else do this work. Another is not me. No one else can do my work but me. Just like no one can go pee-pee for me either," explained the *tenzo*. "Besides, in order to stay the night, I must have the permission of the chief of the temple, and I did not ask for it."

"I can telephone for you," said Dogen. (Ah, this was not possible then.)

"But you are very old," continued Dogen. "Even for kitchen work you are too old. I can see that you are a very great monk. So shouldn't you be reading books instead?" Just that, and a little zazen, and some whiskey? This is what Dogen thought. Dogen thought that the reading of books and sutras, that intellectual work, was more important than manual work. Dogen had felt that in the study of Buddhism reading was more important than practice.

"Pretty boy, pretty young monk," said the *tenzo* (and what he then said has since become famous): "You do not know the true meaning of the word." He said only this—in a loud voice. Then he laughed. "How we practice the way, this you do not know."

Later Dogen wrote that at this moment he was completely impressed, surprised. His entire body was covered in sweat.

"But what is *bendo?*" Dogen asked. "What is the true word? The true way? How do we practice the true way?"

The *tenzo* replied briefly: "Your question itself is the word, it is the practice of the way. Practice your question, and you will become a true follower of the way."

This answer is clear. But at that time, Dogen did not completely grasp it. What is this Chinese man trying to say? Dogen still could not understand the Chinese monk's words.

So, Dogen set a rendezvous with the *tenzo* to visit his temple.

"Surely, if you come I will welcome you. But right now I must leave and return to my temple."

That night, Dogen could not sleep at all. He was completely in *sanran*. Thinking, thinking. His brain was changing—since his childhood, since the time of his ordination; and now suddenly his brain had made a 180-degree turn. Why?

AUG. 3 / 9 P.M.

THE TENZO SAID:

"One, two, three, four."

Chin in! Stretch the neck!

Shoulders should drop. They must not be tense. Inside organs must drop down.

Concentrate on your exhalation.

■

Dogen quickly addressed the *tenzo*: "What is the true essence of the word?" (By this question Dogen meant: What is the true way to read the sutras?)

The *tenzo* said: "One, two, three, four."

(There is laughter in the dojo.)

How do we study the way? How do we study true Buddhism? Everywhere. This is what the *tenzo* had replied. The true way is not hidden.

The tenzo's answer is very simple: one, two, three, four. The true way exists everywhere. It is not hidden.[15]

IMPORTANCE OF THE WORDS

Dogen underwent a complete interior revolution. In *Tenzo Kyokun* he says that, "At this time I understood the true method for studying Buddhism. At this moment I understood how to read the sutras."

Until then Dogen had thought that the word was not at all important. Dogen had studied Rinzai Zen under Eisai, and the Rinzai monks had taught that the word was not important. That the essence of Zen exists outside the word. That, on the other hand, the true way exists only in the dojo, in the temple. That the practice of becoming a monk consists only in ceremonial practice, sutra reading and zazen in the temples. All else they felt (and Dogen too had felt) was not necessary.

Tendai, and many other Buddhist sects too, had rendered the ceremonies very complicated, and so, to become a monk one had only to understand how to practice these ceremonies, read the sutras and perform *kito*.

This is why Dogen thought a duality existed, that a separation existed between the ideal and the real; that these temple practices were one thing, and daily life was another.

But with this reply from the *tenzo*, Dogen's whole mind changed. Everywhere you can practice, everywhere you can learn to become a true monk. The practice exists everywhere. It is not hidden.

Stéphane asked me today why I went to the Santa Lucia the other night. This is why.... But it is not necessary to dance to become a monk. What is necessary is to find where it exists. It exists everywhere. In standing, in sitting, everywhere.

How do we stand? How do we sit? How do we smoke, go to the toilet, dance? Right posture, right manner, is very important. Form influences mind. If form is straight, shadow is straight.

One must realize the word of Buddha. The word of Buddha is also the mind of Buddha. Read the sutras and you can find the exact mind of Buddha.

Master Rinzai and the Rinzai sect have this saying, which has become famous: Do not depend upon the word.

In Rinzai Zen, they say that the true mind of Buddha exists outside the sutras. This is what they say. But Dogen did not agree. Both exist.

If you read mistakenly the sutras, then of course what they say is not true. But if you read them accurately, if you read them truly, then you will find in them the essence of Buddhism.

This is important; Rinzai and Soto differ on this point.

A CELESTIAL WONDER

Anyhow, Dogen was completely impressed with the fervor, with the faith, of this *tenzo*. Had the old *tenzo* not taught Dogen this, then in the later encounter between Dogen and Nyojo, Dogen would not have had satori.

In Soto Zen, the *tenzo* is very important. Until his death, Dogen always visited the *tenzo* before he went to bed.

I do not do it (i.e., *sampai*) for Guy or for Laurent, but if one day they become like the old *tenzo*, then I too will do *sampai* to them.

It was because of this old *tenzo's* teaching that Dogen became the great master that he was. To have met this *tenzo* was a gift from heaven, a celestial wonder.

FROM THE DARK THEY ENTER THE DARK

Monks of the Rinzai sect have climbed up onto the lion's seat and proclaimed themselves great masters of the transmission. And so this Zen of theirs spread throughout China; this Zen which is not at all true. Their Zen is *zusan*.

Zusan means negligent, careless.

What is the difference between Soto and Rinzai? The root is the same. So from where comes the mistake? Of course, their customs differ: Rinzai monks sit differently; they do not sit facing a wall, the position of their hands are different. But never mind, this is not important.

Still, Rinzai Zen is *zusan*. The negligent inspires the negligent. Dogen explains this. The negligent does not know that it is negligent, nor that it is not negligent. A koan. The negligent learns from the negligent, but negligence does not know that it is negligence. Those who are negligent do not know the true way. Nor do they wish to learn the true way. From the dark they enter the dark. This is a great pity.

Since the Soto and Rinzai source is the same, why did Dogen choose to follow Nyojo and not Rinzai?

Patience.
These last moments in zazen are very important.
The last five minutes.
The last minute.

AUG. 4 / 7.30 A.M.

RINZAI - SOTO:

The barbaric and the delicate

Zuzan, zusan—Dogen always used this word to describe Rinzai Zen. *Zusan* means more than negligent; it alo means, not delicate, not complete. Wild, rough, inattentive.

In *Shobogenzo* chapter called "Seeing the Buddha Nature," it is written that, "In China there are presently many who call themselves great masters of the transmission. But it is not so. They are not true masters. All they have done is to recall in their minds the words of Rinzai and of Ummon, believing these words are the essence of Buddhism." But were this true, were these few words by Rinzai and Ummon true Buddhism, then the transmitted line would not have continued until today.[16]

In terms of true Buddhism, masters Rinzai and Unmon were not respectable masters. And modern masters of this tradition are not above Rinzai and Unmon, but below. These modern masters are completely *zusan*. "They do not know true Buddhism. They have not studied deeply the sutras, they have not studied the teaching of Buddha. They are heretic. These masters do not represent the line of the transmission of the family of Buddha." Then, Dogen's final sentence in this chapter: "You must not meet with them."

So while Rinzai is called *zusan*, Soto is called **men mitsu**. *Men mitsu* is the opposite of *zusan*. *Men* means cotton, it means soft, and *mitsu* means thick, intimate, honey. So, *men mitsu* means delicate, careful, attentive, scrupulous.[17]

THE DOJO BECAME A BATTLEFIELD

Like Dogen, I too first received a Rinzai education. At the Rinzai temple in Kamakura. The master's name is Asahina (he is still living today) and at that time he was also a professor of ethics at the University of Yokohama. I met him when I was a student at that university.

Asahina proposed that I come join him at his Rinzai dojo for the summer. So I thought, why not? It's certainly a nice place. I'll be able to go swimming in the sea, I'll have time to read books, and for a change I won't go back to my own home. So I went to his dojo. But there wasn't any time for anything but zazen. We did zazen all the time, from morning to night. It was even beyond mortification. Not once could I rest. So I sat in zazen in a corner of the dojo. But the *kyosakuman* was always hitting me—without my asking for it. The stick he used was very big and very long, and it hurt. Anyway, one morning this *kyosakuman* hit me on top of the head, by mistake. I became mad, like the crazy woman here, and I grabbed the *kyosaku* from him and began hitting him back with it. Everyone in the dojo jumped up to stop me. But at that time, I was second Dan in Kendo—a champion—and I attacked everyone with the stick. Then quickly I escaped from the temple, crying out: "Zen is not true Buddhism! Zen is complete violence!" Anyway, the dojo had been transformed into a battlefield.

A famous master... I forgot his name... would arrive in the morning to give us a koan. Then later in the day we would have to line up outside his door to wait our turn to visit him. We would wait one hour or more, seated outside his door, on our knees in the Japanese style. The pain was terrible, yet if we moved even a little bit, the *shusso*, who sat behind us, would hit us with the *kyosaku*. Then, when it was time to enter the master's room, we would have to do *sampai* three times: once outside the door, once on the threshold, and once in front of the master.

The *mondos* lasted only a few minutes, nonetheless, the only thing we ever felt was fear. The master would growl something which I could not understand. It sounded like a foreign language. So I said: "I can't understand." He replied: "You must do more zazen."

I did *sampai* as fast as I could and got out quickly. The following morning it was the same thing. I would tell him very quickly: "I cannot understand," and then just as quickly escape. And finally I would say to him:—"I cannot understand, I cannot understand"—even before he could ask his question.

This is how it was. Pure formalism. This is why Dogen

criticized the Rinzai method. He said that it was not complete, that it was only formalism.

Anyway, in the middle of the kendo fight in the dojo, I escaped and went right off to see master Asahina—he was not doing zazen with us, he was in bed sleeping—and I told him what had happened. I told him that Zen was pure violence. That it had nothing at all to do with religion. And I said that I was finished with it.

Asahina laughed loudly: "In the history of Zen, only you have attacked the *kyosakuman!*"

My attack on the *kyosakuman* was not good manners. It was an act of violence and I regret it. It is an incident which has since become well known in Japan, and I am not proud of it.

■

Master Asahina is now in his eighties. He is a great Rinzai master and he is presently the representative of all Buddhist sects in Japan. Sometimes he writes to me, and sometimes when I am in Japan I go to Kamakura to visit him. Asahina has done much to help me in my mission and he admires me. But he is Rinzai. He is exactly like Rinzai masters. Still, now that he is old, he has become *men mitsu*, much more delicate.

AUG. 4 / 9 P.M.

KILLING THE BUDDHA

Kyosaku!
(The *kyosaku* is now being given and the sound of it—swack-swack! swack-swack!—is heard throughout the dojo.)

The *kyosaku* must be given strongly. The woman doctor gives it strongly, but the other one, the *monsieur kyosakuman*, gives it very weakly.

In the West, the women are strong, the men are weak.

(Addressing the latter:) *Kyosakuman!* You must hit accurately. Not on the bones, not on the head.

■

Sounds are important in Soto. This bell ending *kinhin* (which has just been struck) has a good sound, and it resounds for a long time. But when B... hit it just now, it went *piff!*

A master can tell if a disciple has satori from the sound he makes on the bell. In Rinzai sounds are not so important... *Kwat!*—this is more important.... Yesterday, M. and C. were on the drums and they were weak. Today the drummers are too strong. *Zusan.*

Some of you are always making bad sounds. When you cough. But make a good coughing sound, and I will do *gassho* to it. Even when you make a *gros pet* (big fart) you must take care. *Gros pets* are not forbidden in zazen. But you must not be *zusan.*

The sound of the *kyosaku* is most important. It is not just a question of hitting strongly. For everyone it is different—for men, for women, for the young, the old, in each case the sound is different.

Sometimes, if the sound of the stick is correct, then you will not even need to receive it yourself, as the sound itself will be sufficient.

For the proper sound, the *kyosakuman* must hold the *kyosaku* at ten or fifteen centimeters from one extremity, and hit with the top fifteen centimeters of the other extremity. Some women are afraid to give it and they hit almost at the handle. So the sound is poor.

During zazen, I do not look, I listen. To the sound of the *kyosaku*. So I understand unconsciously.

■

"Followers of the Way," (the Master reads from the *Rinzai Roku*) "if you wish to get satori, do not receive the influence of others, the doubts of others. If you meet facing behind, or outside...." (The Master stops to address the French translator beside him who has stopped translating:) You do not understand? Again, I repeat: "If you meet facing, behind, or outside, at this moment you must kill everyone. If you meet Buddha, kill Buddha. If you meet the patriarchs, kill the patriarchs. If you meet Rakan (a Hinayana master), kill him.

Even if you meet your father and mother, you must kill them. Meet your family, kill your family. You can obtain true satori at that moment. Be not attached to anything and you can obtain true satori, true freedom.[18]

This statement of Rinzai's does not mean to kill literally. But to be beyond it.

The Rinzai disciples who carried on the teaching of Rinzai made this statement famous by always repeating it. And this is why Dogen criticizes it. This teaching is not mistaken, but it is *zusan*. With statements and sayings such as these, people can make mistakes.

Never in the sutras do you find statements such as these. When people read such statements, they will come to believe that this is the essence of Zen. This is a mistake.

If a master teaches in this manner, then he must show that this question of killing is metaphorical. You must not kill. Commentaries are necessary.

Chukai!

AUG. 5 / 7.30 A.M.

NO NEED OF SECTS

Here in Val d'Isère, the sound of the valley is very beautiful. Particularly during zazen. It is the sound of eternity. It is written in *San Sho Doei* that:

> The color of the mountain
> The sound of the valley
> Everything together
> Is of our Shakyamuni Buddha
> His holy posture and his voice.

Kannon, the Bodhisattva Avalokitesvara in Japanese, means observing sound. *Kan* is to observe, *on* is sound.

Observe the sound of eternity; not the sound of a car.

■

At first Dogen considered Rinzai to be the greatest master. Later, however, he came to feel that Rinzai did not penetrate the ground of satori. Understand, please, that Rinzai is not a super human.

What is the difference between Soto and Rinzai? Why have they remained separate until today? Most people do not know, and if they come across Dogen's words, all they think is that Dogen is just doing propaganda for Soto. This is not important. What is important are the reasons for Dogen's criticism.

Which, finally, is the exact teaching? I want to know. I want to know what is accurate in Rinzai.

In Rinzai there have been some great masters. In Soto there have been many crazy masters. Soto masters are always fighting, and there are very few great ones. And so they have often been criticized. Even in the newspapers. *Soto-shu. Shu* means noisy. It means fighting.

In the forty-ninth chapter called *Butsudo* (*The Way of Buddha*), Dogen speaks of sectarianism and says that it is wrong. In Zen there are no sects, and Dogen himself had no need of sects. He did not like the words "Rinzai" and "Soto," he did not like divisions. Zen is Buddhism, Buddhism is Zen. There is only one truth. So, to know where and to know what is the truth, this was most important to Dogen. He first studied Rinzai Zen, then he studied Soto under Nyojo. Which teaching was true?

In the fifty-second chapter called *Bukkyo* (*The Sutra of Buddha*), Dogen writes that one must not criticize without first giving care and attention to the sutra of Buddha. "Negligent fellows, negligent heros, those who carelessly criticize the sutras of the Buddha—do not listen to their words. Truthful people, true followers of Buddha, please transmit the Buddha's sutras. And become, I hope, the sons of Buddha." Dogen concludes with the practice of zazen, with *shikantaza*. Do not follow the adepts of negligence. *Zusan*. But seek the way of the Buddha. Approach yourself as much as possible to the Buddha's practice, to the Buddha's mind.

I do not want to be different than Shakyamuni Buddha, says Dogen, yet even in 100 million years I could not arrive at my goal and be like him. Rinzai simply says: I am like Shakyamuni Buddha.

Both statements are true, both are necessary. But from an educational viewpoint Dogen's method is soft, it is *men mitsu*. Rinzai's method is hard, it is *zusan*.

UNKNOWN MONDO ON THE SUTRAS

On July 2nd of the year 1225, writes Kenjeki (in his biography of Dogen), Dogen was permitted into Master Nyojo's room where they had the following exchange. This exchange captures the most important difference existing between Rinzai and Soto. They had a secret *mondo*, a *mondo* which has never been studied, a *mondo* which has remained almost completely unknown. And until today no one has touched upon it. No one understands this. It is a very deep point and I have studied it profoundly....

(In Japan, it is very difficult to criticize; it is considered very undiplomatic to criticize, especially Rinzai. But I am not very diplomatic. I like Dogen and so I explain him.)

Dogen addressed Nyojo: In Rinzai Zen their masters say that there exists a special transmission outside of the sutras. Do not use the word, this is what they say. Do not depend upon it. For the transmission is to be found outside the sutras. This is why, for them, Bodhidharma came from the West....

Time is up. I will continue this *kusen* during the *sesshin* which starts in two days.[19] After the ceremony I will give four new *kesas*, to those who have made them. Then we will have a procession outside, and also a group photo. Everyone, please, come for the photo. If I cannot find you in the photo, I will think that you were not here for this *sesshin*.

AUG. 7 / 7 A.M.

SATORI

What is satori? To return to the normal, the original condition. Do not run after, do not escape. Do not escape zazen, do not run after dancing. Not only the body, but the mind too. Neither must escape, neither must run after.

Why does suffering arise? When the body wants something—when it wants to do zazen, to dance, to have sex—and this something cannot be realized, then suffering arises. Conversely, when the mind wishes to escape, and the body cannot escape, then too suffering arises.

Do not run after, do not escape from; this is the condition of satori. One must not seek the truth—so it is written in *Shodoka*. Do not escape your illusions.

Be not in *sanran*, be not in *kontin*—this is *hishiryo*.

The highest way is not difficult; satori is not difficult. Satori simply means not to select.

Through selection we are running after something, or else we are escaping something. So suffering arises. A contradition has developed. The frontal brain and the thalamus are now in opposition. This continues and you become sick, and finally you go mad.

If the body is strong and the mind is weak, the body kills mind. And you become insane. If the mind is strong and the body weak, then mind kills body. And you commit suicide.

Modern civilization is in crisis. Humans are close to madness, close to suicide. Only those who practice zazen are happy.

NO INSIDE, NO OUTSIDE TO THE TEACHING

In China, Rinzai monks are called *kyo ge betsu-den*. *Kyo* means teaching, *ge* means outside, and *betsu* means another transmission, a special transmission. So *kyo ge betsu-den* means the special teaching outside of the scriptures. Bodhidharma, say the Rinzai followers, transmitted *kyo ge betsu-den*.

So, on July 2nd 1225 Dogen visited Nyojo in his room and he asked the master about this, about this special teaching outside the scriptures. "In the Great Way, replied Nyojo, in the way of the patriarchs, in the teaching of the Buddha, there is no inside and there is no outside."

◾

In the tenth year of Eihe (by the Chinese calendar) master Matto (*Kyasapa-matanga* in Sanskrit) arrived in China riding on a white horse, and carrying with him the sutras of the Buddha. It was in the tenth year of Eihe, that is sixty-seven years after the birth of Christ, when Matto arrived in China, with forty-two sutras. And from this moment true Buddhism spread throughout China. Some four hundred years later Bodhidharma arrived in China, and according to the Rinzai teaching, Bodhidharma did not bring any sutras with him, but rather he brought with him a secret Zen. *Kyo ge betsu-den*. This is what Rinzai followers claim, and most people believe it to be true.

But what master Nyojo says, which remains unpopular and unknown, is that Bodhidharma brought with him... transmitted the true sutras, only this. He transmitted the true teaching of the twenty-eight generations from Buddha and Mahakasyapa. This has been certified. Matto (on the other hand) had not received the transmission from the patriarchs. Matto has no certification, no transmission.

Bodhidharma did not deny the sutras, and his transmission spread. Yet it is said in *Rinzai Roku* that Bodhidharma denied the sutras. That they were toilet paper.[20]

So in the year 67, the tenth year of Eihe, Matto brought the sutras to China. And Dogen, who respected the sutras, (subsequently) named his temple Eiheiji—after the arrival of the sutras in the tenth year of Eihe. Dogen also had great respect for Bodhidharma; he felt him to be the embodiment of the true essence of the transmission coming from the Buddha and the patriarchs.

There do not exist two separate sorts of Buddhism in this world, Nyojo had replied to Dogen's question. This is very clear. Bodhidharma alone transmitted the true teaching. And so Nyojo's teaching and not Rinzai's was the true one. The only one. This is what Dogen came to feel. The true truth is unique.

What is the true truth? What is true religion? True Catholicism? True Buddhism? Its essence is one. Its true truth is unique. In religion there is no sect.

But there are many separations, there are many sects.

This transmission outside of Zen, this *kyo ge betsu-den*, is very interesting. It is a koan.

I am always giving conferences; for those who do not understand, I explain.

The Buddha turned the flower in his fingers and smiled, and no one undertood. Except Mahakasyapa. "You alone understand," Buddha said to him, "so I transmit to you the *shobogenzo.*"[21]

So this became a special transmission.

True, true, this is a koan.

But Nyojo's reply to Dogen was not mistaken. In the great way of the Buddhas and the patriarchs there is no inside and no outside to the teachings. There are not two types of Buddhism.

Don't move, don't move. Don't wait for the sound of the bell. Don't run after the end of zazen.

Last night Madame Monnot came running to me: "Sensei! Sensei! The Pope is dying, the Pope is dying!"

"I am sorry," I said. "I can do a *kito* for him."

Don't escape from something, don't run after it either. Especially during *sesshin*.

THE UNDERSTANDING
WHICH COMES LATER

Dogen's *mondo* with Nyojo took place in 1225. But not until 1241 did he write about it in *Bukkyo*. Sixteen years later; a long time.

Objective understanding and subjective confirmation: these two understandings are very far apart. Even if one understands with the brain, true subjective confirmation of this understanding does not arise. When one receives a deep education from a master, one thinks: "I understand." (Nonetheless) this understanding does not become subjective confirmation.

So in 1225 Dogen understood Nyojo's answer; he understood it objectively. But when, on November 14, 1241, Dogen wrote it down in *Bukkyo*, then at that moment he understood it subjectively.

Even if you do zazen, even if you understand it, the merit of it, its effect does not appear immediately. It realizes itself later.[22]

Last year in this dojo a German doctor stood up in the middle of zazen. I thought he wanted to go pee-pee, but not at all. On the way out he cried: "Zazen is not at all effective! I cannot get anything from zazen." And he left the camp. He was an intelligent man, but he did not understand. Anyway, afterwards he came to the Paris dojo, and he also came to talk with me.

If you do zazen here and now, and even if you cannot reach, cannot touch, the point of satori, and you continue anyhow to follow the master (and to follow the sutras—sometimes you must follow the master, sometimes you must follow the sutras, for both are necessary) and you continue and continue but you do not touch—like a hundred arrows which miss the target— it is still possible that after fifteen or twenty years you will be given the *shiho*. It is possible after three years too.

Even though I have continued zazen for forty or fifty years, it is only now that I really understand master Kodo Sawaki's teaching. I understood before, but then it was only an objective understanding. Now I have subjective confirmation. To the bottom of my heart. I thank you very much, my master. Today I am completely impressed with my master, Kodo Sawaki.

Yes, yes, I understood before.... My secretary Anne-Marie is very clear. "Yes, yes, Sensei, I understand."

AUG. 7 / 10.30 A.M.

ONE HUNDRED KUSENS AND NOT ONE HIT

We have the spirit of the way, we practice the way of Buddha, and we do so with great and honest effort, sometimes by following the master's teaching (*waku-ju-toshiki: waku* means sometimes, *ju* to follow, *toshiki* the great intelligent master) and sometimes by following the sutras of the Buddha, and yet we still miss the target. One hundred zazen practices and not one hit.

At this time it becomes possible to hit the target, to touch the essence of Buddhism. The one hundred non-hits can then become one hit.

So, listen to the teaching, listen to the *kusen* (oral teaching), practice the way. Get satori, get confirmation.

Everything is like this. The past *kusens* were not at all effective, there was no hit, just sleep—like some are doing here right now. The *kusen* is no more effective than a dog who hears the words "I love you, I love you." He doesn't understand a thing. Better to give the dog a steak. This way you make a direct hit in one shot.

This works for a dog, but for a human during zazen, he hears one hundred *kusens* and not one of them hits the mark; because he is thinking of dancing. Or of food: "What's on the menu for lunch? Couscous? Spaghetti? We are always eating spaghetti. That's all right for the Italians, but not for me. Potatoes? Good for the Germans."

Sometimes there is a hit, sometimes not. When the *kusens* become too complicated then there is no hit at all.

The American boy, Philippe Coupey, is writing, taking notes. Very interesting. Very good English. But of course he is American. Anyway, sometimes he omits an important point. Too complicated. Better to cut it out. The book will sell better without it. Philippe hopes to make a best-seller. If the book is too complicated, too philosophic, people won't buy it. So, no-hit, no-touch. One hundred non-hit *kusens* which suddenly today become one great hit.

Sometimes one understands now, sometimes the understanding comes in the future. This is satori. One's doubts are resolved.

Master Dogen explained the method for obtaining satori. It is not necessary, this method. Continue zazen, unconsciously, naturally and automatically—this is *mushotoku*, and this is the secret method for the practice and the understanding of the way of the Buddha.

Even if you read books on Zen, such as Professor Durkheim's and Violet's (there are many books on Zen, especially in the German language) the matter only becomes more complicated—

for their direction is wrong—and so, among your one hundred practices, one hundred lectures, one hundred books, you will not score a single hit.

But after following the master, following the teachings, reading the sutras, the *kusens*, after reading **Shin Jin Mei**, *Hokyo Zan Mai*, *Shodoka*, **San Do Kai**[23] and their commentaries, then it is possible to hit the target. One hit comes from the force of the previous one hundred misses.

■

I am looking. Some people come here to seek the way. Some to do zazen. Some come here for a vacation. Some want to dance and they count the days, the hours, right up to the last lunch, before they can again go off to the Santa Lucia. Then they start all over again and prepare for the next *sesshin*. "It is difficult, I am tired. I must escape, I must go once more into town...." But being here is not like being at the Club Mediterranée.

Some have come for one, two, three years and they still do not understand. There is no hit. "Zazen is good. If I continue I can become a 'permanent,' and then I will only have to pay 840 francs for the forty days.[24] That's cheap. Cheaper than other summer camps." These people do not hit the mark. And some of them become even worse! Their direction is mistaken. It is like someone who wants to go to Marseille, heads off in the direction of Paris.

AUG. 7 / 4 P.M.

BUDDHA FINDS THE ESSENCE

Zazen is to be intimate with oneself, with one's ego. Zazen is to discover the true deep deep ego.

■

The old monk of the mushrooms had taught Dogen. And he was completely impressed. So he visited Nyojo's temple, and again he was impressed. This temple was not like a Rinzai temple.

Then Dogen met Nyojo, and at this time the most important thing (obstruction) in Dogen's life vanished—all his doubts vanished.

Dogen also noticed that Nyojo was different than Rinzai. There were no *kwat!* No *mondo*. Only zazen, from morning to night.

Nyojo rarely became angry. And he chanted *Bussho Kapila* at meal times: Buddha was born in Kapila, he had satori in Magada, he taught in Benares, and he died in Kuchira....

This was all there was to Buddha's life. There was nothing in particular. He did not seek after success; he did not seek to become famous; he did not seek glory.

Like the Buddha, Nyojo did zazen from morning till night. There were no discussions.

Nyojo Zen was not at all famous. But Rinzai Zen was; it was completely famous in China at that time. Rinzai Zen was captivating, dramatic, shocking. Nyojo Zen was not. It was Indian Buddhism, and especially its meditation, its zazen, which Bodhidharma had brought with him into China in the 500s.

So the essence of Buddhism, plus the Chinese continental characteristics—its naturalism and its wild, barbaric and dramatic sides—were combined together.

THE INDIAN WAS MYSTERIOUS

In all religions the essence is essential. Why did Buddha appear?

In India at that time there existed the traditional meditations, and they each developed in their own special way. Hinduism. Vedanta. The Indian characteristics had influenced their meditation.

Biographies and places influence people. The geography, the heat. So even today Indians are special. They don't want to work too much. Their food, too, is different. They are very poor, and there are many workers. And their traditional morals are very strong.

So you have the essence of the religion, plus the geography, plus the traditions of the people, plus their customs.

Buddha wanted to revolutionize this. He had discovered the essence of religions.

The Indian religions had become something special. Its meditation had become special and they were no longer a true meditation. They sought after magic powers, and they had become mysterious, mystical, ecstatic and tantric.

So what Buddha did, finally, was zazen. He did *samadhi*, the perfect posture, under the Bodhi tree.

Before this, Buddha had experienced all the traditional meditations of his time. He had experienced Yoga. And he had experienced asceticism and mortification for six years. But in the end he did nothing but zazen. It sufficed him. It was the finale. Zazen is the end of all religions, of all meditations.

This (i.e., the true practice) lasted up until Bodhidharma, the 28th Patriarch, or the 1st Zen Patriarch.[25]

During the time of Bodhidharma many different kinds of Buddhism had developed. There was much dirt. There existed a traditional Buddhism—a traditional mistake. So Bodhidharma wanted to leave India and go somewhere else. To plant in a new, fresh earth. So he visited China.

THE CHINESE WERE DRAMATIC

But then after master Eno, the 6th Patriarch who died in 713, and his successors Seigen and Nangaku, the pure Zen of Bodhidharma began to combine with the Chinese characteristics, with its dramatic and barbaric sides.

The Soto line (however) stayed normal up to the time of Nyojo.

The essence of a religion is very difficult to preserve. And sometimes it becomes necessary to vulgarize for it to spread. But by Nyojo's time, Rinzai Zen which had developed about three or four hundred years ago, had no more sense to it. This Zen had developed into a method for succeeding as a governor.

Zen had penetrated all Chinese culture. It had become a culture. It was no longer zazen. Zen consisted in discussions and in *mondos*, and these *mondos* have become very interesting.... Zen had become a method, a technique on how to swim to live. And Rinzai Zen today is a method for succeeding in our lives.

Dogen respected the Rinzai master Eisai, and he did not criticize him. Because he had received his ordination from Eisai. But Eisai had asked the emperor for offers—this is historical (an historical fact). He had asked to be made a monk of the highest order.

It is said in Japan that Rinzai is the general and Soto the farmer. Rinzai followers are close to the emperor. Their temples are beautiful. Visit Kyoto and you will see the beautiful Rinzai temples. So the Rinzai sect succeeded. They made much money and they held power.

Dogen escaped into the mountains. Nyojo had influenced him.

Before his departure for Japan, Nyojo had said: "As much as possible you must live in the mountains, and you must educate true disciples."

■

Master Nyojo's conferences were not so passionate, and not so interesting: "You must wash your bowls, you must do zazen. And after zazen you must clean your rooms...." This Zen was not *zusan*, it was *men-mistu*.

Nyojo did not often become angry, but when an error was made then he became completely so.

One day the monk sitting in zazen next to Dogen was sleeping, and Nyojo became completely angry. (When Nyojo became this way, which was only once or twice a year, then he became more angry than a *kwat!*) So Nyojo took off his shoe and he hit the sleeping monk. He hit him very hard, and not on an acupuncture point. He grabbed the monk, knocked him off the *tan* (raised platform) and shouted.

Dogen was completely shocked. He had known that Rinzai masters were very strong—and that all Zen masters should be strong—but in Rinzai all this had become mere formalism. The big Rinzai *kyosakus* and the loud *kwat!* But now all this was pure formalism. So Dogen was impressed, troubled.

"*Shin jin datsu raku!*" (Mind and body throw down!) Nyojo shouted and hit the monk.

"A true master!" Dogen thought.

Right after this incident Dogen went to Nyojo's room. And he did totally *sampai*. He did nine *pai*. Maybe he did ninety pai.... This scene was very dramatic. Dogen said: "*Shin jin datsu raku*. My body and my mind have been completely shocked, completely metamorphosed, totally changed." There was nothing left.

After anger passes, one becomes passionate. So Nyojo replied the opposite: *"Datsu raku shin jin!"* (Throw down mind and body!)

Nyojo was very deep. What he was saying was that Dogen must again metamorphose body and mind. He must again do *datsu raku* (i.e., throw away). Nyojo was saying that you must not stop there. There is no satori. Satori does not finish. When you enter the coffin, then it finishes.

Dogen was deeply impressed.

■

Nyojo once wrote a poem called *"Furin."* A *furin* is a little windbell. When the wind blows, the bell rings. I have one in the Paris dojo. The windbell rings, reciting the *Hannya Haramita*. A simple poem but very beautiful.

> The windbell hangs in the sky
> In the cosmos; it is free.
> When the wind comes from the East, (*d'accord*),
> the bell ring: ting! ting! ting!
> When the wind come from the West, (*d'accord*),
> Ting! ting! ting!
> When it comes from the South, ting, ting, ting.
> When it comes from the North, ting, ting, ting.

Nyojo is explaining that we are all free. This is true *Hannya*, true wisdom. Please, *madame*, do not sit here; sit there. *D'accord*.[26]

Mind never stays on anything. This is true wisdom. When a person stays on one point, he is attached to this point and so he cannot create wisdom. Stay on one point, on one thing, and fresh wisdom will not arise. Stay on one point and you become too individualistic, too egoistic. And you are not at all soft. Stay on one point and intuition will not arise.

Zazen is not only tension. During zazen your shoulders must fall. Your thumbs must not be pressed too tightly together, they must not create a mountain. Nor must they be too loosely in contact, they must not create a valley. The chin must be in. Fools always do the opposite. Chin out, thumbs up or down.

■

THE JAPANESE ARE DECORATIVE

In Japan, Soto and Rinzai Zen is essence plus decoration. Only Kodo Sawaki's Zen was true. Before him, Japanese monks did not even know what was a *zafu* (zazen cushion). In their minds they understood zazen to be sleeping while seated.[27] They did not know the posture. What is the zazen posture? Kodo Sawaki reintroduced it.

There are some who do zazen at the Japanese temples of Eiheiji and Sojiji. But their practice is not taken seriously. They do a little zazen, followed by two or three hours of ceremonies.

The practice at Eiheiji[28] is very severe. The *kyosaku* is very strong. And the *rensaku* is always being given, even for the smallest mistake. Formalism.

When Westerners visit the temples in Japan, they become spoiled and they all make mistakes. All those whom I have introduced to the Japanese temples have gone wrong. Even the very strong, like M., like Madame S., and like my old secretary. This is very strange.

There are many who want to go to the Japanese temples. The Paris dojo is not enough for them. Stupid, I tell them. But if you want to go, then go. So I bring them back with me to Japan. I introduce them to the temples. They all got worse!

Before going to Japan my disciple M. was pure. So too was my disciple Madame S. But when later they returned to Europe they were crazy. Why? Because along with the essence of Zen was the decoration.

RETURN TO THE ESSENCE

So I teach only zazen. *Shikantaza*. This is enough.

When I first arrived in Europe I practiced only zazen, only *shikantaza*. And after zazen I sang, alone, *Hannya Shingyo*, in a big voice. My disciple Etienne one day said that he too would like to sing *Hannya Shingyo*. So he typed it up and gave it to others, and then everybody was singing it. Naturally.[29]

What is the essence of religion? Of Buddhism? Of Zen?

After fifteen or sixteen years Dogen's Zen developed and arose in Japan. He had the Japanese trait of delicateness and now his Zen had become completely delicate, *men-mitsu*. His complexity, his delicateness, had increased through the years and all he wanted was to return to the essence of Shakyamuni— the only essence—under the Bodhi tree. Through the posture of zazen Buddha had obtained satori. This meditation was enough. It resolves everything.

Once the martial arts arrived in the West, its essence was completely lost. It became a sport. Westerners like sports. So the master becomes a sportsman. Aikido has become a dance, a martial arts dance. The essence has escaped. I always speak of master Tamura who is a very strong master.[30] He has been trying very hard to introduce the true essence of the martial arts in Europe. Very hard, very difficult. It would be better if he taught gymnastics.

Only force, only power, is important in the West. The essence has escaped. The martial arts today in the west are not at all effective.

Don't move! Don't move! Patience is effective.

After zazen there will be a *mondo*. Everyone is waiting for this. *Mondos* are better than zazen. They wait for the foolish questions....

MONDO

On dreams

QUESTION: What should be done with dreams one remembers? Should one attach importance to them or not?

Master: People who remember their dreams have tired brains. If the brain is healthy you will not remember them.

QUESTION: But what should I do when I remember a particular dream? I want to think about it.

Master: Forget it. Let it pass. Don't think about it. You just perpetuate the dream by thinking about it.

QUESTION: But can't thinking of one's dreams help?

Master: Dreams are of no use, and to think about them is idiotic. They will only make you more complicated. Dreams are recollections of shocks, of impressions received, which arise in sleep. It is the karma of the brain. Your neurons have received a shock, and so you dream. Tired neurons, karma arises.

It is the same during zazen. The subconscious arises, illusions arise. During zazen you can look objectively at your illusions, but during sleep you cannot look at your dream: "Look at this wallet I have found." (The wallet is full of money, but it is stuck in the ice and hard to get out.) "I should get a hammer. But if

I get a hammer then someone else will find the money. What should I do? I will pee-pee on the ice." Psssss. "The ice has melted; now I can pick it up." Then, suddenly, he realizes it was only a dream. He is cold and wet. Pee-pee. Only the pee-pee is real.

You cannot see your dreams. But during zazen you can see your illusions objectively. And your karma too. But not with dreams. Dreams are not real.

During dreams it is the bad karma which arises. To recall them, to repeat them, only perpetuates the bad karma.

■

QUESTION: What do you think of dreams that come true?

Master: A metaphysical problem.

These things cannot be denied. If people think, think, think, then it becomes the seed of the neuron, and so it can be realized. Think always the same thing, think that you want someone killed and this person will be influenced by your thinking. It is possible to kill this way, but it is no good. If you concentrate on some one thing, it is possible. This can even be realized without the use of your consciousness (but unconsciously too). Another question?

Karma

QUESTION: Can you say something about karma?

Master: Always questions about karma. Last year I spoke on karma for forty days. And my disciple Philippe Coupey wrote down my teaching on karma in *The Voice of the Valley*. You must read it. Anyway, karma is action. You create an action and it influences. If you do zazen, this act of doing zazen influences. If you do *sampai*, this too influences. It influences the body.

117

There are three sorts of karma, that of the body, that of the mouth, and that of our thinking. The actions of our body influence our future. If we speak, if we criticize, or tell a lie, this influences the future. If we think with our consciousness, this too influences our future. Our dreams can influence others. This is karma. If you kill somebody and do not get caught, this karma will still manifest itself. The same with stealing. Exactly it arises, in the future. There is good karma too. But the best, the highest karma is zazen. No consciousness. The posture of the body is the best—you don't speak.

So, if you do zazen it sweeps away the other karma. You must not escape from karma. Continue zazen and the bad karma decreases.

Unconsciously, naturally, automatically, karma changes.

AUG. 7 / 8.30 P.M.

PSYCHOANALYSIS:

An inside spiritual mistake

The manifest karma of some of you is coming out. The neck is not straight, the chin is out.[31]

Do not move. Some here are always doing gymnastics. They move their heads about like marionettes. Like A. It influences others. The slightest movement influences. Many karmic influences are in us. Zazen means to throw out the bad karma.

2nd session

■

Zazen is not the same as psychoanalysis. Modern psycho-analysis makes a big mistake. With materialism, with outside materialism, psychoanalysis influences an inside mistake, an inside spiritual mistake.

If people think too much their brains become complicated. Don't move! Don't move!

Western philosophers, western intellectuals, think too much. So Kant's philosophy has become complicated. In Asiatic philoso-phies (however), in their education, in Zen: as much as possi-ble don't think. Think important things. Selective memory.

My mother educated me when I was a child. When I had a bad dream she would say: "A dream is a dream. It is not impor-tant. There is no reason to be anxious over it." She was very intelligent.

Dreams are not at all important. You must abandon the past. You must concentrate here and now. But this is not the way with psychoanalysts like Freud and Jung.

"What did you dream?" the western mother asks her child. "You must remember it." So all day long the boy tries to recall his dream. This is a total mistake. Psychoanalyists are, I think, the cause of the crisis in modern civilization.

■

Do not run after something, do not escape something. This does not mean that one does not think. It is possible to think during zazen. *Hishiryo:* absolute thinking, beyond thinking. This is the secret of zazen.

We always dream during sleep. We sleep deeply for two hours, then we dream. Then we fall again into a deep sleep, for another two hours. The brain again awakes and again we dream.... Sometimes it is the body which wakes up, and not the brain. When this happens the body moves, its scratches itself, rubs its nose, massages its genitals. But when the mind is awake and the body is asleep, dreams appear. The dream is realized, the devil is coming, and the mind wants to escape. But the body which is asleep doesn't move, doesn't follow the mind, and the person suffers.

Zazen is the opposite to modern psychoanalysis. Surely the psychoanalyists will not be happy if I spread zazen. They will lose their work. So surely they will be against me. But it is not me, it is the essence of traditional Zen; it is this which I spread.

Pascal says that man is a *roseau pensant* (a thinking reed). This is the European-style philosophy.

■

Thinking is necessary. Do not negate thinking. But here and now, what is thinking? This is important. It is not necessary to recall past thoughts. Of course, when it is necessary to make use of past memory, here and now, then we must think.

Without thinking, when there is no thinking, then another thinking arises. A fresh thinking. Wisdom.

Most people think of the past and of the future, even during zazen. Most people are in a dream state.

■

Concentrate on your posture. And *hishiryo* consciousness will arise. Infinite wisdom.

Chukai! (i.e., stop the *kyosaku*.)

Don't run after, don't escape. Concentrate here and now and the time will pass quickly. Then there will be no pain.

Kaijo! (i.e., hit the drum.)[32]

(At the end of zazen everyone participates in the chanting of the Sutra *Hannya Shingyo*. The *kyosakuman* delegated to the big bell begins the chant by striking the bell three times and then by intoning, alone, the first words: *Maka Hannya Haramita Shingyo*. This ancient custom is practiced in all Soto temples.)

"Maka Hannya Har...."
Big voice! It is not necessary to decorate.
"Maka Hannya..."
Again.
"Maka..."
Again.
"Maka Hannya Haramita Shingyoooo!"

AUG. 8 / 7 A.M.

THE SOFT WORLD OF NYOJO

(Everyone is moving in *kinhin*.)

Stretch the neck. Stretch the knee (of the forward leg). Chin in.

■

Our body is delicate and complex. It is influenced by climate and weather. Today it is cold and snowing.[33]

In daily life it is difficult to observe your body. But during zazen, if you do it with exactitude, with the correct posture and with the correct breathing, and if you continue to practice this with your concentration focused on your exhalation, then you can observe, intimately your body and your mind.

■

In comparing Rinzai and Dogen Zen, we must not only compare Rinzai's Chinese characteristics with Dogen's Japanese ones, but we must also compare Rinzai's characteristics with Nyojo's. For these two lines first existed in China.

The world of Nyojo is very soft. Sometimes it is strong and direct. Sometimes it is like the celestial arch, at other times it is direct and simple like fresh iron. It is soft and it embraces everyone just as the sky in spring, very simple and without decoration.

It is like raw iron; you cannot taste it, you cannot bite it.

Dogen met with Nyojo, and he received a strong education, and when Nyojo roughly hit the sleeping monk sitting beside him, Dogen received a very big shock and he went right to see the master in his room, and he said: *"Shin jin datsu raku."*

"Datsu raku shin jin," replied Nyojo.

This great *mondo* between the master and the disciple consisted in only this.[34]

Then there was Nyojo's poem on the sound of the windbell. The mouth of the bell is very big. The sound is very free. And all his body became this mouth. This *furin*, this windbell, explains forever *Hannya* infinite wisdom. There is no thinking of the future. *Ici-et-maintenant* (here and now) is what is most important.... And Dogen was again impressed.

If the wind comes from the West the bell rings. If the wind comes from the East it rings. It rings with the South wind, too. And it rings with the North wind. And it explains forever *Hannya Haramita*.

One day Dogen and Nyojo were driving in an ancient Chinese car, and Dogen said: "Dear respected master, this poem has utterly impressed me. This poem alone expresses the deep wisdom, the deep *Hannya*."

"Others too have admired it," replied Nyojo. "But not so deeply as you. You alone understand my poem. If you explain this poem, if you explain *Hannya*, you must make such a poem."

■

Nyojo had influenced the mind of Dogen; Nyojo had certified the mind of Dogen.

Nyojo's seed was planted in Dogen; this seed was placed
deeply in Dogen's mind, and this seed became a fresh bud. It
opened into a flower. It spread leaves and it became a big tree
and its flowers opened and it gave fruit.

This happened fifteen or sixteen years later, after Dogen had
returned to Japan. The process of growth was very long.

Even if you understand with the brain (if something has
influenced you, you can understand), but for this understanding
to become true bones, true blood, and true flesh, much time
is necessary.

Since my first meeting with master Kodo Sawaki at Sojiji,
forty years have passed. And now, today, I can compare Rinzai
and Soto Zen exactly and deeply.

■

Dogen returned to Japan in 1227. Then some years later he
received the *Nyojo Roku* (*Record of Nyojo*), consisting of the late
master's conferences and *kusens*. And it was at this time, fifteen or sixteen years later, that Dogen began to compare the
Ronzai and *Nyojo Rokus*.

It was also at this time that Dogen left Kyoto. He moved from
the temple of Koshoji to the temple of Eiheiji. This move took
place after he had read *Nyojo Roku*. Why did Dogen leave Kyoto?

When Dogen returned from China he wanted to spread the
true Zen throughout Kyoto, and so he built his dojo in Uji, just
outside the big city. But in Kyoto Dogen quickly ran into strong
criticism from the traditional religions, Tendai and Nembutsu.
This, plus (the fact that) a nun, who loved Dogen, offered him
the temple of Eiheiji, contributed to his leaving.

But what influenced Dogen the most to leave this city were

the words of Nyojo, which came back to him fifteen years later, on reading *Nyojo Roku*: "When you return to Japan, please, spread the true Zen there, and give profit to as many people as you can. But if possible, do not live in a place where there are any castles, and do not approach the governor and do not approach his ministers. And when possible do zazen and give *sesshins* in the deep mountains and the profound valleys... " (Val d'Isère is very good for this) "... and if you do not succeed in spreading Zen to many people, if you transmit it to one person, then my true Zen will be caught and it will spread into the future. Zen is finished in China."

Dogen spread Nyojo's teaching throughout Japan. But in modern times its essence has been lost. Today in Japan there is too much decoration, too much karma. So I have brought the true teaching to the West.

Today it is snowing in Val d'Isère. The sound of the valley is covered in snow. This is good for zazen. You cannot go out. You cannot escape to the Santa Lucia. Now you can look deeply into yourself.

Surely Nyojo's world, Nyojo's words—his roar from China to Japan—has woken up the sleeping dragon.

Today during the ceremony we will do a *kito* in homage to the Pope.

Kaijo!

AUG. 8 / 10.30 A.M.

FUKE HAD THE AIR OF AN ASS

(The bell has been struck twice and the people begin *kinhin*.)

Chin in. When the chin is out it means that you are tired. So take care to always keep your chin in.

If during *kinhin* your hands are placed too high on your chest, you will become tired. The hands must be placed just under the sternum.

(The bell is struck once and the people return to their places. The bell is then struck three times and they resume their postures.)

Kyosaku!

If people are sleeping during the *kusen*, then today I will allow the *kyosakumen* to give the *kyosaku*.[35] It is necessary here. This is a very sleepy *sesshin*. My *kusens* have become music to sleep with.

■

Rinzai Roku terminates with an account of master Fuke. Fuke was not a monk, nor was he a layman. Fuke's name has remained famous even until today.

A **Fuke sect** existed in Japan up until the Meiji revolution. In Japan at that time there existed the Obaku, Rinzai, Soto and Fuke sects.

In the Fuke sect they never practiced zazen; they practiced the flute. Fuke followers always carried a flute with them, and they entered samadhi by playing it. Before the Meiji revolution, about one hundred years ago, the Fuke monks held a lot of power. They were used by the Japanese government, and they became government spies. But after Meiji their sect was forbidden. Their masters continue today as *shakuhachi* monks. But they are not monks. They are now professors of *shakuhachi*. *Shakuhachi* is not Zen.[36]

■

Fuke and Rinzai were good friends. In the Fuke sect they even claim that Fuke educated Rinzai. But this is not true. Obaku was Rinzai's master.

Fuke was even more *zusan* than Rinzai. Fuke was completely wild.

He always carried a bell, like a windbell, about him, and he would run after people on the road, ringing his bell behind their ears. When the people turned around, Fuke would stick out his hand and ask for money. He was an amusing monk. He was not a monk. He was a beggar.

(The Master picks up *Rinzai Roku* and opens it.)

"So, one day Rinzai and Fuke went to a vegetarian banquet given by a vegetarian believer. During the meal Rinzai asked Fuke: 'A hair swallows the vast ocean, a mustard seed contains Mount Sumeru. Does this happen by supernatural powers, or is the whole body (the substance, essence) like this?'

At that Fuke kicked over the table. He was not *men-mitsu*.

So Rinzai said: 'Rough fellow.' "

(The sound of the *kyosaku* can be heard over the Master's words.)

It is not necessary to give the *kyosaku* while I talk!

"Fuke replied: 'What place is this here to speak of rough and of refined?'

The next day they returned to another vegetarian banquet. During the meal Rinzai asked: 'How does this food compare with yesterday's?'

'I understand,' Rinzai said quickly before Fuke could kick over the table, 'I understand what you are doing, but you are a rough fellow.'

'Blind fellow,' replied Fuke, 'is there anything of refineness or of roughness in the Dharma?'

Rinzai stuck out his tongue."[37]

"Another time Rinzai and two old teachers were sitting in the hearth pit of the dojo. Rinzai remarked: 'Every day Fuke plays the fool in the market place. Does anyone know if he is a vulgar person or a sage?'

At that moment, before Rinzai even finished talking, Fuke entered the room. Rinzai addressed him: 'Are you a vulgar fellow or a sage?'

Fuke: 'You tell me.'

Rinzai gave a *katsu*, and Fuke thereupon pointed his finger at the others present and said: 'Kaijo's style is of the newly married, Mokuto's is a grandmotherly Zen, and Rinzai's is of a little servant. All three are blind.'

'Robber,' replied the master.

Fuke left yelling: 'Robber! Robber!' "

"One day Fuke was eating raw cabbage before the dojo. Rinzai saw him and said: 'You have the air of an ass.'

Fuke brayed.

'Robber,' said Rinzai.

Fuke left yelling: 'Robber! Robber!' "[38]

Chukai!

MONDO

Helping the Pope to paradise

QUESTION: Why did you conduct a ceremony this morning for the passing away of the Pope? What was its meaning?

Master: As a gesture of respect towards Christianity. Once when I was in the Vatican, I was welcomed by the Pope. I met with him. This ceremony is not a contradiction. Why do you ask?

QUESTION: I would like to know what is the spiritual aim of this homage ceremony.

Master: Respect. In Christianity they always want to go to paradise. So I prayed, I did *kito,* so that he would go there. It was to help him get there. This is true.

Mushotoku and the martial arts

QUESTION: Is a martial arts master *mushotoku* (beyond object) when he practices his art?

Master: During the practice of all the martial arts you must be *mushotoku.* If you think "I must win," then you cannot win. When we abandon everything, when we become completely *mushotoku,* then we can win. It is the same when you paint; if you think "I must paint a beautiful calligraphy," then you will not succeed. This is true with everything. In art, in the martial arts. Abandon ego. *Mushotoku* is necessary.

In Japan before the Meiji revolution, it was the custom in

the martial arts dojos to supply food and bed and even some sake to all those who did combat there. Food, bed and sake for one night. Even for the losers.

One day a diviner—his divining business was going very badly—so he decided to present himself at a fencing dojo for a tournament. He was not a samurai and he knew nothing of fencing. But he had a strong face and he also had a large sword. So he arrived at the dojo and he told the samurais there that he wanted to have a combat with their master. The master was in the bath and when one of the disciples came to tell him that someone was waiting in the dojo to do combat with him, the master said: "Now I am tired. After my bath I want to sleep." The disciple warned the master that this samurai waiting for him in the dojo was very dangerous looking.

"Ah?" replied the master. "Well, tomorrow; tomorrow, he must come back."

"We told him that," replied the disciple, "But he said: 'No, now!' He refuses to leave until you do combat with him."

So the master got out of his bath, dried himself, and went to meet his opponent in the dojo. The master looked at the man's face, and he was surprised. The face was strong and wild looking, and his mustache was long and thick.

In any case, this diviner was completely *mushotoku*. It was not necessary for him to win. All he wanted was for the master to give him one good blow to finish with it. Then he could have some sake.

So the master began to think: "If I attack him this way from the left, he will get me from the right. But if I attack him the other way, surely he will catch me here." This master's brain had become complicated.

The diviner was not at all afraid and when he approached, the master retreated. He kept retreating. And finally he did *sampai*.

"Never until today have I seen anyone use such a style! Never have I experienced this technique. I do *sampai* to you. But please, tell me, what school do you belong to? I have studied many different techniques, but I have never seen anything like this."

The diviner who was very honest, laughed and said: "My school is to eat and to sleep. For one night."

Mushotoku. This is the secret of the martial arts. When you are *mushotoku* you are afraid of nothing. With *mushotoku* everything comes to you.

I am *mushotoku.* When money comes, I get it. Yesterday I received from Japan a *fuse* of a million yen.

AUG. 8 / 4 P.M.

THE RENSAKU UNTIL THE STICK BROKE

Many people have not come today. There are many empty *zafus*. The *kyosakumen* must look into the rooms and find out who did not come. There will be *rensaku*. (The Master sends the *kyosakumen* off to look.in the rooms.) It is alright if you notify the office first. You tell them why you cannot come. Those who do not come to zazen because of sickness, alright.

There is only tonight and tomorrow morning left. There are not many zazens to go.

■

2nd session

People who are now seated in zazen are true seekers of the Way. All of you have good postures. Your faces are clear. There is no fatigue.

(The *kyosakumen* return with five or six people, mostly permanents.)

It is not necessary to remain sleeping in your rooms. For those who have come back to do zazen, I will give a discount. Only three *rensakus* for you. A rebate.

(A *kyosakuman* whispers to the Master that one of the rooms is locked. A second *kyosakuman* then appears and whispers something else to him.)

Room 79 is the residence owner's room. The first *kyosakuman* had thought that there was a couple in the room making love. So he stood in front of an empty room, looking through the keyhole.

(The Master addresses those who are about to receive the *rensaku:*)

The *kyosaku* is not a punishment. It is to wake up you. It is a good massage and it will make your fatigue disappear.

During *sesshin* in Japan those who remained in their rooms without permission received a big *rensaku*. My master Kodo Sawaki always went after those who stayed behind in their rooms without permission. Kodo Sawaki would get very angry. More than Nyojo. When he caught one he would give him the *rensaku* until the *kyosaku* broke. Some of them ran away—they ran right out of the dojo. One once ran out and hid in the bell tower. Since Kodo Sawaki could not climb that high up the tower, he rang the big bell. Everyone stopped zazen to look. It was very humorous.

(The Master addresses one of the people presently receiving the *rensaku:*)

It is not necessary to look at the *kyosakuman*. It is not necessary to look.

Sometimes humor is better. In the Zen tradition monks are humorous. Dogen too sometimes, but not in his *Shobogenzo*.

A PRIZE FROM THE SHOGUN

One of Dogen's disciples one day went to visit the governor in Kamakura. After his visit he returned to Eiheiji and told the master that he had obtained some big prizes (large land from the Shogun, from the Prime Minister), and Dogen became completely angry. "You are foolish, dirty," he said and he kicked the disciple out of his room with his foot. He excommunicated him. Then he dug up the ground under the disciple's *zafu;* he dug a hole two meters deep, and threw away the dirt.

This story is recounted in some books. That it is true is not so certain. But it still captures Dogen's character.

TWO POEMS

Fuke was in the habit of going about the streets and the marketplace ringing a bell and shouting his poem:

> I hit the brightness when it approaches the darkness.
> I hit the darkness when it approaches the brightness....

(This is Fuke's famous poem; it is in the *Rinzai Roku,* Chapter 47.)

> When it comes from the four quarters
> and the eight directions of space
> I attack it like a whirlwind.
> And when it comes out of the empty sky
> I flay it like with a broom, ding, ding, ding!

An intellectual comes and I attack with reason: I discuss. A fool comes and I reply with foolishness. (There are some here who are very intelligent, but not many. I hear the questions. They are always rational, always reasonable.)

When it comes from the four quarters and the eight directions of space, I hit like the wild wind, and when it comes out of the empty sky, I give it the *rensaku*. This is Fuke's poem.

Nyojo's poem *"Furin,"* like Fuke's, consists of seven ideograms and four phrases:

> All bodies are like a mouth which hangs in the
>   empty sky.
> Do not ask, it doesn't matter.
> The east wind, the west wind, the south wind, the
>   north wind—
> They are all the same; all winds are the same.
> The mouth talks, it tells of *Hannya,*
> It tells of the highest wisdom,
> Ding, ding, ding."

Fuke's and Nyojo's poems are both very famous. But Nyojo's is deeper. Fuke is a bit wild, a bit barbaric. Always *kwat!* Always hitting, kicking. Nyojo on the other hand, when he became angry, he became truly angry. Then later he would apologize. "I did not want to hit you. My mind did not want to, but my hand moved. Pardon. I do not want to hit you, all I want is to educate you. I want to produce in you the great elephant, and the great tiger."

A strong education is necessary. The lion who wants to produce a strong one of his own kind, hits the little lion and throws him down. Right down the mountain into the valley.

So after Nyojo hit the disciple, he apologized and he cried. And the disciple was impressed. Nyojo was always crying in his inside mind. Kodo Sawaki as well. When he hit someone there were tears in his eyes. I saw them. He was a true educator. In modern education, though, there is too much importance put on words, on discussions, and on being diplomatic. One must penetrate not only the frontal brain, but right through to the thalamus. Otherwise the education you receive is not effective.

Nyojo's poem is direct and simple and very delicate. Like a bell. Like maybe a cute little bell. Anyway, if you go into the provinces of Japan, you will see little bells hanging from the doors and houses.

TWO PROUD HORSES KICKED EACH OTHER

Here is another Rinzai koan: An old monk who came to consult Rinzai, instead of going through the usual formalities, asked quickly: "Is it making *sampai*, or is it not making *sampai*?" Rinzai gave a *kwat!* and the old monk did *sampai*. "A good robber of the green wood," said Rinzai, to which the old monk left shouting: "Robber, robber!" Rinzai then remarked: "To think that there is nothing further to seek is a mistake."

Rinzai then went looking for his *shusso*, and said: "Was there a fault or not?"

"There was," replied the *shusso*.

"Was the fault with the host or with the guest?"

"Both were at fault."

"What was at fault?"

The *shusso* escaped, and Rinzai said: "Better not to think that there is nothing further to seek."

Very funny.... Later a monk related this exchange to master Nansen. (Nansen is the master who cut the cat in two).[39] And Nansen criticized it. He said of this encounter that "the governor's two horses kicked one another."

In this discussion between Rinzai and the *shusso*, the *shusso* was more clever than Rinzai. Rinzai was too young—that is what Dogen said of this encounter. The calm and the quiet are more effective. Silence is the strongest education. The horses of officers are very proud. And not at all scared. This story is about two proud horses who kick each other. It is the same as theater.

MONDO

Greater than the atom bomb

QUESTION: Many times I think without wanting to think. Where do these thoughts come from?

Master: From the subconscious. Jung called it the collective unconscious. It is a dream. It is illusion.

Thoughts arise from the center, from the thalamus, from the neurons in the thalamus. They are illusions, delusions, and *bonnos*. They are dreams.

Jung wrote that if someone were to dicover a method for bringing out the subconscious, this would be a great discovery. Greater even than the atom bomb.

This discovery: zazen did it. It is the biggest discovery of the twentieth century. But Jung and the psychoanalyists do not know this, and so they are still searching.

Good question.

Half a person

QUESTION: Will Zen continue after you are gone?

Master: There is no reason for you to think of "after."
It will continue, exactly. There are many disciples.
One person, one-half a person, is enough to continue it.

This is not a conference

QUESTION: Why do you give *kusens* (oral teachings)?

Master: You don't like the *kusens*?

Answer: Yes, but they are a little disturbing. I prefer the first part of zazen when you are not speaking.

Master: Ah, so you can think, yes?

When you are completely quiet then you think: "I want to eat a beefsteak." So my *kusens* are better than your thinking.

Sometimes it is necessary to teach, to educate with words, otherwise you will not progress. If you only do zazen, if you only practice *shikantaza*, then wisdom will not be realized.

For myself it is better not to give the *kusen*, to do nothing at all. The sound of the valley, the flow of the river; they are very quiet.

But for you the *kusen* is necessary. It is the teaching during zazen.

Answer: Yes, but the *kusens* make for thinking.

Master: Not necessary to think. To be natural is better. Think from the bottom of non-thinking, think not from the bottom of thinking. This is *hishiryo*, the secret of zazen.

If you continue to practice, then you hear with the thalamus and not with the frontal brain. You hear it with the body. This kind of an education is fundamental. It is not like with a university conference.

You don't like the *kusens*?

Answer: They're not so bad.

Master: Because you cannot sleep as you would like, this is why you do not like them. Next time you must put some cotton in your ears.

Pain and the fat man

QUESTION: What should we do when we are in pain?

Master: Think about pain and it gets worse.

Stretch your backbone, stretch your neck, raise the top of your head. Or else change legs, cross them the other way. Without disturbing those near you.

In any case, for fat people like you it is always difficult. Because the body is heavy. I experienced this when young. I stopped eating. It was very difficult, so I have compassion for fat people.

Like Marco Polo the American boy. He is very heavy and he says that zazen is too painful and that he cannot continue. But he continues. He came all the way from New York for this *sesshin*. Very expensive. I will give him a special certificate. He does not want to hear my *kusens*, but I will give him a certificate anyway.

AUG. 8 /8.30 P.M.

THE RINZAI TENZO DID SAMPAI

Twenty more people arrived today. There are no more rooms and so they are sleeping in the garage, where it is very cold.

If you want to do a *fuse* (give a gift) during this *sesshin*, it is important to whom you give it. A *fuse* given to a pitiful thief has little effect, but give a *fuse* to someone who practices zazen and the merit will be greater than if you had given a *fuse* even to Buddha. So for those who can, please, do not put on your heat and this way the heat will be concentrated in the garage.

Once I did zazen for an entire night in the snow. I did not get cold. During zazen the body temperature rises.

In a sutra it is written that if you want to have a second bowl of soup and at this moment you decide not to have it, then this will become a great *fuse* for all humanity. If you wish to change your tiny room for a big apartment and you do not, then this will become a great *fuse* for all humanity. And not just for one day or for one year, but more merit for always. It spreads throughout humanity. So surely the merit of such *fuse* will change your bad karma. To decrease your desire becomes a great desire, a desire of high dimension.

So tonight, if you can, please do a good *fuse*.

And so all together we wish to arrive into the world of satori. This is Mahayana Buddhism.

■

I will now continue the theater of *Rinzai Roku*:

"Rinzai had been invited to an army camp (not a summer camp) for a vegetarian banquet." (Again mistake! In military camps you do not have vegetarian banquets. Books in English are full of mistakes.) I continue: "At the gatepost Rinzai happened to meet two officers. Pointing his finger at the post, Rinzai asked: 'Is this the column of a sage or of the common people?' (This too is a complete mistake in the English translation... Anyway, that Rinzai spoke this way does not matter, but afterwards that his disciples and others interpret such statements is not good.) The officers did not reply, so Rinzai hit the post and said: 'Whatever you say, it is only a piece of wood.' "[41]

Only this. Nothing more.

◼

"Later Rinzai asked the *shusso*: 'Where do you come from?'
Shusso: 'From the prefecture where I sold rice.'
Rinzai: 'Did you sell the lot?'
Shusso: 'Yes, yes, all of it.'
Rinzai drew a line in front of the *shusso* and said: 'Did you sell this, too?'
Shusso: '*Kwat!*'
Rinzai hit him."[42]
Good theater. One always needs two to play it. Rinzai and the *shusso*.

◼

This next koan on the *tenzo* (chief cook) is very interesting. It is only because of this koan that the *tenzo* has become famous in Rinzai.

The Soto *tenzo* has also become famous, because of Dogen. I have already given an account of Dogen's experience with the *tenzo*, so you can compare the two. By these examples alone you can come to understand which is *zusan* and which is *menmitsu*, which is deepest.

"When the *tenzo* approached, Rinzai related what had just happened.

Tenzo: 'The *shusso* did not understand you.'
Rinzai: 'How did you understand it?'
The *tenzo* did *sampai*. Rinzai let out a *katsu* and hit him." (General laughter.)[43]

I understand the deeper meaning, but it is still theater.

Time to stop. You must all be sleeping by now. So I will give you a discount. I am compassionate with you. Because I too am tired.

Stretch the neck, chin in; push the sky with the head, push the earth with the knees.

AUG. 9 / 7 A.M.

MASTER HAKUIN

(The master reads from *Rinzai Roku*:)

"Rakuho, Rinzai's secretary, who was standing next to master Rinzai, said to the scripture teacher" (this is a mistake; it is not a "scripture teacher" here, but a "Tendai master").[44] "So Rakuho said: "How do you understand it?"

Secretary: *'Kwat!'*

When the Tendai master had left, Rinzai asked his secretary: 'Was that *katsu* for me or for the Tendai master?

'Yes, for you.'"

He was very *zusan* so the Master hit him.

"Secretary: *'Ka!'* Rinzai hit him again. Secretary: *'Ka!'* "

THE KA-PA KOAN

In Japan, master Hakuin used this koan and it became known as the *"Ka-pa* koan."

Master Hakuin asked a disciple: "What is the meaning of this koan? You must solve it."

The disciple replied with a *Ka!* and then he hit himself. When he hit himself it sounded like *Pa!* (General laughter.) This is why the koan came to be known as the *Ka-pa* koan.

When master Rinzai used this koan it had a deep meaning. But Rinzai followers later turned it into theater.

■

"You must speak," said a Rinzai master. "What is the secret essence of Buddhism? You must tell it to me in one phrase.

And with your hand covering your mouth...." Some Rinzai masters and their disciples talk this way during *mondos*.... So the disciple jumped up and covered the master's mouth and said: "You must tell me first!"

THE FORBIDDEN BOOK

In modern Japan most Rinzai temples are in the line of Hakuin. (There is another line called Takusui, but it has very few followers.)

I have an old book here with me, *A Critic of Rinzai Zen*, and it concerns Hakuin.[46]

The Rinzai people do not like this book and they managed to have it suppressed. So for many years in Japan this book remained unpublished and forbidden. But if I translate it into English and publish it in America, the Rinzai sect would be very angry. The book says that Hakuin made many mistakes and he was not a great master.

Hakuin Zen is a concentrated Zen to cure sickness. And this is very sad; it is not *shikantaza*.

For a full year, beginning students do not eat and do not sleep (says the book). They are always receiving the *kyosaku*. And meanwhile they are given koans to solve. Every day the students repeat this, and they become very tired. When the student is on the point of becoming completely mad and neurotic, he is permitted *kensho* (i.e., satori). For the intellectual student it is very hard, and by then (i.e., when he is ready for *kensho*), he is thinking only of escape. So at this moment, the master tends him a bit of sugar saying, "Maybe now you have a little satori." So they have a comic *mondo* with a foolish koan, and the intellectual, who is now like someone falling into hell, wakes up. And nothing. This is the state of mind of satori. Right before the intellectual falls into madness, he wakes up—and this is satori, this is enlightenment.

This is how it is in all Rinzai temples of the Hakuin line. And it is a complete mistake. My master, Kodo Sawaki, also said that this method is completely crazy and dangerous:The weaker people who follow this method end up in the hospital.[47] There has been much written about this in the book.

(The Master continues to refer to the same book:) In the next room to Hakuin's sat a nun (the nun Hakuin always consulted). She was waiting there to test the new disciple. The disciple entered and the nun, who was seated in a chair, said to him: "Without using your two hands, lift me up." The disciple, who was young and strong, kicked the nun in her sexual organs, and she quickly stood up.

There are many humorous scenes in this book but if I read them, none of you would stop laughing until the end of the *sesshin*.

■

Concerning the koan, "What is the essence of Buddhism?" Hakuin in the end replied. Hakuin's answer became books; it became a collection of koans.

What is the essence of Buddhism? Hakuin answers: "The sparrow goes *tzu! tzu!* The crow goes *ka! ka!* The dog goes *wan! wan!* The cat goes *nyan! nyan!*"

Disciples who wish to pass these koans quickly, buy Hakuin's book of koans. But as westerners do not make the same animal noises as do the Japanese, they would not be able to pass the test. In Japan cows go *mo-mo*; horses *hin-hin*; and cocks *ka-ka-ka*.

I finished this book in one night. It was better than a comic book.

■

I am now comparing Rinzai and Soto Zen. Rinzai and Soto are of the same source, only Buddha's way, only Bodhidharma's Zen. But then they separated.

I am Soto, so surely Soto is best. This is my conclusion.

Dogen was searching for the true way, the true Buddha's way. The true Buddha's way is only one. The ways leading to the top are numerous. But through *shikantaza* Dogen sought the true way. Why did Dogen begin *Shobogenzo* by writing that the direct gate, the front gate, to the top of Buddhism is *shikantaza?*

If you, here, understand both Rinzai and Dogen, and if you compare them both, and if you have the right knowledge of Zen, and if you educate others, then this work will become historic.

AUG. 9 / 10.30 A.M.

THE BUDDHIC SPIRIT OF RINZAI, DOGEN
and all great religious leaders is the same

(The Master enters the dojo once everyone is seated, does *gassho,* and takes the high seat. Then reaching over, he hands the editor of this book a piece of paper. On it is written: "Zazen is eternal life. Zazen is the perfection of the true Dharma *(sho-bo).* Zazen is the Buddhic aspect which is realized in man. Zazen is the state of mind which is only one, which is aloneness. Zazen is to be intimate completely with oneself.")

This is the last zazen of this *sesshin*. Concentrate to the end. I will now examine your last zazen postures. I want to take a photograph of each of you in zazen to keep for the future. (The Master begins taking photos. His secretary helps him with the camera.)

I wanted to take more photos of you, but my secretary just broke the camera. She dropped it.

Now that I am again seated the camera is working again. But I took photos of most of you anyway, and I will see. For ten years I have been taken by you in photos, and now it is I who take photos of you. I will keep them. Historic.... But if you want I will give them to you.

■

Last zazen. Most of you will be leaving today. So those who leave, and especially the new people, do not forget your postures of zazen and *kinhin*.

■

Like with Dogen, Rinzai did not make any mistakes. Later though, the Zen Rinzai took another direction. But now you can see which one is the true meditation.

Rinzai, Dogen—everyone—search for the true way. But no one is the same, and everyone has a different karma.

Master Hakuin spread Rinzai Zen throughout Japan. He had a very deep influence, and he too believed in zazen.

Even if you do zazen only once, your bad karma will disappear for a long time afterwards. The spirit of each of us is the same, it is the methods which differ: *zusan, men-mitsu.* Jodo Shinshu, Nembutsu, and Master Shinran too. Here too the spirit of Buddhism is the same.

If you invoke the name *Namu Amida Butsu,*[48] and if you concentrate on this name, then it is the same as when you concentrate on zazen. Without purpose. *Mushotoku.*

All karma of the three worlds (i.e., of past, present and future) transforms and decreases. All great religious people have transformed the bad karma of all mankind. Each one of us has a bad karma. Our lives are not so good, not so bad. Sometimes a storm comes, sometimes a rain comes, and sometimes it snows and sometimes it is a fine day.

In the voyage of our lives, sometimes waves, sometimes the calm. In *Shodoka* it is written that we walk alone. The voyage of our lives is alone, and when we enter the coffin we are alone. No one follows.

But for those who have experienced zazen, to be alone is not so bad.

In the end we are alone and in solitude. I have always said that the state of mind in zazen, the last state of mind, is in being intimate with oneself.

For those who continue to practice zazen: when we are alone we are completely calm. Not anxious and not frightened. We reach completely the supreme peace and the highest pleasure. When we practice zazen alone in solitude, we find deep calmness and peace. This is the world of true religion.

We are alone, our lives are in solitude. But people who have reached satori, these people can be with others, these people can play with others on the way of **nirvana.**

So those who have continued zazen here together and have together experienced this *sesshin*: these people are eternal friends, they are of an eternal family—Dogen said this. We can be together, we can step together, we can make a procession together, towards the eternal world of nirvana.

I hope that you continue zazen. Until death. To pile up the satoris. I hope that you get many satoris. Not one time, but ten times, a hundred times. A thousand infinite satoris in the eternal world.

Chin in. Last chin-in. Last stretch-of-the-waist. Last patience. Last ceremony.

Now we will chant the *Hannya Shingyo*.

Dai kaijo![49]

editor, Philippe Coupey

3rd session

AUGUST 12 – AUGUST 20

AUG. 12 / 10 A.M.

Today begins the preparation for the third *sesshin*. The permanents here must do zazen with the others. If they do not, then the new people here will not want to do zazen either. The permanents pay much less than the others and so they must not become lazy. This is not the Club Mediterannée. So those permanents who have not come for this zazen must receive the *rensaku*.

C. and N., you are the *shussos* and you are responsible for those who have not come. Who has not come?.... They do not know.

Kyosakumen, stand up! You must go and see who have not come for zazen.

The last *sesshin* was not so bad. But by the third and fourth *sesshins* the permanents are always tired. Not from doing zazen, but from exterior activities. Too much drinking, too much dancing at the Santa Lucia. This is why the atmosphere of the *sesshin* is bad. For those permanents who went to the Santa Lucia last night they must receive the *rensaku*.

During *sesshin* that which is most important is *samu*. Between *sesshins* the permanents had one day of rest and one day of preparation for the new *sesshin*. But their *samu* yesterday was not good. The cleaning was done poorly. On the balcony in front of my room there is dust, dirt, plastic bottles and cups. And the wind made it all stink. A garbage heap. It is only zazen one must practice during *sesshin*. From the moment one rises to the moment one goes to bed, one must be attentive to all one's actions. This is *sesshin*.

Those who are here now, why have you come?

■

SIT

Zen Teachings of Master Taisen Deshimaru

For new people zazen posture is most important. Stretch the waist, the backbone, the neck. Chin in. Place your mind in your hands. Don't let the thumbs fall. Don't push them up either. Shoulders should be down. The internal organs must fall naturally. Concentrate on the exhalation, not on the inhalation.

(The *kyosakumen* return with five permanents.) Give them the *rensaku*. Five times on each shoulder. Also, the *rensaku* for those who have arrived late in the dojo.

■

(Everyone is now in *kinhin*. A woman falls unconscious and the *kyosakumen* carry her out.) Zazen and *kinhin* postures are very strong, and those who have weak hearts and weak nervous systems show a strong reaction. But it is not necessary to become anxious. Soon you will become quiet, soon you will return to the normal condition and you will be more healthy.

Stretch your knees, stretch your neck.

(Zazen:) During *sesshins* we must concentrate not only on zazen but on all the actions of our daily lives. Right from the moment we rise in the morning.

Don't move, don't move.

Everyone during *sesshin* must do *samu*. Do *samu* every day and it will become a great merit, a great *fuse*. If you wish to eat a good beefsteak and you do not eat it, this means that you have given a *fuse* to all humanity, you have given a beefsteak to all humanity. And its merit will completely return to you in the future. If on a particular day you wish to dress up in beautiful clothes, but instead you dress in a black *kolomo*, this merit will return in the future. It means that you have given these beautiful clothes to all humanity. If during *sesshin* you want to sleep with someone…, this is not easy to do. During a proper *sesshin* people sleep on a *tan* (raised platform) in the dojo, and it is not so comfortable as here. Here it is even better than the Club Medierannée, for each room has its own bathroom with bathtubs and toilets, and this is not like in a real *sesshin*. In a real *sesshin* we all eat together in the dojo, without alcohol, without wine, without meat or fish. But here sometimes we have wine, meat and fish. I have prepared this *sesshin* so that it will be soft.

Chin in. Don't move.

Lunch is at 12:30. Take care of the sound of the *han* (the wood) and don't be late.

In modern times people have become individualistic and egotistic, and so we have the crisis of this civilization.... But follow exactly the others and harmonize yourselves with them and certainly later on, when this *sesshin* is over and you return to the social world, your actions, without words, will influence others and you will become great educators, unconsciously, naturally and automatically.

Patience is important. When the pain in your knees becomes unbearable, and you continue to be patient, the effect of this patience will be great. The virtue of patience is far greater, far more effective, than the practice of any mortification.

Kaijo!

AUG. 12 / 8.30 P.M.

Someone was singing today in the toilet in a loud voice, in a very loud voice. I have said before that when here one must be silent. This is not the Santa Lucia. Those who wish to sing must do it outside.... For his honor I will not mention his name. But he must receive the *rensaku*. It is necessary. *Kyosakuman*!

In a dojo, in a temple, singing is not permitted. Only the chanting of the sutras, not songs.

■

(*Kinhin*:) The *shusso* and the columns (those seated in the corners of the dojo, facing out) must put order in the lines.[1]

Don't stand still. Some here are like trees, waiting for the dog to come pee-pee on them.

■

(Zazen:) Don't move. During *sesshin* someone moves, even a little, and it influences the atmosphere. People who are different and who do not harmonize, break the atmosphere.

■

During the first and second *sesshins* we had some crazy girls here. I don't think we have any crazy people here in this third *sesshin*. But if there are, then certainly they will soon manifest themselves... like the one last week who knocked on my door at two in the morning. When I opened my door this girl hugged and kissed me and I was completely surprised.... Mad people on the streets do not cause much influence, but when they come into the dojo their influence is so great that no one can continue zazen.

■

During zazen we must understand true ego. We must put off all bad karma, we must become completely pure. *Shin jin datsu raku*. *Shin jin* is body and mind, *datsu raku* is bad karma metamorphosed. This is *sesshin*: to decrease the bad karma. You have not much time to do this, just nine or ten days. But it is

possible. You can decrease your bad karma during *sesshin*....
Some increase it. There are some here who have experienced
many of these summer sessions. When they arrive they are
with one madame, and when they leave they are with two
madames.

GENJO:
The highest realization

Last night the American Zen center in California sent me
their English translation of *Genjo Koan* by Dogen. I read it. A
completely childish translation. Superficial. It is translated into
good English but the sense is not at all deep. They do not understand what is *genjo* koan.

I have already experienced *kwat* koans and *katsu mondos*.
What is *mu*?

Master Rinzai created the koan. Master Dogen created the
kanji (ideogram) *genjo*.

The word *genjokoan* is very interesting. Dogen created this
expression. *Genjo* is not a modern Japanese word; the Japanese
themselves do not understand this word.

Dogen used this expression 271 times in the ninety-five
volumes of *Shobogenzo*. I counted them. Dogen never used any
other expression so much. Dogen was fond of it. Rinzai used
"*koan*" and "*katsu*."

The word *genjo* has many meanings. In Chapter Two, *Maka
Hannya Haramitsu*,[2] here *genjo* means to realize. It is actualization, realization. *Maka Hannya Haramita* is the realization of
Buddha himself. So here in this second chapter *genjo* means to
realize. In chapter seven, *Senjo* (which means toilet), Dogen
writes on how one washes his behind after he has gone to the
toilet. It is to realize, it is the realization of infinite merit. When
the dignity, the manner, of the Buddha or of the patriarchs is

realized in this place, the devil, and heresy (of a mistaken religion) escapes. (Recites.) Now the teaching of Shakyamuni Buddha is spreading in all directions throughout the world. *Genjo* is the actualization of the body and mind of Buddha. *Genjo* must be realized here and now; and the study of old koans is formalism, theater and antiquity.

In the chapter called *Kajo* (which means "in daily life"), Dogen explains the method for eating. Table manners.... I once did such a demonstration for Professor Levi-Strauss, who has himself written on table manners, and he was very impressed.[3]

Dogen writes that such manners have been transmitted since the Buddha and the patriarchs and that these manners are realized here and now.

Before we eat we sing *Bussho Kapila*. Then there is absolute silence.... But when I'm not with you at the table, you all talk. The talking starts with the *shusso* (i.e., the head monk). But this is not possible; there must be absolute silence during *sesshin*.

In the chapter *Kesa Kudoku*, Dogen uses the expression *genjo*. The *kesa* made from old rags, becomes the highest cloth. (Recites.) Here the true *kesa* is realized.

THE GREAT SAGES AND THE TRUE MOUNTAIN

Genjo, genjo. In the *San Sui Kyo* chapter (the Sutra of Mountain and Water; *san* is the mountain, *sui* is water, *kyo* is sutra), Dogen says that everywhere where there are the big mountains, Buddha and patriarchs have appeared, water is realized. *Genjo*. (Recites.) Where water arises, all Buddhas, patriarchs and great masters everywhere are realized. This is interesting. You are all great masters. Everyone. You are doing zazen. You become Buddha, God. For exactly water comes. So with the sound of water. The sound of water comes. (Recites.)

Mountains are beyond antiquity, beyond actuality. Mountains

have the shape of great sages. Ever since ancient times the great sages have always liked the deep mountains. They have made of their bodies a mountain. So, by the wise, by the great sages, true mountain is realized. *Genjo.*

This is the *genjo* koan of mountain and river. In the mountains great sages are assembled. In the Alps, in its mountains and valleys, the great *genjo* is realized. It is realized now, during this *sesshin.*

It is not realized through dancing at the Santa Lucia.

Why have you come here? To dance at the Santa Lucia?

Do not interrupt me with your coughing. (There is much coughing in the dojo.) Always cough, cough, cough. You eat too much, this is why you cough.

But do not catch cold. Do not sleep nude in bed.

AUG. 13 / 7.30 A.M.

SATORI VISITS YOU

Zazen is not mortification. Zazen is the Dharma gate to penetrate the truth. For beginners it is difficult; they have not the habit and it hurts. So they should sit on a high *zafu.* Put lots of kapok in your *zafus.* Those who are in pain can bring a blanket with them. In Japan they use *tatamis* and it is softer to sit on. My master Kodo Sawaki used a mat which he placed on the *tatami.* One hour of zazen makes no difference, but it makes a difference if you sit for a long time, for three days or for a week.[4]

155

■

Last night after zazen a young American girl came into my room. She asked someone to cut her hair for her—a little man, but I won't say his name—but he cut her hair too short (for her taste) and she was angry. I told her that her hair would grow back. "Some people cut off all their hair." But she was angry, angry, in front of me. She has done zazen for many years now. But this morning she is not in zazen. Angry. She thinks hair is a decoration. When Anne-Marie became my secretary I cut her hair short and she was not angry.

■

Genjo means cosmic order, cosmic power, realized in front of oneself, without seeking.

It is not necessary to seek after anything, there is no need to seek satori. If you do zazen, satori visits you. There is no need to think about koans.

In the Rinzai sect they seek satori. They seek to obtain *kensho*. In Rinzai they are always searching for something. With their personal wills. This is not correct. In the end they are tired.

When we are not running after, or away, when we are only doing *shikantaza*, doing zazen, and we are no longer thinking from the frontal brain, the subconscious arises, the collective consciousness arises, it arises from the central brain.Don't avoid this consciousness. Don't run after personal consciousness. Then we connect with the cosmos. We become natural.

You can hear the voice of the valley. The voice of the valley is the voice of nature, the voice of the cosmos.

■

Abhidharma Sastra: Vasubandu[5] wrote *Abhidharma Kosabhasya*. *Abhi* means true wisdom, to observe oneself; *dharma* is the rule, the law, Buddha's teaching; it is all existences, the highest, the cosmic truth. Fundamental cosmic power. The prefix *abhi* means facing, going toward, approaching, mastering, formation, realization of the true wisdom or true truth. So *Abhidharma* means to observe the Dharma; it is the realization of the Dharma.

In *Udhana Sutra* this is called *Pathamabhi-sambuddho,* and in English this means: first into satori. This is *abhisambuddha,* this is *genjo*. It means to realize. One who has come to the realization of the highest wisdom.

In the Pali-English dictionary they use the word "enlightenment" to explain this. And so does Professor Suzuki in his English translations. But this is not enlightenment. Satori visits. Satori enters into us. Satori does not come from us.

So it is one who comes from the realization of the highest realization—realization of the public theme. Realization of Buddha, realization of the *kesa* here and now. The true *kesa* is realized. *Genjo*.

Kesa genjo, satori *genjo,* koan *genjo*. All this means without thinking. It does not mean thinking with our self-conscious, as (does) a public theme, a koan.

Koan is a public theme. It is an eternal truth, the true truth. So sometimes koan means satori.... In Rinzai a koan has become a difficult problem, a mysterious problem.

A disciple presents himself to the master and the master gives him a koan—like you give a child chocolate. What is *mu?* What is your originality? What was your mind before you were born? You cannot answer, so it becomes a koan. And in the end it becomes theater.

What is the essence of Buddhism? Give the answer with one word, without using your mouth. Not possible. So the disciple stood up and placed his hand over the master's mouth and said: "No, you must answer first!.".... Koan, koan, koan. In China the koan had become *à la mode*.

When I first arrived in Europe everyone who knew a little about Zen was always asking me about koans. "Please, master, give me a koan." They did not know what koans were. During Dogen's time too the situation was the same. This is why Dogen wrote *Genjo Koan*.

AUG. 13 / 9 P.M.

WITH NO-MIND COMES EVERYTHING

What is satori? The return of body and mind to its original condition. The body and mind of most people are not in their normal condition. They have been over-influenced by others, by their surroundings, and through their daily lives. But through zazen one can come back to the normal condition.

For master Dogen satori is *genjo*.[6]

Satori realized through zazen. So zazen itself is *genjo*.

■

In Rinzai they seek the solution to a koan. But seek something and it will escape. Like a cat or a pigeon—seek them and they will escape. If a boy runs after mademoiselle, mademoiselle will escape. (In modern times it is mademoiselle who runs after the boy and it is the boy who is scared and escapes.)

When we are unexpecting, when we are **mushin** (no-mind), when we are *mushotoku* (beyond object), then at this time everything suddenly comes. This is *genjo*. True fortune comes unexpectedly, in a visit.[7] But if we desire it, then it will not come. It will escape you.

In most religions, theologies, and European philosophies, they seek to understand the truth. And sometimes (in doing so) intuition arises. But then they begin thinking, with the frontal brain, and matters become complicated. They wish to study further, to write philosophical books, to make categories, and in the end they become complicated. Like Kant's philosophy. And like Nietzsche. In the end Nietzsche went mad.

■

Hishiryo is not thinking, but thinking. (Recites *Fukanzazengi*.) Think from the bottom of non-thinking. How?

This is *hishiryo*. It is beyond thinking, it is absolute thinking. It is passive knowledge, as unexpected realization, an experience.

Satori is a passive, intuitive recognition. It is not active. It is not thinking with the frontal brain, it is not epistomology. Satori is zazen plus intuitive wisdom. *Genjo*. The actualization of satori.

STAYING ON SAMADHI

I always say that naturally, automatically, unconsciously through the *samadhi* of zazen, intuitive wisdom appears. This is *genjo*. *Gen* means actualization; *jo* means to become, *jo* means perfect, complete…. But stay on *samadhi* and wisdom will not arise. (Marco Polo said during the last *sesshin* that he wants to stay calmly in *samadhi*. He does not want to accept. He wants to stop, to close.)

During zazen it is better to stop the frontal brain. (But this does not mean sleep, the stopping of everything.) Then the thalamus will become completely active, and it will receive the vital thrust.

THE PHILOSOPHER'S METHOD

Bergson speaks of intuition as the only means of understanding duration in terms of the life experience—he calls this the vital thrust.

Kant talks of things which can be fitted into categories of our understanding, and of those which cannot.

So intellectual thought became the absolute method for philosophical research, and Kant's, Schilling's, Fichte's and Hegel's philosophies are very complicated.

Hegel created with theories and with concepts a very complicated system.

Bergson understood the value of intuitive recognition. He understood intuition (*chokan*), but intuition and intellectual thinking (logic) are opposed, in contradiction, and so finally Bergson was thinking and seeking always through his frontal brain.

European philosophers who have not experienced body-thinking, practice finally nothing but active knowledge. These philosophers did not know zazen.

Surely in Europe, through my disciples, a true philosophy will appear. Surely people who practice zazen in the West will become great. They are realizing a new renaissance. An historical revolution in western history and philosophy. I think so.

■

In Rinzai Zen, satori means mental action. Intuition beyond common sense. They play with koans. They are concerned only with koans. They, too, seek with the frontal brain; through *mondos* with the master: "What is the essence of Buddhism?" "*Kwat!*" This is repeated and repeated, and always in the same way and finally the disciple becomes tired. He has not enough food and not enough sleep and so he becomes like a crazy person. He suffers, suffers, even in his dreams he suffers, like someone in Naraka. Then the master gives him a hint, and he wakes up from his dream and his suffering is nothing, and he becomes very happy. Happy like after a bad dream.

ZAZEN:

The content of Buddha under the Bodhi tree

Satori in Sanskrit is *bodhi*. The original source of *bodhi* is Buddha. Buddha is the Sanskrit word for satori. So Buddha means he who has gotten satori.

Buddha abandoned mortification after doing it for six years. He stopped this step-by-step training, which is mortification, and sat under the Bodhi tree. Last night I explained this. Zazen is perfected nirvana. It is *genjo*, the realization of perfect nirvana. It is the content of the satori of Shakyamuni Buddha while sitting under the Bodhi tree.

■

If we stay on *samadhi,* as in Yoga—most meditations wish to stay on *samadhi*—then **prajna** (*Hannya*) will not be created and wisdom will not arise.

Hishiryo does not only mean to stop thinking. *Shikan: shi* means to stop, *kan* to observe.

In western philosophy it is only a question of *kan*. Of observation. Without nirvana, without *samadhi*, without zazen, without *hishiryo*. To seek the truth: only observation, only thinking. To seek the truth assembled through intellectual knowledge, through categories, through concepts, created by ourselves.

So it is, too, with existentialism and with psychology: observation only. These people do not experience true meditation and so they cannot truly understand their own selves. They cannot experience the subjective, so they run after, they search, they seek. They look only from the outside, objectively.

Genjo is the truth which comes. It is not necessary to run after it. The truth is automatic, unconscious, natural. And it appears unexpectedly, of itself. This is *genjo*.

Genjo koan means the realization, the actualization of the koan. A koan by itself is not at all effective. A koan only complicates the brain. If truth is not effective in our daily lives then it is only knowledge, know-how.

Genjo is the actualization of satori in our daily lives. By the wisdom of *prajna*, of *Hannya Haramita*. And by observation of *ku*.

It is from this point that is realized, produced, created the true deep method for the living. It is the ideal living method. This is the *genjo* koan. The actualization of satori. It is satori, *genjo*.

Chukai!

AUG. 14 / 7.30 A.M.

Don't move, don't move.

Kyosaku!

If you want to move you must do *gassho* first. If you move without first doing *gassho*, the *kyosakuman* must give you the *kyosaku*.

The *kyosakumen* must hit with the end of the *kyosaku*. Hit the shoulder within the last ten centimeters of the stick. Some here hit within thirty centimeters of the end, while others hit with the handle. The sound is not good. Its sound influences others.

Kinhin!

Two bells: *kinhin*. Three bells: zazen.

After the two bells, after zazen, and before *kinhin*, the columns[8] must open the doors and the curtains.

(*Kinhin* has ended and everyone is returning to his place.)

Those who sit by the window are always last.

They are still walking! Who is responsible there? Who is the column?

No, leave the curtains open.

If you wish to look out at the landscape, you can. The color of the Alps is wonderful.

AUG. 14 / 9 P.M.

DOSHU: TO EXPRESS

At night the curtains are always to be closed! The columns are responsible.

Please, listen to the sound of the valley, to the voice of the valley....

Satori visits from outside. But it does not come from one direction. Satori enters into us when we are concentrated, when we abandon the ego, when we are in *samadhi*. At this moment when we are completely in *samadhi*, satori enters us. This is *genjo*.

SIT

In Rinzai Zen satori is to observe the nature of the ego: *kensho*. In modern times Rinzai satori is the observation of the nature of Buddha, of one's own self.... To understand the nature of the ego, or of Buddha, the method of the koan and of the *mondo* are used.

In Dogen satori, the method is passive recognition.

This is not *kensho*. This is *genjo*. Satori visits from the cosmos, from the cosmic order, it visits automatically, naturally, unconsciously.

In western philosophy as in European epistomology, understanding comes through conception by cognition; it is intellectual knowledge from the frontal brain.

By always seeking and running after the truth, cosmic truth escapes.

In Dogen Zen, in Soto Zen, satori is an unexpected realization. So sometimes it is the same as intuition, sometimes it is *kan sho* (of the heart, enjoyment—*kan* means to observe and *sho* means to shine), and so at one moment I say "concentration" and at another I say "observation."

The German word for *kan sho* is *genuus betrachtung.* (Laughter.) I know German. My pronunciation is not so good, but I remember the words.

Genjo in the heart. Aesthetic ideality, aesthetic solitude, aesthetic objectivity, aesthetic reality. In German it is called *aesthetische tiefe.* (More laughter.) It is not necessary for the translator to repeat my German!

Anyway, it doesn't matter—German people do not know this German word, they have forgotten it. Nor do they know of Moritz Geiger who wrote *Tiefen Wirkung.* His dates are 1880 to 1937.

So even in art, aesthetic enjoyment and natural appreciation are not the same. Aesthetic enjoyment is intellectual, objective and active; but natural appreciation is subjective and passive. Unexpected realization is a passive recognition. *Erkenntnis* is the German for passive.

European philosophy is active; they are always running after something, always seeking.

But if you do not run after the truth, true truth will arise. True satori arises from *mushotoku* (without purpose). It comes from the outside, from the cosmos. The cosmos gives. It is like God-giving. It is automatic, natural and unconscious.

■

Dogen used the word *genjo* many times. In *Shobogenzo* he used it 261 times. (In *Rinzai Roku* it is the word *katsu*. *Katsu* is used hundreds of times.) But more than *genjo*, Dogen uses the word *doshu* He used *doshu* 299 times. *Do* means the way, and it means to say; *shu* means take. Dogen's *doshu* means to express.

The words *genjo* and *doshu* were created by Dogen. (*Genjo* existed in China before Dogen's time, but Dogen used the word more deeply, and he gave it many meanings.)

The relationship between these two words is very important; *genjo* without *doshu* is not complete.

Sometimes the *kanji do* means the way, and sometimes it means to say, to speak. *Do* can also mean: the word, the language. The Greek word *logo* is very similar to the *kanji do*.

As you know, the New Testament begins with the phrase: "In the beginning there was the word." This signifies *logos*.... I read the Bible in Chinese. The Chinese ideograms are very interesting. This phrase in Chinese is written: *Gen shi yo do*. *Gen shi* originally meant: in the beginning. *Yu* means: exist. And *do*: the word.... So this is the second meaning to the word *do*. The word *logos* has only one meaning and so it is not as practical a word as *do*, which means both "of the word" and "of the way."

So this double significance (of logos) is expressed in the one ideogram *do*. This is interesting. *Kodo* (as in Kodo Sawaki) means to develop the way. The *do* in *Shodoka* means satori.

So the relationship between *doshu* and *genjo* is deep.

■

After the sound of the wooden clappers at night you must be quiet. You must not box. The American girl knocked out the little French monk last night. This American girl is very strong. And she has a good posture. She always sits in the lotus, and she has followed me for a long time. She's a good girl, but sometimes she's a little… a little…. Well, anyway, she should take care. She's the American female champion here. She k'o'd the French monk. She also smashed his glasses, and now he can no longer see.[9]

Marco Polo is the American male champion here. He was always writing me postcards from America, "I am very glad to be able to do zazen with you, and I will come again and do it even longer," he wrote. But now he says he wants to return to America. He had been waiting since last year for this Val d'Isère *sesshin*, but now he wants to leave, before the end. Because his knees hurt. Now he has doubts…. Patience is necessary, but he says that he can no longer be patient.

I hope this modern Marco Polo will surpass the ancient Marco Polo. The ancient one visited Asia and was very famous, as you know. He wrote interesting books about China and the Orient. But he knew nothing of zazen (even though zazen had spread through Asia during his time). His books are interesting but they do not touch on Zen, nor on oriental religions and oriental culture. Marco Polo was only a tourist…. Had he studied zazen or Buddhism in Asia, then surely European civilization would have changed, even in those times.

Anyway, I hope the American boy and the American girl will continue zazen. America is very fresh and young. Zen is spreading there but it is *zusan*. This is why Rinzai Zen is successful in America. But you Americans who have come here for Zen, I hope that when you return you will educate Americans in Dogen's Soto Zen.

AUG. 15 / 7.30 A.M.

THE NECESSITY OF EXPRESSION

Transport the ego to the cosmic order, to the order of all existences, and this is *maya*, illusion, and not satori. But when all existences of the cosmic order visit the ego and certify the ego, then this is satori.

Go towards all existences of the cosmic order, go with the desire to certify all existences of this order, and this is not satori. Seek truth with the frontal brain: maya, illusion.... But if (during zazen) all existences of the cosmic order visit the ego and certify it, then this is satori unconsciously, naturally and automatically.

Genjo (the realization of satori) is expressed by the body, the mouth and the consciousness. This is not categorical; this is *doshu*.

How we take the way, how we express the way, this is *doshu*. Expression is necessary: through body and mouth. Through sentences. Everyone is now expressing *doshu*: through their coughing in the dojo.

Everyone has different sounds, different expressions. If I hear the voice, I can understand the satori. Everyone has a different degree of satori.... Some here make very strange sounds, of all sorts. Expression is important.

ZAZEN POSTURE:

The expression of satori

The posture of zazen and the posture of *kinhin* is the expression of satori, of *genjo*.

SIT

It is only in the posture of *kinhin* that some here realize completely their dignity: satori, *genjo*. The posture expresses it: *doshu*.

(The Master chants *Bussho Kapila* in the manner everyone chants it at mealtime.) By this voice alone I can understand the degree of your satori. The sound of the voice, when chanting *Bussho Kapila*, is the expression of *doshu*. When the body does not move in zazen—*doshu*. The action of our body, of everything, is an expression of *doshu*; and so it is *genjo*.

Dogen repeated *genjo, doshu, genjo, doshu*. With Rinzai it was *katsu*. Or the raising of the *hossu*, or the lifting up of the finger..., and then quickly the *kyosaku* is given.

Rinzai Zen cannot express the true essence of Zen, of Buddhism.... It is true that Rinzai himself created. But his line only imitates him, and so it has become theater. This is why Dogen repeats in his *Shobogenzo* that this is a mistaken Zen, a big mistake.

It is for this reason that people in the West think that Zen is very funny. But this is a mistake and this is not Dogen's Zen.

SHOBOGENZO:
An elaborate expression

Zen cannot be expressed in words and sentences. It is for this reason that *doshu* is so important: how we express ourselves, how we express *genjo* koan, the actualization of satori; how we express ourselves, this is *doshu*.

Dogen writes of the importance of how we express ourselves through words, through language.[10]

In Rinzai Zen words are not so important. Always *katsu*, the *hossu*, and blows with the stick. This technique is of more importance in Rinzai *mondos* than are words. In Rinzai, words are of little importance.

But for Dogen it is possible to express yourself not only by the body, but also by words and by writing. This is *doshu*.... So

Dogen wrote ninety-five volumes of *Shobogenzo* and many other books. This is an expression of *genjo*, of satori. In these volumes of *Shobogenzo*, Dogen writes on existence and time, on life and death of humans, about the good and the bad, on how to catch the true truth.

In the end truth comes. Like this. But how? How does one express this—the method? The expression of it is very delicate. It is very elaborate, very rational, very *men-mistu*. Dogen's *Shobogenzo* is a very elaborate expression.

EYES HORIZONTAL, NOSE VERTICAL

Gen-no-bi-choku. Gen is the eyes, *no* is horizontal, *bi* is nose and *choku* is straight, vertical. The eyes horizontal, the nose vertical. So **gen-no-bi-choku** means the normal condition. (Push the sky with the head, the ground with the knees.) Anyway, Zen is *gen-no-bi-choku*.

(Recites from Eihei Koroku).... What I have just recited is a famous sentence of Dogen's. (Translates:) "I did not experience much zazen in the dojos of China," says Dogen; he was humble—"But I did have the fortunate chance of meeting with master Nyojo's *tenzo*. This was a great moment in my life; and I understood that I could do *doshu*. I could express *gen-no-bi-choku:* the nose is vertical and the eyes horizontal. I understood this, and since that time I have not been abused by others.... I returned empty-handed to Japan. There is nothing concerning Buddhism." So there is nothing. Only following the cosmic order. True freedom. "Every morning the sun rises in the East and every evening it sinks in the West. Clouds pass on and the mountain appears. The rain passes on and the form of the mountain, the color of the mountain, becomes clear. So what is the essence of Buddhism? What is the true truth?"

This is the *doshu* of Dogen.

Chukai!

Kaijo!

AUG. 15 / 9 P.M.

THE WISDOM WHICH VISITS

What is *doshu*? The subjective *genjo*.... When we express *genjo* objectively it is *doshu*, wisdom.

Wisdom is *genjo*, wisdom makes *genjo*.[11]

■

Wisdom and knowledge are not the same. In science knowledge is very important. In Zen Buddhism it is wisdom which is important. *Maka hannya haramita*. We are always repeating the sutra of *Maka Hannya Haramita*.[12] The perfect wisdom which visits us. *Genjo*, realization.

But we must not search for wisdom, for if you do, then it will not appear. You must not search outside for it.... I have said that satori comes from the outside; so some here are surely looking for it outside. Open the door. Where is it?.... This is an error.

When you abandon ego, when you become empty (*ku*), wisdom comes. But if you have a strong ego wisdom will not come.... In Japanese the word "wisdom" means to float.

Wisdom, satori, *hannya haramita*: sometimes these words have the same meaning. What is satori? It is perfect wisdom, *maka hannya haramita*. What is *maka hannya haramita*? It is Buddha himself.

■

So if the ego is strong wisdom will not come.

This afternoon the female American champion offered me a necklace. A beautiful necklace, a Buddha statue decoration.

She made it herself. But for me this necklace is not so interesting.... Anyway, I visited her in her room. She was not happy.
Her face was not Buddha. She was sulking. Why? She has not
changed at all since the other day. Even if she stays angry, her
hair will not grow back faster. She has no wisdom. Her ego is
strong, but if at this moment she were to abandon her ego, that
which was unfortunate before would become fortunate now.
Unhappiness becomes happiness. Through wisdom you can
change your state of mind. But this American girl has a strong
ego.

I always say that hair is a decoration. So when I give you
the ordination, I always say that at this time: cut the decoration.

If we are too attached to vanity, we sulk.... Two summers
ago I cut my secretary's hair short. She smiled. Her inside was
not so happy, but she did not sulk. If we abandon the ego and
attachments, satori, wisdom, arises—it floats. But if we are egoistic and have desires, and especially desires for the impossible, then this is not wisdom. This is foolishness. Most people
in daily life are attached to impossible desires. One's hair cannot be any longer, so we sulk. Wait half a year and it will be
longer. Cut your hair during the summer and by September it
will again be long.

■

To express *genjo*: this is *doshu*, wisdom. *Doshu* is wisdom.

To realize *genjo*: this is intuition. Intuition from the outside.
When intuition arises, understand it, control it, construct it,
and at this moment it becomes wisdom.

How can we obtain wisdom? People are always asking me
this question.... Kant did not reach wisdom. Western philosophy has not reached it.

Western philosophers always speak of reason and of understanding. The German words for this are *vernunft* and *verstand*.

German words are very precise…. These two words have different meanings. In English they mean, respectively, reason and understanding, and in French, *la raison et l'entendement*. Kant discussed this in his *Critic of Pure Reason*. Understanding is an intellectual faculty coming from the frontal brain. Reason is rationalism, logic; it is the faculty to know, to judge, to act.

Now in Buddhism we have intuition and wisdom, and to compare them is very interesting, very important. Intuition, wisdom, *Hannya Paramita, hishiryo*.

Zen and western philosophy are not the same.

■

Satori and intuition are not the same. Satori is sometimes the same as intuition, but it is not enlightenment. Intuition is spontaneous. Intuition means: to look outside, to look at the visible, to look at the cosmic order. So when you stop the frontal brain, *hishiryo*-consciousness arises. (At the bottom of non-thinking is thinking, non-thinking. How do we think non-thinking? This is *hishiryo*.)

But even if we do realize intuition (spontaneity), if we do not control this realization, if we do not put it into order, structure it, then this intuition finishes and only *genjo* (i.e., realization) remains.

In this way understanding becomes reason. Only *genjo*: only inside, individual certification.

Starting from intuition, from understanding, one must use control and structure; then it will become intellectual, or active. In order to speak one must use order. It is the same with writing. To express oneself through writing, it is necessary to be intellectual. So we have the expression *doshu*.

At this time we need wisdom. Knowledge comes from thinking, not from intuition—they are not the same—but reason becomes wisdom.

COMPANIONS IN SATORI

It is written in *Agama Sutra*—it is very difficult to translate this primitive sutra, but anyway, here's what Buddha said after he had sat under the Bodhi tree (in this sutra the Bodhi tree is called the Nirodha tree, which is its true name): "Indeed, without a partner, without a companion to respect, to venerate, to continue living is very difficult. With which Brahman (Hindu monk), with which Shaman (Buddhist monk), should I be intimate and respectful?"

This was Shakyamuni Buddha's doubt.

After sitting under the Bodhi tree he received a big satori. From the outside. It arrived, this satori, while he was looking at the morning star. *Mushotoku*. Without his waiting for it, spontaneously. But later, had Shakyamuni kept it to himself, then it (i.e., his awakening) would have only been *genjo*. It would not have been sufficient, not satisfying. So he wished to communicate it, to share it, with a companion. He wanted to have a spiritual companion. To express himself, to express his satori. *Doshu*.

Complete solitude is difficult. Complete solitude becomes individualism. And Buddha had a need to help others, to share his satori, to certify it through expression, through *doshu*. This is very important in Mahayana Buddhism: not to be alone in solitude. "*Gyatei, gyatei*," says the sutra. Go, go, together to the other shore of satori.

Originality is always solitude.... Buddha had his true originality. In *Shodoka* it is written that we always go alone, that the steps we take are alone. But companions in satori play together.... Alone our lives are solitary. During zazen we are alone. But we are also with others in the dojo. And we do zazen together. Our inside mind becomes solitary: we become quiet. With two hundred others.

Companions in satori can play together. So, the holy solitude of originality (of *genjo*) must be accepted by other spiritual, sympathetic companions. One needs to express one's originality of *genjo*.... It is this *doshu* which promotes my mission, which educates and which edits books through intellectual reasoning. Inside *genjo* must be expressed outside.

So Buddha got up from beneath the Bodhi tree and soon (thereafter) he met five Brahmans, five friends who had followed him when he escaped from the palace....[13]

When the subjective *genjo* is expressed objectively, then at this time Buddha's satori is certified perfectly.

Chukai!

(B., the *kyosakuman*, intones the *Hannya Shingyo*:)

"*Maka Hannya Hara...*" Stop. Now again. "*Maka Han...*" Again, again! "*Maka Ha...*" Again. But from the belly, not from the nose. "*Maka Hannya Haramita Shingyo-o-o-o...*'

AUG. 16 / 7.30 A.M.

Listen to the voice of the valley.

(The door giving out over the river Isère, at the far end of the dojo, is open and one can hear the murmur of the current running over the stones in the riverbed, and the master says: "Listen to the voice of the valley, the voice of the river." Just after he says this, someone gets up and closes the door. "Ah? Stop! Now we can no longer hear the voice of the valley!")

The flowing stream never stops. The stream is never tired. Its water is always changing, always impermanent. The bubbles float on the stagnant pond, sometimes vanishing, sometimes arising, and never remaining in one place.[14]

Our lives are like this. So are our minds, like the stream.

Open the door to the current. So we can hear the sound of the water. During zazen we can compare it with our minds. (The door is opened.)

■

In Buddhism Kannon is a very important Bodhisattva. Kannon is the Japanese for Avalokitesvara. *Kan* means observation, *non* means sound. He observes the sound.... of the drum of B. last night singing *Hannya Haramita*.

Do not make foolish sounds! (Sounds of many people blowing their noses.) There is no need to compete with one another in making these sounds. Make holy sounds. B.'s sutra voice is not so good, not so strong; but now he makes big noises.

The atmosphere of this dojo is not good. The *shusso* is responsible but he is no good. I just asked (i.e., signaled) the *kyosaku-men* to stand up but they haven't stood up. The *shusso* must direct them.

People who have not received the permission to take photos in the dojo must not do so. (A new person has gotten up to take photos.) This is not a photo studio.

BUDDHA FINDS HIS COMPANIONS
and his realization becomes expression

In our lives it is very difficult to live alone. Not just because of material reasons, but for spiritual reasons too. Even for those who go into the mountains to live it is not easy. Because most of us need love, compassion, sympathy, comprehension from others. Without this most people's lives would be of no value. Philosophy, literature, art cannot be created by themselves alone. Even if *genjo* exists, one is not happy if others do not see it. If *genjo* is not certified it has no value. Of course there is Saint-solitude. It exists. Complete solitude, ecstatic solitude. But this too must be certified objectively before its value is perfectly realized.... Poems, literature, art, thought, religion too, must be created from *genjo*—then they can be communicated (shared) with others by *doshu* and so spread through society.

So, after his great satori under the Bodhi tree, under the Nirodha tree, Buddha went off to find his friends (the five Brahmans who had escaped with him from the palace), but they were not so impressed with Buddha. These Brahmans were completely ascetic monks..., and Buddha had drunk milk brought to him by Sudiata. And too, he had touched the skin of Sudiata, a farmer's daughter. (Sudiata had brought help to Buddha; every morning she came to see him—she did not come at night—and she helped him.) So, the five Brahmans refused to follow Buddha's teaching. Because he was not pure. He had given up the practice of asceticism. He had broken the Hindu precepts. Nonetheless, in the face of this, Buddha was peaceful. He had obtained a great satori. He did not certify himself, but the great satori had visited him, had penetrated him. In the end these five Brahmans became disciples of Buddha.

■

So Buddha gave conferences and spread the teaching and this became *doshu*. His great satori, his original solitude, his aesthetic solitude became *genjo*, became *doshu*. This is expressed in his conferences. We sing it every morning when we sing *Bussho Kapila*. (Chants:) *Bussho Kapila, Jodo Makada, Seppo Harana, Nyumetsu Kuchira*.... Buddha's life was very simple: He was born in Kapila, he got satori at Magada, he taught in Harana, and he died in Kuchira. This is all. *C'est tout.* His life was entirely **dokan.**

Dokan means: repetition, repetition in daily life. To repeat zazen, ceremony, *samu*, zazen, ceremony, *samu*. And so it becomes a habit. The body becomes spontaneous. And so you have wisdom. There is no need for the frontal brain.

■

Zazen is not a matter of steps. It is not a training in steps. Yoga people are always saying that zazen is of too high a dimension; and that steps are necessary at first. Mr. Blitz,[15] who is involved in the education of forty people at Zinal this summer, said to me that yoga is a step towards zazen. Steps are necessary, he said. First step, second step.... I replied that zazen is a cablecar; it takes us rapidly and automatically to the top, it takes us seated to the top of the mountain.

It is not necessary for us to use our own proper will power. Use the cablecar, and with its power we are quickly on the mountain. Unconsciously, naturally, automatically. Zazen is not *shuzen*,[16] zazen is not mortification, it is not a training in steps.

(Recites *Fukanzazengi*.) I always repeat this statement from *Fukanzazengi* during the final two *sesshins*: Zazen is not *shuzen*, it is the Dharma-gate to peacefulness, to true liberty. It attains to *Bodhi* (wisdom). Practiced and certified, it attains to *Bodhi-satori*, to perfect wisdom.

■

Koans are eternal truths. Even eternal truth exists. Even God exists. If you do zazen then *genjo* is realized; the koans are realized; Buddha is realized. Our freedom then becomes exactly like the dragon who enters the water, or like the tiger who enters into the mountain. Such will be your freedom; it will be complete.

Those who wish to receive the *kyosaku*, please ask for it.

Today we rest for the *sesshin*. Tonight it is not permitted that you go to the Santa Lucia. You must sleep. Those who are tired during *sesshins*, the cause is not from too much zazen, but from too much drinking. And too much dancing. Some of the permanents drink and dance until five in the morning. This is not possible. I must give you the *rensaku*. This is not the Club Méditerranée. Some here become strong through zazen, and then they lose their energy by going in many directions. Control is necessary.

Time is like an arrow, like the stream in the valley. It flows by quickly.

Chukai!

Kaijo! (Drum.)

Everyone here is completely tired! Drum! Drum!

AUG. 18 / 7 A.M.

The next two-and-a-half days is the *sesshin*. A true *sesshin*, not a preparation. This is the third *sesshin*, and after this one there is only one more left. The permanents and some others have been here since the beginning of July, along with myself. But most of you are only attending this third camp, and you will be leaving in three days.

Why have you come here, why have you taken the train up here to Val d'Isère?

THE WAVES STRIKE AND THE WAVES BREAK

Our lives are just like a trip to the coffin. From one hole to another. Out from the mother's opening, and into a hole in the earth. During the trip much phenomena arises. But you are thinking only of food and of sex and you forget about the hole at the end.

When we look at the landscape from the window of the train, it appears as if it is the landscape moving—we forget that it is the train itself which is moving—and so we forget that our object in traveling is to arrive at the station at the end of the line....

During these last ten days of preparation for this *sesshin*, there was no preparation....

I want to give the first *kyosaku*: the *rensaku*. To three people. One is for the young American female champion. But she hasn't come to zazen today. She is sleeping.

One person makes a mistake and it influences the others. With enough mistakes this will become like the Club Méditerranée.

Another girl here cut the American girl's hair.[17] So they fought. The cause for the haircutting and the fight was over a young American boy. All three should receive the *rensaku*. The cutting of hair has to do with the seeking of the way, but they never think of this.[18] They only cut hair for play. This is not good.

The American girl wants to leave. She has forgotten her goal. If the train stops for a bit in a tiny station on the way, and we step down on the quai for a moment, we forget the train.

■

Don't move, don't move.

Don't forget the course of the train. Don't forget the object, don't forget the station. You have only two-and-a-half days left here.

Some of you are sleeping, sleeping. Do not continue as though you were still in your beds. Those who are sleepy must receive the *kyosaku*.

(*Kinhin:*) You must not look at the others' faces when you are in *kinhin*…. Stretch your knees, stretch your necks.

(Zazen:) Last night was the full moon. It was very beautiful. It rose above the top of the mountain and I could see it from my window. It rose over the top and lit up the mountain. Then clouds passed in front of it and covered up the light of the moon.

We all possess Buddha's nature. Original mind is exactly like the light of the moon, of the full moon. Completely bright, shining. But sometimes clouds come and some minds become dark, dark.

(Chants from *Sanshodoei*.) This is Dogen's poem entitled "Zazen." What is zazen?

> Upon the water of my mind without dirtiness
> The moon which is clean
> The water of mind without dirtiness
> Even the waves break and they become bright
>   with light.[19]

The first phrase is zazen. The moon means the zazen posture, zazen mind, *hishiryo*. The waves mean *bonnos*, delusion, the subconscious, bad karma, which arise during zazen. For example *kontin* and *sanran*.[20] The light means satori. The waves arrive and illusion comes, and so we think of many things. Of what we are going to eat for lunch and so on. But continue zazen and the waves will break; they will pass on, pass on, and there will be light, illumination.

The light means satori; but this does not mean enlightenment. Satori is not enlightenment—as the word (enlightenment) is used and understood in Christianity. Satori is the return to our original, normal condition. This is *hishiryo* consciousness.

Chukai!

After the ceremony we will have a procession outside. Everyone is to follow, quickly. The *kyosakumen* are to take up the rear to keep the order.

Kaijo!

AUG. 18 / 10.30 A.M.

MONDO

Big satori or small?

QUESTION: You said that Buddha had a great satori. What I would like to know is if there are degrees in satori.

Master: Degrees are not necessary. What is my degree now? It is of no use to think of degrees, nor to compare yourself with others. Because there are many kinds of satori. And besides, what is a big satori, a small satori? Which satori is the deeper? To make a comparison here is not possible.

"I must wash the toilet and arrange the shoes outside the dojo"—this is necessary, and if you realize this necessity and practice it, then this too is satori. A little one, but a great one. Understand this objectively and it will be big and deep.

Some people only understand the necessity of arranging shoes, and subjectively they have a great satori. But objective and subjective understanding is not the same, and one cannot compare the two.

Master Kyogen got satori objectively when he heard the sound made by a stone hitting a bamboo. But objectively speaking the sound is not so important. He got satori.... Master **Gensha** hurt his toe while traveling, and he wondered: "From where comes this pain?" and he got a big satori. Everybody wounds themselves, but they don't then get satori. But he did.

Such a thing cannot be measured or described in degrees, subjectively or objectively. Understand?

In Tibetan Buddhism, in Yoga, in most religions they make steps. But not so in Zen. If you obtain true understanding, subjectively, then no steps are necessary. Another question? Monsieur?

Now is an inhalation, an exhalation

QUESTION: The important thing in zazen is here and now. What is the temporal time dimension of now?

Master: It is the instant, now. This moment now. But this instant now has already passed. This instant does not in reality exist.

So during zazen: now I breathe in, now I exhale. Concentration is on one breath after the other.

The instant, the right now, does not exist. Because the moment we think of the moment, it has already passed. The true now does not exist. This is important. So I say "point." Like connecting points in geometry—they make a line. If we concentrate on this point, which is related to the other points (in the line), it becomes a great concentration. Another question?

Christian enlightenment

QUESTION: Earlier you made a comparison with Christian enlightenment, saying that it was negative in Christianity. But what understanding do you have of Christianity to make such a comparison?

Master: Yes, I compare…. We all have a good occasion now to grasp the difference…. Yes madame, you must explain it to us.

Madame: Enlightenment is the meeting of God and the creature of God.

Master: Ah yes, communion. I studied it.

Father Lassalle[21] wrote books on this subject, but he too is mistaken. Lassalle is not so deep concerning the true satori of Soto Zen.

I know both, so I can compare. But which is better, ah this I cannot say—nor did I say. Because the object is not the same.

In Christianity one wishes to communicate with God, yes? So when one communicates with God one gets satori. This is enlightenment, yes?

Madame: You are wrong. One cannot use words to describe this matter!

Master: If we do not use words we cannot discuss this matter. Yes? So what does enlightenment mean, what is true enlightenment?

The words enlightenment and satori are different in meaning and they cannot be translated.

But I do not translate the words enlightenment and satori. Satori is satori, enlightenment is enlightenment. Which is better? On this point I make no comment. For those who believe in enlightenment, enlightenment is better. Understand?

Madame: Yes, of course I understand!

Master: So there. These words cannot be translated.

On this point, though, many masters have made mistakes. Enlightenment is enlightenment.

To think during zazen that, "I must get enlightenment" is foolish.... But during prayer, perhaps it is alright to think this way. It is the Christian method.

A good question, madame.

Even Father Lassalle is mistaken here. During zazen he always seeks to communicate. "Ah, today it almost happened!" He wrote me this. It was very funny! "Now, now it is possible to get satori. Right now it is arising. Ah no.... I don't understand." (Sensei laughs.)

Me too, I don't understand what he is talking about!

If you continue zazen without eating, without sleeping, continue the *sesshin* for one week, for ten days, then surely you can see God. If you create an image of God—"This is my God, this is my Christ"—if you imagine this, and if you wish to meet with Him, then you can. It is very easy.

The brain becomes very sharp, and then it becomes tired and sick. And it is at this point that illusions arise, illusions of Buddha. Many people have experienced this. It is not so difficult to do. In one week or in ten days you will realize this. "I must meet with my father, with my mother." It is possible.

I experienced this. For three months I did zazen with only *genmai* (rice soup) and without sleep. My mind became special and anything was possible. Even a sound, a drop of dew falling....

But this is not true zazen. It is a bit crazy. It is only the arising of special mental phenomena. But sleep well and everything will return back to normal and it will all have seemed like a dream. It is like a dream.

Anyway, madame, after the *sesshin* is over you will no longer meet with God, with Buddha. Beefsteak will be better then. Understand? No? She cannot understand.

If you wish to meet with God, then it is with your imagination that you will meet with Him. But you must first have an object, an image of Him. If you do not imagine this in your head, then you will not meet with anyone, with anything. "This is God which has come to me." What has come to you? Only something of your own category.

Madame: It is not a question of seeking outside, of ideas. It is a question of grace, given by the outside.

Master: For it to be given, you must first imagine it.

If you do not seek something, will you experience it? (No reply.)

In the end they are both identical. This is better than seeking. For then surely it will come.

Even if we do not seek grace, today it comes. You feel God. Automatically and spontaneously. Which is the better of the two? It is better, I always say, when it comes from the outside, when God is realized spontaneously. It is possible; but this is your subconscious thinking. Grace which comes from the outside is a subjective matter. Psychologically speaking it is an objective matter. Yet they can be the same.

When the subconscious realizes, then you can see. The same as a dream. It is realized by the brain, by the subconscious. And so too with enlightenment. Even if you do not want to see, you see. Buddha is realized. I have experienced this.

In religion this is a very high stage: to communicate with Buddha or with God. But this is a special condition of the brain, and you must be beyond this. Such a state is not true wisdom.

I always say that we should return to the true normal condition of the brain, then true wisdom can manifest itself. See Buddha or Christ and our brain is not in its true normal condition, but in a special one. But people like this state. "I see Buddha! I have attained enlightenment!" This is a special state which is never permanent—it is not the normal condition. We cannot perpetuate special mental conditions; from such conditions true wisdom cannot arise.

Here is one of the differences existing between Christianity and Zen. Western philosophers and theologians are always transcending a special consciousness. They always seek to go up, up, up.

But in the end they fall down. They become crazy. If you understand this then you will be able to understand Dogen's Zen.

Most people wish to arrive at a special condition. During my three months *sesshin* my mind became completely pure and even the merest smell, of a toilet, of the blood of someone entering the room, became strong. The mind is so pure (when in this condition) that you can understand the minds of others.

You can even see behind yourself. Everything is then possible.

This is not transcendental consciousness; yet this is the level people seek. And when they are there (Sensei taps his forehead), they are fit only for the mental hospital.... Most people cannot understand that one must be beyond this state, and so they search for it, search for it, and finally, because they cannot always continue in this state, they become completely sick in the head.

Buddha experienced this too. For six years. But in the end, when he was completely exhausted and half-dead, he realized that this was wrong. It is from this experience that Buddhism came about. Do you understand?

Madame (assuming a stance of defiance): Of course I understand. But this is not what I am seeking.

Master: What do you seek? (No reply.) You must clear your head of prejudices. Prejudices are not good in religion, in Christianity, in Zen.

Madame: I read your book and I came here without prejudice.

Master: But you have plenty. It is not necessary to compare, but (rather) to grasp the essence. What is the essence of religion?

Buddha, too, sought complete purity. For six years he practiced without eating, without sleeping, right up to the point of death. But he could not find what he was looking for and he completely fell down, almost dead. Sudiata, a farmer's daughter, arrived at this time carrying a jug of milk on her head. She looked at his face and saw that it was noble, and she took him in her arms and carried him under the Bodhi tree. She massaged him and gave him milk and he awoke and sat up.

It was from this moment that Buddha's mind changed. Due to the milk. Milk is utterly forbidden in Hinduism, and by drinking it, Buddha had completely wiped away six years of mortification. And his stomach and intestines were happy. His body too. And his mind as well. His mind had completely changed....

He continued zazen every day, and every day Sudiata came to see him. And he looked at her. (During his mortification Buddha was not allowed to look at a woman's face.) But now he looked, and he thought: "She is very beautiful." He had returned to the normal condition. He smelled her: "A fine smell, a nice perfume." He touched her skin: "Not so bad, either." Buddha understood that he had returned to his normal condition, and in this condition a deep joy arose. At this moment he had satori, and it was then that he saw his practice of mortification was a mistake. "I was expecting something, something special, an enlightenment. It was a mistake." And this is why Buddha separated himself from Hinduism. Do you understand, Madame?

Not yet? Continue to do zazen, this is better. Then you will come back to the normal condition and you will understand. Your question, Madame, was good. This is a point that many Christians have not been able to resolve. Satori and enlightenment. If you resolve this matter (not with your head) then you will be able to compare, and you will be able to understand true enlightenment.

The normal condition

QUESTION: What does it mean "to come back to the normal condition?"

Master: It means the normal condition. When the brain physiologically, psychologically becomes truly quiet.

But when you are a little crazy you are not in the normal condition. In the last *sesshins* some people in the *mondos* here were in a completely abnormal condition. And in this *sesshin* it is the same. There are some who are not normal here, like the American champion. It is their karma arising.

Everyone has karma, in the brain too, in the subconscious. Thoughts, anxiety, fear, become implanted more and more deeply in the neurons of the brain. These thoughts come to the surface during the day, in dreams, and particularly during zazen. Once these seeds have arisen, then there is nothing: finished. But to come by this is very difficult, because these dreams of today go back for instance to seeds implanted ten and twenty years ago. So it is not easy to have a completely pure brain.

But with the frontal brain at rest (not thinking) the subconscious surfaces and its contents (seeds) escape, the neurons become quiet, the brain is at rest, and the normal condition appears.

To seek for something during zazen is not good. If you seek for something, the seeds in the neurons of the brain only increase.... But if you practice my teaching exactly, if you concentrate on the posture, your thinking will stop. (Sensei, who is sitting with the *kotsu*[22] in his hand, puts it down and takes up the zazen posture.) Concentrate on the posture, with the hands exactly like this, and rapidly your thinking will stop. When you are like this the alpha waves appear on the electroencephalogram.[23]

The subconscious arises. Because you can no longer think. You try to think: "I must communicate with God," but you cannot. It is no longer possible to think like this, because if you do, then without a doubt your thumbs will drop. (Sensei drops his thumbs.) Like this. The moment you begin to imagine things, this happens. (Sensei rolls up his eyes like a caricature of someone thinking of God.) Others think the opposite, that God is not coming to them, and their thumbs are like this. (Thumbs up.) "God is not coming," he thinks and he is not happy.

So it is not possible to keep the posture and think at the same time. The subconscious arises, you become clean, you are back in the normal condition. Automatically and spontaneously.[24]

This is why after zazen everyone is brilliant. Their brains have rested and their karma has decreased. Their eyes are bright, and their faces too. People who continue zazen change. Those who escape zazen, their faces change too.... Another question?

Originality is individuality

QUESTION: I knew nothing of zazen three months ago. But then one night I had a dream that I was looking at one of your books, and at your name on the book, and this is why I came.

Master: I am very happy. What were you doing in this dream?
Answer: We were talking over matters together and you said to me: "You have had enough with individuality! Now you must learn with others collectively." I replied that I did not agree with you about "finishing with individuality."
Master: This is the karma of westerners. So?
Answer: So, you did not reply.
Master: A good dream, an historical dream. Write it down.

What's your name? Ah, Monique. Monique's are always good. The first person to receive me in Europe was named Monique. At the Gare du Nord. But you are very beautiful. Where are you from? Ah yes, Brussels. How old are you? Thirty-seven? You had a good experience. Have you a question?
Monique: Yes, on this question of individuality, on the question of becoming more yourself....
Master: Individuality and a strong ego are not the same. To return to your originality is individuality. Originality is not karma—it is not bad karma, it is good. But each person is different, and you are only you. You are your own originality. This is what I call true mind. If you cut the bad karma, good karma remains: your originality. You must discover your own originality. This is zazen.

You must not abandon your originality.

In modern education everyone is educated the same, and so his true originality cannot be realized. With mass production, mass education, even the parents themselves cannot find the true originality in their own children. But it is difficult to find. The educators cannot find it.

Zen Teachings of Master Taisen Deshimaru

But I can find it—by looking at you from behind. Everyone has his originality, and I can seize it.... Continue zazen and our true originality will realize itself. Realize this and you will become strong. Anyway, this is the duty of religion, the duty of the true educator (i.e., to help people find their originality).

Most people make mistakes concerning "I," "me." These people have too strong an ego, a bad ego, and they are too attached to it, and this is why they cannot find their true originality.

Find your true originality and you will become truly distinguished.

Modern education has forgotten this, that each person is different. In the universities they teach only the sciences....

You had a good dream, Monique. Another question?

By looking in the mirror

QUESTION: When, during zazen, we become afraid of abandoning this ego, what is the correct attitude of mind to take?

Master: "I must abandon the ego"—it is not necessary to think this. Just do zazen and you will abandon it.

But if you think: "This is my bad karma," and you realize this, then this is good karma. Then little by little you will come to understand. You will understand: through my *kusens* (oral teachings); by looking in the mirror. You see the form of your face appear.

4 P.M.

THE WRITINGS OF DOGEN, THE MONDOS OF RINZAI

Today is fine weather. Like on the Mediterranean coast, in Cannes or Nice. Which is better, to sit by the sea or to continue zazen in this dojo? Those who seek their pleasure by the sea or at the Club Méditerranée will not know, right up until they enter their coffin, what is the true life, the true cosmic order. But you know.

■

Here is a *mondo* with Mayoku (or Hotetsu, a disciple fo Baso). One day Mayoku was using a fan when a monk said to him: "Wind is everywhere; it is not necessary to use a fan, so why are you using one?" Master Mayoku replied: "Although you know that the nature of the wind never changes, you do not know the meaning of blowing everywhere."

"Well, then," said the monk, "what does it mean?"

Mayoku continued to fan himself and did not reply.

This is how Dogen writes.... (Now here is a *mondo* from *Rinzai Roku:*) Master Mayoku came to Rinzai for an interview, and spreading out his *zagu* (prostration cloth), he asked Rinzai: "Of the twelve heads of Kannon which is the true one?"

Rinzai, who liked theater, came down from his seat, picked up the *zagu* with one hand, grabbed Mayoku with the other, and said: "The twelve-headed Kannon, where is she now?"

Mayoku twisted his body and made as if to climb up on Rinzai's seat. Rinzai then lifted his *hossu* and hit him. Mayoku grabbed the *hossu* and both went up together to Rinzai's room.

THE KATSU MONDO

Rinzai asked a monk about the four kinds of *katsu*. (Rinzai's *katsus*, i.e., shouts, are very famous and there exist many kinds of sounds.)[25] "So Rinzai said to the monk: 'Sometimes a *katsu* is like the precious sword of the Vajra king; sometimes a *katsu* is like a golden-maned lion crouching on the ground'"—this means that the first *katsu* is sharp like a sword and can cut everything, and the second *katsu* is like the roar of a lion. When the lion roars one hundred animal-brains break—this statement is from *Shodoka*.[26]

The third kind of *katsu* is a... is a... (Sensei lifts the *Rinzai Roku* text closer to his face, then reads the phrase verbatim:) "...is like a probing pole to which a grass bushel is fastened to cast shade." (General laughter.)[27]

Oh, I cannot understand this English! English books are no good....

What this means is to test, to measure. Rinzai uses this *katsu* when he wants to see the other's face; this *katsu* is the measure by which he tests another. When Rinzai utters a *katsu*, he studies the partner's face so that he can see, can understand, the other's mind.

(When I, myself, shout, some people are quickly afraid and run away. Some smile. My secretary is used to this now and sometimes when I shout she says: "You want something, Sensei? You want some tea?")

So, Rinzai asked the monk: "How do you understand this?" The monk hesitated and Rinzai gave a *kwat!*: "Which of those four *katsus* is this one?" Rinzai asked.

This is a koan. It is the koan known as the Foolish Koan. This is what Rinzai Zen is like. Always *kwat!* Like ducks. It is a training method.[28]

∎

Here is a *mondo* between Rinzai and a great nun. (Nuns in the past were not so weak; they were strong like French women.) "So Rinzai said to the nun: 'Welcome? Not welcome?'"

(Sensei addresses one of his disciples sitting in zazen:) Mireille, if Rinzai spoke to you this way, what would you reply?

"Anyway, this nun replied with a strong *katsu: Kwat!*

Rinzai held up his stick and said: 'Quickly, speak, speak!'

The nun replied: '*Kwat!*'"[29]

In the end this nun was not so clever. Why hadn't she taken away Rinzai's *kotsu*, since it was clear that he was going to hit her with it?

A famous book of commentaries on *Rinzai Roku* written by an historic Rinzai master asks this question. And Dogen, too, writes on this *mondo*: he says that nuns should not use *katsus*, but that they should remain more quiet. Quietly, quietly, and so teach from behind. This is the true woman.

■

Patience. Some people here are in pain. Some are sleeping, sleeping.

Don't move, don't move.

AUG. 18 / 4 P.M.

MONDO

Layman P'ang

QUESTION: What is your opinion of Layman P'ang?

Master: Who?

QUESTION: You don't know Layman P'ang? Dogen has written about him.

Master: I know Dogen's work. It must be your pronounciation.

QUESTION: Dogen wrote that Layman P'ang was foolish.

Master: Foolish?
Philippe Coupey (interrupts): Sensei, this woman is referring to a book called *A Man of Zen* which deals with a Chinese Buddhist layman called P'ang who lived around 800 and who is famous for having put all his things—all his money and furniture—in a boat, which he sank in the middle of a lake. Then he went off begging.
Master: Yes, now I understand. No, Dogen admired P'ang. This story about P'ang impressed me too. I remember now. Philippe Coupey explained it clearly to me and now I know whom you mean.

P'ang never became a monk. He received the bodhisattva ordination. And before that he had been a great governor and very rich. But he continued to practice zazen and he was always making bamboo baskets.

"You have so much money," people were always saying to P'ang, "You should give some of it as a *fuse* to the temple. You must help the poor." "No, no, no," P'ang would reply. And in the end he took all his money and possessions and threw them into the ocean. Interesting, yes?

People are always wanting to give, give, give. But he was even beyond that.

So later, after he had thrown away his entire fortune, people said to him: "What you did was not at all useful! Why did you do that?"

"Because I do not want to spoil others. I did not give it to the temple because I did not want to spoil the monks; and I did not give it to the poor because I did not want to spoil them either."

So this is why P'ang threw his fortune down to the bottom of the ocean. This is very deep; it is historical.

When P'ang was a child, one of the other children with him fell into a huge glass watertank. The child began to drown and none of the other children knew how to swim, and no one knew what to do. What would you have done? P'ang broke the tank with a big rock and the boy was saved. The tank was very expensive and it was huge and it held a lot of water, but what P'ang did was wise. It is a deep koan.

A relationship exists between the breaking of this watertank and the sinking of his fortune in water. It is a deep koan.

In any case, gifts sometimes spoil people. "You must help the poor. Help the hippies; they are so pitiful, help them, help them." Yes, P'ang's was a deep education.... Sometimes a slap is better. Another question?

■

Master: Alors? Mademoiselle, a question?

Mademoiselle: Yes, could you please explain to me the connection between thinking everyday of death, and to be living here and now?

Master: The same. Life and death are the same.

But think, "I must live, live, live," then you are attached to life. But think: "Now I must die," and your life will be deeper. Do you understand? Yes. Very good.

■

QUESTION: How must we educate our children?

Master: It is like flying a kite. It is difficult to fly a kite. Pull the string too hard and the kite will fall. Let the string go too loose and it will still fall.

In modern times parents spoil their children. Many of you here are spoiled—you were spoiled as children.

But too much severity is no good either.

Another question? Philippe? What is it?

Companions Everywhere

Philippe: You said that after Buddha got his big satori, he had a need for *doshu* (he wanted to express his satori), and for this he needed companions....

Master: Yes, yes, companions.

Philippe: When you first arrived in this foreign country you were alone and without any satori-companions. Well, were you lonely, was it hard?

Master: I had many, and now even more. Madame Monnot arrived. She sat for my first conference. And the next day she visited me and I gave her a massage. Madame Monnot was impressed, and not just by the massage. And then many others came to me right after her. The famous singer, the actress, then Etienne, Malika, Liliane. Everywhere companions are possible.

Though I couldn't understand the language, I thought that the French were better than the Japanese. There is no karma.... It is more difficult to educate your own family, because with your own family you are too intimate, and karma is complicated.

Everyone in Japan understands Zen. They do not understand it, but... Europeans are fresh, they connect with zazen quickly and directly.... It is the same with love. With your own family it is not possible.[30]

Here it is fresher. Only the essence. (Sensei opens his fist in a gesture of a bud bursting into bloom:) *Paf! I shin den shin.*[31]

Earth becomes old and planting becomes very difficult. But when the earth changes, it is fresher. In India, in China, in Japan, the earth became old. So the planting is not fresh. I brought the true fresh seed to Europe. After (Buddhism grew weak in) India, Bodhidharma brought the seed to China. At this time India was completely down. While China, its culture, was very high. The Chinese civilization was the highest of all civilizations, and much higher than now. Its intellecual level was the highest in the world.

Buddhism is high dimension and it needs high-class people. So after the Indian, Chinese and Japanese civilizations, comes the European one (Sensei makes the gesture of climbing a ladder, then he makes the gesture of planting a seed, and then of the speed sprouting:) and now *pop!*

This was my plan.

But American people are a bit, a bit.... (Sensei taps his forehead and looks at Philippe) What do you think?

Philippe: Well, I think the American earth is the freshest of all!

Master: Yes, yes, America is fresher. America accepts.

I am very interested: which one **accepts**, America or Europe? Japanese people are very interested in this. It is an interesting problem.... But you came here! You came from America. Why?
Philippe: Because you're here.
Master: You write books. Your work is very important, it is historical. Your position is completely historical.

AUG. 18 / 8.30 P.M.

FUKE'S KOLOMO WAS HIS COFFIN

Tonight's kusen is on the last chapter of *Rinzai Roku*. This chapter deals with Fuke and Rinzai.

Fuke is famous today in Japan for his use of the *shakuachi* (flute), but originally Fuke was famous for his use of a little handbell which he rang in the streets.

Fuke wanted to become a monk, so he went about the streets asking people for a black *kolomo* (monk's robe). Many people gave him *kolomos*, as a *fuse* (gift). But he was not pleased with these *kolomos*, they were no good. So he went to Rinzai's temple and Rinzai, who was waiting for him, said to Fuke: "I have made a special *kolomo* for you. It is for your ordination. It is a very beautiful *kolomo* and certainly you will be able to wear it."

Fuke: "Where is this *kolomo*?"

Rinzai: "Come into my room and I will show it to you." And Rinzai showed Fuke the special *kolomo* he had made for him—

it was a coffin of superior quality. "Here," Rinzai said, "this is a good *kolomo* for you."

When Fuke saw the coffin he was very happy. "Yes, this is a very good *kolomo*." (Fuke was completely abnormal.)

So Fuke carried off this *kolomo*, this coffin, on his shoulders. He returned to the marketplace calling out loudly: "Rinzai made this *kolomo* for me. So now I am going off to the East Gate to enter transformation (to die)."

Many people came to watch. But once at the East Gate, Fuke said: "Today's not so good. Tomorrow. This East Gate is not so good either, so tomorrow I will go to the South Gate."

The next day everybody was at the South Gate waiting for Fuke. They were certain that today Fuke would die, so they waited. Fuke arrived with his coffin and sat inside it. Then he said: "The direction of this gate is no good either," and he got out of the coffin.

This pattern went on for three days. No one believed him anymore (he was just a liar) and on the fourth day, when Fuke arrived at the North Gate, there were no spectators waiting for him. (Nevertheless) he went out beyond the city walls, put down the coffin and climbed in. A traveler happened by and Fuke asked him to nail down the top of the coffin over him. "I want to die in this coffin, so when I am laying down inside you must nail it closed."

"*D'accord* (okay)," said the traveler.

"And tell them in the streets that Fuke died today at the North Gate."

The news spread quickly and soon a crowd of people arrived. They opened the coffin and found that the body had vanished. But from high up in the sky they heard the ringing of his hand-bell.

This is the last sentence of *Rinzai Roku*. Very interesting. Only the ringing of the bell.... Where is Fuke now? A mystery. Magic.

No, this is not a mystery, this is not magic. This is literature.

Poetry.... *Rinzai Roku* is not so bad sometimes. This last sentence is very interesting.

◼

Rinzai always criticizes Fuke: "He is too *zusan*, too *zusan*." And Dogen always criticizes Rinzai the same way: "Too *zusan*, too *zusan*."

Where is the true Zen? You must decide.

AUG. 19 / 7 A.M.

THE ESSENCE OF BUDDHISM:
Inside or outside the sutras?

(*Kinhin*:) Stretch the knees, stretch the neck. When you exhale, press down on the intestines, on the *kikai tanden*. During the exhalation, press the foot down on the ground, stretch the waist and press the hands together.

◼

(Zazen:) Master Rinzai has said that the Buddha's sutras are but toilet paper, and that one must not become attached to them. This is somewhat true. But the sutras are not toilet paper. Sutras should be read and they should be believed and respected. (Herein) lies the difference between Dogen and Rinzai.

Kyoge betsuden: the true essence of Buddhism exists outside the sutras. This *kyoge betsuden* was the slogen of Rinzai Zen.

Do not depend on the word, on the letter, on the phrase: true. One must not become attached to the word, to the sutra. Dogen recognized this. *I shin den shin* is the essence of Zen. Yet both are necessary. Sometimes one must follow the sutras, sometimes one must follow the master. This is a method for obtaining satori.

THE GREAT ZEN CLASSICS
and the Shin Jin Mei

Sosan, the 3rd Patriarch after Bodhidharma, wrote *Shin Jin Mei* and **Yoka Daishi** wrote *Shodoka*. They wrote these texts to show the true Zen of Bodhidharma. These two texts are the same in Soto as in Rinzai; they are both important. But after the 6th Patriarch the line separated, and the Nangaku line became that of Rinzai.

Sandokai by Sekito and *Hokyo Zan Mai* by Tosan (both of which were written after the split in the line had occurred) are the true bibles of Soto Zen. These two works are chanted every morning after zazen. Then they are followed by *Hannya Shingyo* or some other sutra. This is so throughout the ten thousand Soto temples in Japan.

In the Rinzai temples they read *Shin Jin Mei* and *Hannya Shingyo*.

■

Shin jin means faith. (*Shin* is to believe; *jin* is mind, heart; and the *mei* of *Shin Jin Mei* means inscription). So *shin jin* is to believe in the essence of Buddha's nature in our minds, to believe in the essence of mind, of true mind.[32]

From this comes many things. In the *mondo* a woman asked which was better: to believe in Buddha's mind or to believe in God's mind? To compare is impossible. Buddha's and God's

201

mind are very close. But people want to make categories and so mind narrows, narrows.

Shin Jin Mei consists of 584 *kanjis* (ideograms), of 146 phrases (one phrase consisting in 4 *kanjis*), and in it is included the essence of five thousand or six thousand sutras. The source of the koans of the Chinese patriarchs—of seventeen hundred koans—is *Shin Jin Mei.*

In Rinzai **Hekigan Roku** is a more useful and a more important collection of koans than in *Rinzai Roku.* And many koans in *Hekigan Roku* come from *Shin Jin Mei.* For example the second koan, the Joshu koan; and also the fifty-seventh koan, the fifty-eighth, the fifty-ninth—all these koans are just phrases taken from *Shin Jin Mei.*

Shin Jin Mei is the oldest and most sacred work in Zen.... Bodhidharma did not write a book. Nor did Eka. But Sosan wrote *Shin Jin Mei.*

Master Dogen used many phrases from *Shin Jin Mei* in his *Shobogenzo.* If we cannot understand *Shin Jin Mei,* then we cannot understand *Shobogenzo.* So master Keisan, the 4th Patriarch after Dogen, wrote his commentaries on *Shin Jin Mei;* they are very deep and are now very famous.

Master Shinran[33] says in a poem that people who have true faith (*shin jin*) are the same as Buddha.

The great *shin jin,* the believing mind, is the Buddha's Way. This is God. Buddha's nature is God itself. (In Christianity God and man are always separated, always in dualism. In Buddhism all people have Buddha's nature—so people become Buddha.)

SOSAN'S BIOGRAPHY

Shin Jin Mei appeared thirteen hundred years ago…. Sosan,[34] who was completely covered with leprosy (he had a very bad karma) went to visit Eka's dojo. "My karma is not good," he said to Eka. (Bad karma becomes exactly leprosy.) "I want to confess everything," Sosan said to Eka.

"You must let out your crimes," Eka replied. "What is a crime? What is good, what is bad? The cause is not karma. There is no crime, there is no karma. Do not be attached to them, to your crimes, your sins…" And Eka gave Sosan the ordination.

Sosan then did zazen every day. And through zazen his leprosy left him, and his body completely changed. This is Sosan's biography, only this.[35]

Later a great and famous Emperor in Chinese history, Emperor Genso, gave Sosan the name "Great Master Kanshi." Kanshi Sosan.

"*Hishiryo*" comes from *Shin Jin Mei*. What is *Hishiryo*?

10.30 A.M.

FAITH IS NON-DOUBT

The **shin** of *Shin Jin Mei* has two meanings; one is to believe and the other is faith. The faith of enlightenment, of satori, of Buddha and of God are the same and are not the same. *Shin* is active faith, active belief; it is also mind, passive mind. For me

God and Buddha are the same, while for others, for Christians, they are not at all the same. The names are different.

People who are attached to God, escape Buddha; people who are attached to Buddha escape God. But be unattached and all can be embraced.

I have faith in zazen, I have faith in the *kesa* (monk's robe). Your living postures are better than Buddha statues. On entering the dojo after you are all seated I always do *sampai* (prostration), not only for the statue of Kodo Sawaki on the altar, but for your postures, for your living postures.... I do not have so much faith in your physical comportment (i.e., outside of zazen), but when we do *sampai* together after zazen and before breakfast then we have a respectful mind. Then we can feel each essential mind in each mind.[36]

■

In Buddhism God and Buddha are not the same. In *Maka Hannya Haramitsu Sutra*, *ku* (emptiness), which is its essence, means existence without numenon, without substance. So Buddha has no substance, only *ku*. But the Christian God has substance—one fixed soul which lives for eternity.

Non-doubt, this is faith. I am connected with the earth, with the cosmos, with all existences. This is true faith in Zen.

It is not necessary to see God, to imagine him, we are already connected with him. God lives always in our mind. This is faith.

We must believe in this connection. So I say that the zazen posture itself is Buddha. If you steal something from someone, at this time you are immediately a thief. It is not necessary to go to prison to be a thief. For exactly at this moment you are already one.

So with zazen. When you do zazen, at this time you become Buddha. Believe in God and at this time you are connected with him. This is Buddha's mind, God's mind.

Right unto the coffin some people doubt. So God escapes.

■

If we use philosophical or Buddhist words to express mind then it becomes more complicated. So Rinzai said that sutras are but toilet paper. The essence of mind, finally, cannot be explained at all. Because it is the *ku* of *Hannya Shingyo*, which is existence without substance.

So Rinzai says: *Kwat! Kwat!*

And then the disciples imitate Rinzai and it all becomes ceremony, formalism.

When a disciple intimates Rinzai's *kwat!* it is a trace. When a horse walks he leaves hoof tracks. A dog leaves paw tracks, a cock or a duck leaves cock or duck tracks. There are many tracks. Kant tracks, Hegel tracks, Spinoza tracks.

Even if they run after the trace, they will not catch their true substance.

In *Kongo Kyo* (*The Diamond Sutra*), it is written that when we do not stop on a trace, then at this moment true mind arises.

Rid ourselves of our dirt, of our bad karma, and true purity is realized.

What is true happiness? Our mind thinks that happiness is to become rich, to eat fine food, drink old wine, have a second house, a beautiful car, go to Cannes, and travel around the world. Mind is mistaken.... Think during zazen that it is very hot today and that "we would like to go to the swimming pool, and our *bonno*-mind, our desiring mind, makes a mistake.

■

Four monks were doing zazen around a candle in a mountain hermitage. The idea was to maintain absolute silence. But then a gust of wind blew out the candle and the youngest monk said: "It's dark in here."

"Don't speak!" another monk answered.

"This is no good," cut in the *shusso*. "Both of you have broken the rule of silence."

"You three are no good," then said the master. "I am the only one who kept the rule of silence!"

All four of them spoke. Most people in the social world are like this. Even monks, too, are like this.

TRUE SATORI IS NOT KNOWING IT

Mind, what is it? One cannot give it a true name.[37] Language is not always convenient for expressing mind. Gestures are sometimes more effective. The use of the thumb, a finger before the lips. *Immo* is a word often used in Zen and it means: that.

How do we look at Buddha, how do we communicate with Buddha?.... If I think, "Now I am sleeping," then this is a dream. When in sleep we cannot know we are in sleep. This is *shikantaza*. When in zazen we do not know we are in zazen.

"I have satori." This is not true, not true satori. "I communicate with God"—this too is not true. In true communication we do not know true communication. Many people mistake this. When we have true satori, we do not know this and this is true *shikantaza*. But think you are in *shikantaza* and it is not true *shikantaza*.

Usually a name is temporary and it is wrong. All existences, form, figure, aspect, all of this is not true, not the true aspect. They are only temporary aspects and so they are false.

This is why Bodhidharma answered the emperor with the words *fu-shiki*.[38] This means "I don't know," or "don't think." It can also mean "beyond thinking."

Eka said *fu ka to ku* which means: impossible to obtain.

Eno said *honrai muichi butsu* which means: the original nothing, everything is nothing in its originality.

■

I am explaining to you the true essence of Zen, the essence of Soto Zen, of Dogen's Zen. It is only zazen. And its true essence is *hishiryo*, beyond thinking. The actualization of beyond thinking. This is not a conception, not a category.

■

In *Hokyo Zan Mai* it is written that:

> The snow gathers on the silver plate
> The heron is hidden in the moonlight.

So everything is white, the same, equal. Yet the plate is silver, the moonlight is the moonlight, the heron is a heron.

Stéphane became the master on stage the other night. Off-stage he is Stéphane. In my youth I was interested in the theater. On stage a king, off-stage a servant. Off-stage the king serves the servant.

■

I did a calligraphy in my room last night. "Open the door and receive the monk."…. A monk comes to visit a temple in the mountains and the chief of the temple opens the gate and welcomes the monk. This is a beautiful scene. But Stéphane (in reading the Japanese *kanjis*) thought the calligraphy meant something else. He thought it meant: Open the door, the *manko* welcomes you. (*Manko* in the Japanese ideogram means the female sex organ.) This is a good koan. The ideograms are the same, yet everybody imagines them differently. Japanese and Chinese ideograms are very convenient, they have many meanings.

SIT

Zen Teachings of Master Taisen Deshimaru

ABANDON THE SELECTING MIND

In *San Sho Doei*, Dogen wrote that:
>The white heron in the snowfield
>The winter grass is invisible
>The snowfield hides his silhouette.

This has a very deep meaning. It means the posture of *sampai*, the posture of zazen.

We cannot look at our own mind. When we observe, when we limit, then it only becomes an imitation, a trace. We can catch the traces of the mind. But then at this time the traces become a category. A man in the *mondo* asked me about time. About here and now. The present is important. When we decide now at this moment, this now is past.

So in the first phrase of *Shin Jin Mei* it is written that the true way, true mind, is not difficult; one must just not select. Selecting mind produces a mistake. Selection means attachment. In Dogen's *Shobogenzo Zuimonki* (written by Ejo, the eldest disciple of master Dogen[39]) it is said that if we abandon the mind which selects, then at this moment we can have true satori. This is true mind.

Some people here are sleeping. Sensei's kusens, his words, make for good music.

Chukai!

Continue with patience and the ego will vanish. This is so with everyone. The bad ego will end and the ego itself will become pure. Nothing is of much importance. You are tired, but you are not tired. You will become strong.

To move is easy, to not move is difficult.

10.30 A.M.

MONDO

God and Buddha

QUESTION: What relation do you see between Buddha and Christ?

Master: The same and not the same. Time is not the same, place is not the same. Buddha came before Christ. He was born in India and Christ in Israël. Their karma is different. But their holy and essential mind was very near.

I cannot compare them now; it would require a long conference. What do you want to ask?

QUESTION: During your *kusen* you said that Buddha is God and is not God. So can we say that Christ is God and not God?

Master: Christ is everything, so he is God. In Christianity, in the Christ-God relationship, God is always important. But in Buddhism God can become another thing. We respect Buddha, but we must not be attached to the form of Buddha. We must be beyond Buddha. But in Christianity it is impossible to be beyond God.[40]

When I first arrived in Paris, Monsieur Joly believed completely in Hinayana Buddhism. One day, Madame Lambert said to him that God and Buddha were the same. Monsieur Joly became very very angry. (Sensei speaking like Joly:) "Not at all the same! Not at all the same!" Monsieur Joly was not at all *Joli* (French for "pretty"). He had too much attachment to the Buddha form. Madame Lambert's thoughts were larger, more international, universal. Joly's were more narrow. So I did not discuss it with them. Both are correct.

As with the Madame in the *mondo* yesterday—the one who spoke of communion, communication. It is the same. Had I said that God and Buddha were the same, she would have said, "No, no, no."

So it is a very big problem, this exchange between Buddhism and Christianity.

The late Pope (Paul VI) wanted to make this exchange, to become friends. But he wanted to use Buddhism, he wanted to use Zen.[41] In the past Christianity was completely exclusive. There was only Christianity, and all other religions were a complete heresy, they were not true.

God and Buddha are the same in (the sense of) the fundamental cosmic power. I think so.

In Buddhism, Buddha is sometimes Shakyamuni (like with Christ) and sometimes Buddha is the Buddha before Buddha. In India, Buddha means all the masters, all the patriarchs.

Buddha's Buddha was the absolute Buddha. Like God. The absolute does not exist, but Shakyamuni Buddha does.

There are many kinds of buddhas. The succession since Bodhidharma, Eka, Eno, everybody, all the patriarchs: buddha. Dogen: Buddha. When I die: buddha…. Buddha, in Japan, sometimes refers to dead people. It means you are dead, you are buddha.

But in Christianity God is very simple; the category is very exact. What is God? Christian theology is very explicit.

Anyway, the category of *ku* in Buddhism is the same as God. The fundamental power of the cosmos. This is God, this is *ku*, the essence.

QUESTION: After Christ died someone opened the coffin and there was nothing. Yesterday you said the same about Fuke. What happened?

Master: Mystery! People like the mysterious. After Bodhidharma died they opened the coffin, and there was nothing. So they said that Bodhidharma walked back to India after his death. This is literature, poetry, the infinite. It is a metaphysical question. Mix metaphysical with physical problems and you become a little crazy. In Zen Buddhism these problems are not mixed.... To continue zazen is better. It isn't necessary to make categories. From non-thinking, intuition arrrives. Wisdom arrives. This is better.

The American supermarket

Philippe: Last year, in talking about the American Zen master [...], you said that his teaching was true Soto Zen....
Master: No, not now.[42]
Philippe: Last year you said yes. Anyway, what is interesting here is that this master, I've heard said, has recently come into serious trouble with the Soto Shu (the official Soto hierarchy and headquarters) in Japan. He is the only Soto master who is non-Japanese, and I am wondering if this had anything to do with his problems with the Soto Shu?
Master: This is not the cause, not the problem. He escaped from Soto Zen, so he is not a true Soto Zen master. Yes, Master [...] practiced Soto Zen and I believed him to be pure, before; he was a true Soto missionary in America.

Sometimes he welcomes the Tibetan master into his dojo, so when the Tibetan master comes, they practice Tibetan meditation. Another time a famous Yoga master comes, so then they have Yoga meditation. There are many many kinds of meditations in America, and he welcomes them all. Sometimes zazen, sometimes yoga.

The method he uses is very free, but it is not Soto Zen, not Dogen Zen. For people who like zazen, they give a conference on Dogen Zen. For those who like Yoga, they have conferences on Yoga. It is very clever, but it is not true. He has not one true thing. This is not *shikantaza*. It is a supermarket. It sells many things. But *shikantaza* means only zazen.

Yasutani was also like this. He was born in a Soto temple, he became a Soto Zen monk, and he practiced Soto Zen. He also practiced Rinzai Zen—he liked satori. So a great Rinzai master told him once: "You've got satori." Therefore he wanted to use both Rinzai and Soto, and this is why Rinzai monks did not like him. And Soto too excluded him. So Yasutani escaped to America.[43]

Sit on two chairs and you will fall down. Run after two rabbits and both will escape you. You must concentrate on only one. Then one becomes all.

My Zen is exactly Dogen's. *Shikantaza*, only one. This is true Buddhism. And not sectarian. And Master [...], even if he is beyond Soto Zen, beyond the Soto sect, his Zen is not true.

American Zen is mistaken. There is Alan Watts' Zen, Rinzai Zen. There are many kinds, many flowers. They are beautiful; but American people do not understand true Zen.

So, Philippe, your book is very important.... My book! You did the writing. It is very important. This book will influence the Americans. American people are very clever so they will quickly understand. It is interesting this book *The Voice of the Valley*.[44]

Dokusan

QUESTION: Some years ago I had the occasion to participate in a retreat in a Christian monastery in Belgium. Each day and whenever we so wished, we had at our disposition a Spiritual

Father with whom we could speak of our problems, of what we were living and experiencing, and I found this to be very beneficial. Do such meetings exist in Zen?

Master: In Zen: *dokusan.* Who was the master?
Answer: A different one every day. They were called Spiritual Fathers.
Master: And what did you ask?
Ans: We could ask anything we wished. But in particular we told him what we were experiencing, what we were feeling.
Master: They do this in Rinzai. But not so much in Soto. People in Soto ask their questions like this, in a public *mondo.* It is better.

But if you want to ask me a question in private, it is possible to visit my room. This is *dokusan.* I use it.[45]

But now in Soto as well as in Rinzai, *dokusan* has become formalism. In Rinzai, after the morning zazen, you go and visit the master with your koan: "What is *mu?*" asks the master. *"Kwaaat!"*

In Soto *dokusan* is the same. The disciple enters the master's room, does *sampai,* asks something of the master, and the master gives him the *kyosaku.* Only this. Pure formalism.

I created this (form of *mondo*). It is very effective. They never have *mondos* like this in Japan. Because the master himself cannot answer the questions. So they answer with a *kwat* or with the *kyosaku.* But I am very kind, exactly I answer you.

Language is very difficult, so if you want to ask me a secret question, madame, by letter would be better. Write a note and give it to my secretary and I will answer it. This way I will keep your secret a secret.

The death of Buddha, the death of Christ

QUESTION: Christ died young and with much spectacle and violence, and his death had a deep signifiance for humanity. Does the death of Buddha also have a deep significance?

Master: No. His death was natural. Buddha had just eaten some pork, and his intestines were sick and he died very naturally. He was about eighty-five years old and there was nothing spectacular or special about it.

It is not good to eat pork in India, and for the Hindus it is even forbidden. But Buddha ate pork—I read this in a true sutra.[46]

It happened while he was at a believer's house in Kusinagara. The believer (Cunda, a blacksmith) had invited Buddha, and the dinner was very delicious and everyone ate a lot; and Buddha, whose intestines were unhealthy, died. He died in a forest, a beautiful forest, between two lovely trees, Sala trees.

Many disciples, all his believers, all the animals (one thousand of them, the forest was full) came around him.... Buddha had a completely good posture, and in the end he gave them the Testament Sutra, *Butsu Yuikyo Gyo*. After giving this *kusen* (oral teaching), he fell into a deep sleep. This is a very famous scene; you can see it in the Nirvana picture (which depicts Buddha lying on his right side).

This death has no significance. His testament though, is very famous. Master Dogen has written on this testament in the ninety-fifth chapter of *Shobogenzo*.

Buddha died naturally, he was smiling and peaceful. This is nirvana. Nirvana, completely quiet, only this.

It wasn't the same with Christ. Christ's death was very dramatic. And so the religion too.

Buddha experienced life until he was more than eighty years old, and so his teaching changed. Buddha lived fifty years more than did Christ; and he changed. Kodo Sawaki too—when he was young, and later at fifty, sixty, seventy, and then just before his death when he was in his eighties—he changed, changed. My teaching also has changed. My old disciples know. From the time I arrived here to now, it has changed. It has become deep.

So Christianity and Buddhism are different. A person who lives until eighty becomes deep. His experience becomes very deep.

But for younger people Christianity is very effective. I, myself, in my younger days experienced Christianity. I was very impressed by it. But Buddhism is deeper. So after practicing Christianity, to practice Buddhism is very effective: one's personality becomes deep.... Another question?

Mind is always the same

QUESTION: This morning you said that true mind does not choose; but in everyday life we are always confronted with decisions to make. We have always to choose. How can we harmonize these two necessities?

Master: Good question! It is a physical-metaphysical question. To seek the true way: don't select

In daily life it is necessary to select. Macrobiotic people always select. (Sensei imitates someone examining the food before him.) "This is no good, I don't eat this! Oh, this is very good, I eat this!"

Mind is important. I don't select my disciples. If one escapes, *d'accord!* If one comes: welcome!.... Mind is always peaceful.

Most peoples' minds are always selecting. But these minds are not practicing. This is a contradiction; and so life becomes difficult.

Mind which does not select is in its normal condition, and

for this mind everything is *d'accord*. I have no money, never mind. Mind does not select. It is decision. Decision is very important.

Consciousness always makes karma. "You must do it like this!" or "You must do it like that!" But the cosmic order is not so exact (i.e., the cosmic order is not like this).

So it is not necessary to select. Bad things in the end become good, and good things bad. If we get something, we lose something. It is always this way; mind is always the same. Do you understand?

This is satori. Inside mind. Everything.

Wisdom is necessary. Want too much and it escapes. The cat, the madame. But when mind becomes quiet, everything comes. Even money.

Business without profit is foolish. In business it is necessary to get money. In business, in life, wisdom is necessary.

8.30 P.M.

NOTHING IS SO IMPORTANT

The true way is not difficult, but people want to select and so it becomes complicated. Satori is not at all difficult. It is simple. It is to return to the normal original condition of the brain.

Nirvana means total death. Enter the coffin and this is complete satori. Zazen is to enter into the coffin. It is very simple. There is no decoration. The family furnishes the decoration. After our death we don't need decoration, nor food nor sex. It is very simple, very pure.

Christ said in the Bible that all existences return to death. But then God makes them all relive again.

Think while you are in the coffin, then you will understand that nothing is important. During zazen—if you have done it for a long time—things are not so important. The source of anxieties decrease. Desires decrease.[47]

Sometimes they arise again: "What's become of my family?"

Even if you are in pain, if you are suffering in zazen, even if you die now, never mind. It is not so important. Just continue zazen, and at this moment everything will finish. The philosophies, the sutras, fears, anxieties: they are not so important. Do zazen like this for a week and everything in the end will finish. There will be no more questions in the *mondos*. The brain will have become simple.

But were I to say: "If there are no questions we will continue zazen," then surely someone will say to himself: "I must think up a question." So thoughts arise and the brain becomes complicated, and more and more thoughts arise.

A little difference in the beginning becomes a big difference in the end. As big as between the earth and the sky.

Zazen is nothing, it is simple. But even that can become complicated. Some continue zazen for five or seven years and their zazens have become complicated. Karma is different, and thinking and seeking are not the same.

When I was a child my mother wanted to make me into a little monk. She was very religious, like Kannon (Avalokitesvara), and she respected monks. So once she even shaved my head. Very good; I had a nicely shaped head. But my mother was also very economical and this way she could save up on barber fees.... Then in my twenties I became neurotic: I read philosophy books, literature, books on Buddhism and on Christianity and I became complicated.

Then I went to study Rinzai at Engakuji. Next I went to visit (the Soto master) Kodo Sawaki at Sojiji temple, and I told him that I wanted to become a monk. Foolish, he said. He knew my character. If he were to give me the monk ordination too soon, then surely I would escape. Better to give me the ordination just before his death. This way I would not escape.

■

I give the monk's ordination to everyone. All they must do is ask for it and I say, *"d'accord, d'accord."* The body gets it. Not the mind. But later the mind gets it too. Body and mind, surely....

■

Satori means that there is no world to escape from, no world to run after. This is true zazen, *shikantaza.*

AUG. 20 / 7 A.M.

GENSHI AND THE LIGHT OF THE MOON

If you do not know the principle of the deep way your brain will tire in vain.

Genshi. Gen means deep or bottom; *shi* means principle. *Genshi* has a deep meaning, a deep originality. It means the true way. If we look only at the finger which points to the moon, we cannot see the moon of *genshi*.

Each person is different. Each have different dimensions. Between that of the little girl and the man: I love you. The little girl does not know this.... If dimensions are different then it is very complicated. But if the dimensions are the same, then one can quickly understand. Man with man, woman with woman, horse with horse, homosexual with homosexual.[48]

The shadow of the moon arises anywhere, and the light reflects in any place. But its shadow lives in the minds of those who look at it. The shadow of the moon is only one, the same. But in the mind of each beholder it is different.

Genshi, the deep principle, the fundamental source, fills the whole cosmos. And yet like the moonlight, it is in every town, every village. The fundamental cosmic power is everywhere, here and now. So too in zazen right now. But we cannot look at it; we cannot seize it, touch it. Because each has his own karma. The dimensions are not the same. This is satori, this is enlightenment, communion. Each person has his conception, his category, his own norm. Each chooses for himself.

Listen to the voice of the valley. When you return to your homes try and remember this sound.

The voice of the valley, the current in the valley, the color of the mountain: this is from Sotoba, a great poet of ancient China. Well, one night while he was doing zazen in his hermitage he heard the voice of the valley, and he woke up completely. Unconsciously, automatically and naturally *genshi* penetrated to the deep bottom of his *ki kai tanden. Genshi*, the deep principle. *Genshi*, the root, the source.

■

All phenomena are but a dream, a bubble, a shadow, a thunderclap, a dew drop—it is the same.

The flowing stream: it is impermanent, always changing. But it is permanent, it is the stream, always flowing, never stopping, and the water is always fresh. Bubbles on the surface of a stagnant pond: sometimes they disappear, then they reappear. Our life is like this. There is no need to run after or to escape.

Kaijo!

Don't move! Whenever I say *kaijo*, you move. You run after the drum, after the sound of the drum.

(The drum is struck nine times—to indicate the hour.)

The sound of the drum is very deep and at the end of zazen it is very effective. It touches your *ki kai tanden* under the navel. So it becomes strong.

(The wooden block suspended at the entrance to the dojo and the metal plaque suspended in front of the kitchen, a good two hundred meters off, are struck with steadily increasing speed, causing the sounds to interplay and to blend together.)[49]

The traditional sounds you hear in and after zazen have a deep meaning.

10.30 A.M.

THE LAST ZAZEN:

The flower has fallen and the mountain is tranquil

Push the sky with the head, the ground with the knees.

■

If our mind becomes normal, becomes tranquil, it vanishes naturally and automatically. This is satori, this is *hishiryo*.

Here is master **Keizan's** commentary:

> The white clouds disappear, the blue mountain
>   stands alone.
> The souring power of the many mountains vanish,
> Only one—the highest, the one which reaches to
>   the sky—is standing.
> Nobody arrives at its summit, nobody knows its
>   name.
> Even Buddha and the Patriarchs cannot explain
>   it (*doshu*),
> Neither in conference (*kusen*), nor through silence.
> In the realm, arrived at through deep study:
> All the day long you look,
> Yet there are no eyes with which to see it;
> All the night long you listen,
> Yet there are no ears with which to hear it.

Keizan's poem is beautiful; I like this poem. What is zazen? It is this.

> The music of a stringed instrument without
>   strings [50]

It moves the sleeves of even the wooden people.
A flute without holes even harmonizes with the
    iron man.[51]

Shinpo kyochi. Shin is mind and *po* is object. So the subject and the object vanish together. *Kyo* is the surroundings, the objects, and *chi* is wisdom. *Kyochi tomoni minzu:* surrounding wisdom together vanish. So together, without arrangement (there is no planning, no comparison, no thinking) the wind stops blowing, the waves have disappeared and the ocean is again calm. The flower falls and the mountain grows more peaceful.

The flower falls and the people have gone away. After the flower has fallen and the people have left, then the mountain is more peaceful. This is the aspect of mind during zazen. This is how it should be understood. It is not only a landscape, but also zazen-mind.

It is a Val d'Isère landscape. The landscape and the last zazen are the same. Do zazen and you do not have to go to the mountain. Zazen and the mountain are the same. The real mountain is inside mind. Please, look at the mountain in your mind.

This is the relationship between life and death, and it can be experienced during zazen.

The flower falls means that all finishes, the good and the bad.

Some here are always criticizing: about the food, about other people. And even during the *sesshin* they are saying: "It's cold today and we must have some heat." Or they think of how to win money on the stock market. All this is bad karma.

But when the wind comes, the flower falls. All falls. There is no darkness, there is no light, there is no running after, no escape from. There is no anxiety, no fear. The mountain becomes completely peaceful. This is zazen.

■

Kyosaku!
This is the last present. The *kusen* is soft, the *kyosaku* is strong.

◼

Zazen is dry wood without thinking. The deep wisdom arises.
The blue mountain stands alone. There are many mountains, and their soaring is finished. There is only one: the highest, the one which stretches into heaven. This is zazen mind.
You must become a dry tree during zazen. This is from a poem by master Daichi:[52]

Dry Tree

Throw out the body
Stand on the edge of the precipice.
The wind polishes, the rain washes—
How many thousand of times?
The bark of the trees fall off,
And there is nothing left but the pure truth.
And even an ax cannot cut it open.

This poem not only speaks of a dry tree, it expresses zazen.[53]

◼

The wind has stopped, the flower has fallen and the mountain is tranquil—this is the last *kusen*.

SIT

Zen Teachings of Master Taisen Deshimaru

4th session

AUGUST 23 – AUGUST 31

AUG.23 / 10 A.M.

THE HARD KISSES OF MASTER KISS

Kinhin is the same as zazen. It is standing zazen, it is moving zazen. (Everyone is now in *kinhin.*) *Kinhin* is harder than zazen. (Someone collapses.)

Kinhin and zazen produce a strong reaction. Those who are weak, who have bad nervous systems, quickly fall down. But afterwards they will become strong.

◼

(Zazen:) Don't move, don't move. When you move you must do *gassho* first. Those who have not the patience, or who are sick, or who are about to faint, they must do *gassho* first. And then the columns must accompany them outside. (Someone else is being carried outside.)

◼

A *sesshin* means to touch, to make contact with our true mind. We must look towards the inside. We must do this in the calm, in the silence.

But a *sesshin* also means to decrease desires.

People in modern civilization have too many desires. Complicated desires which they cannot realize. So they fall sick. People have too many desires and therefore they cannot be satisfied. So all they can do is use their imagination. If their desires cannot be realized, they become sick or they become mad or they commit suicide.

True peace is not to have too many desires inside. In this way realizing one's desires becomes very easy; and there's no anxiety. Inside is quiet.

It is difficult to decrease desires. But continue zazen and it will happen unconsciously and automatically.

The atmosphere is very quiet, the others are calm. If you follow the rules of the dojo, of the *sesshin*, you will receive the influence of the others. From the atmosphere you will become quiet and your inside desires will decrease.[1]

■

In ancient times in Japan traditional *sesshins* lasted one, two and three months. In modern times only ten days or a month.

In those times *sesshins* were only for monks. When a monk came for the first time, he would not be allowed to enter the dojo. He had to wait in the waiting room. To be trained and tested. Some waited a week before they were allowed into the dojo. In the history of Zen many great masters had first been tested in the waiting room. (Here there is no waiting room, only a garage.) In the waiting room there was no sleeping. The food was reduced.

■

In the history of Rinzai Zen there was a monk, coming in the direct line from Nangaku (the great Chinese patriarch), who was called Sekken Kiss.[2] (*Sekken* in Japanese means soap; but it also signifies a mountain in China.) And his first disciple was named Fusan Ho-on.[3] (Fusan is the name of another mountain in China.)

Ho-on had once gone to a Soto dojo under Taiyo Kyogen,[4] a famous patriarch of the Soto line, and Kyogen had later wanted to give the *shiho* (transmission) to Ho-on; but Ho-on had refused it because he had already received the Rinzai ordination.

So Ho-on, who had also received the Soto education, returned to the Rinzai master Kiss. Kiss was very strong.

There were many people in Kiss' waiting room during the

preparation for a *sesshin*, and every morning Kiss brought a bucket of water along—one bucket for each person. Kiss then threw the bucket of water over each of their heads, completely soaking them. It was during the winter and it was cold and everyone was angry. This master was mad.

(I am very kind. I welcome you. You are all very welcome. I embrace you, even though my name is not "Kiss." Master Kiss never gave soft kisses.)

So Kiss was testing their ability to pursue the *sesshin*. And everyone escaped. Except Ho-on. Ho-on alone was patient. "I come from the Soto dojo of Taiyo Kyogen and I want to stay here. Even if every morning you throw water on me. Because I have come to seek the way."

To seek is not so easy, it is not so hard.

So Kiss was impressed. Most people only come to eat, or to dance, or to find a sexual partner. "But this is not the Mediterranean Club here," said Kiss.

Ho-on became the *tenzo*.... Kiss was very strict. He had only one hundred monks in his dojo but they were all strong monks. Because only the strong ones stayed.

There was never enough food. There was only *genmai* soup in the morning and *genmai* soup at lunch. There was nothing for dinner, and, besides, the *genmai* soup was mostly water. So the desires of each deminished: their only desire was for food. They were very very hungry. (This is good for zazen; eat too much and zazen becomes difficult.)

Then one day master Kiss went away (he went for a walk), and the *tenzo* Ho-on, who had compassion for the monks, wished to give them more to eat than just *genmai*. So he looked for the key to the storeroom in the master's quarters, and he fetched out some noodles which he gave to everyone.

Kiss returned at this time, and he called in the *tenzo*. Laurent, Guy, come!⁵ Kiss was completely angry. "In my absence you stole! You stole the key!"

"The monks said they were starving, so we stole the key."

"You are the same as a thief! You can no longer live in this dojo. Get out, out...."

Ho-on went off traveling. But sometimes he would return to the dojo to sleep in front of the gate. Kiss became angry again: "You must go away. A thief cannot sleep here."

Ho-on went off begging. He begged around the temple. And during Kiss' absence he would do zazen in the garden under the trees. When Kiss saw this he said: "This is a temple garden. You must pay for the place you take up." (Kiss was very economical.) So Ho-on gave him the money and the rice he had received from begging; and so he continued to do zazen in the temple garden, in the place he was paying for.

Then one day Kiss came across Ho-on on the road begging, and he said to him: "You are doing this for the way. You are seeking the way. Very good."... And in the end he gave Ho-on the *shiho*.

This story is famous because Ho-on had first received the Soto training. Soto Zen is not so negligent. Patience is necessary... and Ho-on had already decreased his desires.

■

Kaijo!

Don't move, don't move. The last moments of zazen are very important. You must have patience.... Stéphane! Socks are no good.[6] You are negligent, you dress negligently. This is why you have caught a cold. Everyone must take care not to catch colds during this *sesshin*.

■

4th session

AUG. 23 / 8.30 P.M.

UNDERSTANDING RINZAI

(The darkening sky beyond the open window, the blue mountains, the sounds, the wind in the pines and the river below; with everyone engaged in mutual listening, hearing the world talk, never repeating itself, always the same, fading down the mountain side, off in the silence....)

When we hear the sound of the valley, of the river, true religious mind arises.

The American boy Philippe Coupey wrote in English *The Voice of the Valley* now being published in New York. The book had to do with my talks last year in Val d'Isère, when I spoke about the karma in man, of concentration and of observation. And now this year I am comparing Rinzai and Dogen Zen: *Shobogenzo* and *Rinzai Roku*.

Each religion is different and each religious mind is different. Why did Rinzai arrive? Why did his sect arrive?

I have already talked about Rinzai's visit to the Obaku dojo. And how for three years Rinzai did nothing but zazen and never even had a *mondo* with the master.

I have studied many books on this and at last I have understood the true story. It is not explained in other books, nor in *Rinzai Roku*. And no masters have ever written profoundly on this matter.

In his younger days Rinzai had studied deeply the psychology of Buddhism. He had studied the *Yui-Shiki*, the Visryana of Mahayana Buddhism. *Yui-Shiki* is more complicated and much deeper than modern psychology.... So Rinzai only read

231

books. He did not do zazen, and he became too intelligent, too academic.

Then he became a monk and went to visit Obaku's dojo. (Rinzai found Buddhism very complicated, and this is why he went to Obaku.)

But what he underwent was the complete opposite to Buddhist psychology. Everyday was just the *kyosaku*. Everyday it was the big voice of master Obaku. So he asked himself many questions. But since questions are not possible, he had no questions. So the *shusso* told him to ask one. "What question should I ask?" Rinzai said. "Ask the master what is the essence of Buddhism," replied the *shusso*.

Rinzai was scared. Yet he went and asked the question anyway. He did not get the answer. He got the *kyosaku* and escaped. The *shusso* sent him back and this time he received the *rensaku*—and not on the acupuncture points, but on the top of the head.... (Like myself; when I visited the Rinzai master Asahina at Engakuji in my younger days, I too got hit on the head, and I too escaped; but I didn't return.⁷)... Rinzai, though, was very patient and he went back. He went back twice and he got ninety blows.

Anyway, he was filled with doubt. "I want to go for a walk," he told the *shusso*. "Not to escape, just for a walk."

"In that case," said the *shusso*, "I will introduce you to a great master, and you can go there. Master Taigu, master Great Fool. This great master is a great fool."⁸

Rinzai found this very interesting. So within a few days he arrived at the Taigu temple and there he met the Great Fool. "Why have you come?".... Rinzai told him: "When I ask Obaku a question on the essence of Buddhism, I only get the *rensaku*. Have I made a mistake?" He was full of doubt.

"You have not at all made a mistake. But why can't you understand? Because you are foolish."

"Why am I foolish?"

"Because Obaku gave you the exact answer; and, too, he taught you with kindness."

At this moment Rinzai got satori. "Oh, the essence of Buddhism is very simple," he said.

When Rinzai returned, Obaku asked him: "You understand now the essence of Buddhism?"

"Yes, I understand," he replied getting up and hitting Obaku in the face.

Obaku told him not to come too close. "My mustache is very strong. You must not touch the mustache (whiskers) of the tiger."

In his youth, before he had become a monk, Rinzai was very intelligent—he had read many books. So Obaku cut it. Obaku's stick was very effective.... For the very intelligent, cries and the *rensaku* are very effective.

For everyone it is different, but for Rinzai it was effective. So he always used this method on his disciples. And this is why Dogen criticized Rinzai Zen: too negligent.

(Two people have fainted and are being carried out by the *kyosakuman* and by one of the columns.) In the beginning many people fall. Four or five have already fallen today. This is because they are returning to their original condition of mind and body. So for those who have a weak nervous system, this is very good: just before they commit suicide or before they die, they fall down.... (But for people who are intrinsically mad, this is not so. To cure the truly sick is difficult.)

Still, for people who are too nervous, who think too much, who take too many drugs, and for those who are spoiled by their parents, their education and their surroundings, Rinzai Zen is sometimes effective. But Rinzai education is not a normal education. So Dogen criticized Rinzai Zen, saying that it was *zusan;* that it was rough and barbaric.

■

233

About this non-thinking, please, think from the bottom of non-thinking—this is how you must think. Don't think from the bottom of non-thinking, said Dogen. Don't think about thinking. Think don't think. Both. This is *hishiryo*. This is the secret of Zen.

What is *hishiryo*? During zazen everyone practices *hishiryo*. The influence which comes from the posture is necessary. If the posture is wrong, you cannot create the state of *hishiryo*.

For Blaise Pascal, it is the *roseau pensant* (thinking reed)— this is religious thinking. I don't know Pascal's mind. But if Dogen were living, he would say that Pascal was very delicate, very fine, and not negligent.

■

Our life is very limited, just like the wind. Just like the river. It passes very quickly. Time passes and the flowing stream is not at all permanent. It is always changing. The river remains, but the water is never the same. The river and the earth are always the same, but the water is always changing…. In a stagnant pool the bubbles sometimes appear and sometimes disappear. The *roseau* in the moonlight: the autumn wind comes, and it is always thinking, and then before the winter it dies. He (the *roseau*) is very weak. But he thinks. (The true *roseau*, though, does not think; man thinks.) This is religious consciousness.

■

What is the religious mind?

Mind returns, it sinks, to the root of birth. This is thinking: thinking about our roots, our source, our birth.

Man is born out of one hole and he finishes in another hole. He goes from hole to hole. This is man's life. *C'est la vie*…. The salmon returns to its source, to the source of its birth. And there she deposits her eggs; she fertilizes them, and then she quickly dies. Anyway, all sentient beings wish to return to the source of their birth.

But for man it is not necessary that he return to his source (to his mother's orifice) because man has developed his frontal brain, his intellect, and he has a memory. So he thinks about it.

Sometimes this can become animism. Like people who want to go to nature, who want to go into the mountains, to hear the sound of the valley.

Man seeks the cause. Why? Why? From source to source. Why? Why?

Logical, mathematical-thinking people discover infinite progression. It is the law of series. People who realize that the cosmos is infinite, but that the ego is not, understand. Life is short. Life passes by, passes by, like a river, like an arrow. We must proceed quickly to the coffin and quickly we enter into it. This is the true religious mind.

So people want to create a reasonable request (that which would put them) beyond their limited lives.

THE GREAT WISDOM OF PREHISTORY

Ceremonies of simple morals and manners

In prehistoric and in ancient times people were not like animals, but different, and they created simple morals and simple manners. This is the root of civilization; it was primitive but very simple. This was the great wisdom of humanity of prehistoric times.

The ceremony: the prostrations (sampai) and the chanting of Hannya Shingyo are very simple. Simple morals, simple manners. This is the root of our civilization.

Why do we do sampai? It is written in the great sutra Hannya Haramitsu that we do sampai for Buddha. This is Maka Hannya Haramitsu, the Great Wisdom.

This is *prajna,* wisdom. We do *sampai* together every morning after breakfast, the master and the disciples together, on the concrete (terrace in front of Sensei's quarters). Everyone knocks his forehead on the concrete. A deep meaning. It means creating wisdom. Knock your frontal brain on the concrete and without question wisdom will arise.

Do *sampai* for Buddha, as respect to Buddha; offer flowers, offer a candle, offer incense, read the sutras—all this is ceremony.

Why do we do *sampai*? To create wisdom.

Kyosaku! Give the *kyosaku* to those who want it.

And for those who are too intelligent.

Chukai!

AUG. 24 / 7.30 A.M.

THE FIVE REVOLUTIONS OF HUMANITY

During zazen: no hearing, no looking, no thinking. No looking with the eyes, but looking. Thinking, no-thinking.[9]

This morning there is no curtain over the window, and people are looking out at the landscape. Or they are looking at the woman's hips before them.

Hear the sound of the valley. Hear but not hear.

Someone in a black *kolomo* is wandering about outside.[10] He cannot follow the system. He is a cancerous cell.

Normal cells become abnormal. They become mad and so they affect the other normal cells.

He is now walking across the bridge.

Stéphane, it is not necessary to look! You too are a cancerous cell. Do not look at others during zazen.

(Everyone is now standing in *kinhin* and the master says:) If the form is straight, the shadow is straight; and so the mind becomes straight.

(Zazen:) In the future civilization, in that of the twenty-first century, the revolution will not be materialistic, like the Communist one, but it will be an interior spiritual revolution. A revolution of the mind.

People mistake consciousness. People don't think at all, except on the material. Materialism has developed and man has forgotten the mind. Only you, who are looking at yourselves, know (the mind).

In the process of humanity I count five steps, five revolutions. The first one was in prehistoric times when man came to a standing position. Then there was the agricultural revolution: the development of food. Next was when people went to the cities. First they lived on boats, now they live in Paris. In the fourth through the sixth centuries B.C., a spiritual revolution appeared. A spiritual renaissance. (In England the renaissance was industrial, in France it was cultural. In India Buddhism arose.) The present revolution has been a scientific, an industrial one. Modern times are completely material. The material controls man's mind.

This is a big problem for the twentieth century. How do we be here and now? How, in our own mind? People have forgotten about mind.

In the fourth stage appeared the spiritual revolution. It occurred four to six centuries before Christ, and it touched all of humanity: India, China, Greece.[11] Humanity produced this great spiritual revolution.

And now mankind must return to this. Man must find the value of consciousness; he must find the value of the mind of humanity itself.

The first three revolutions of humanity were all of them visible. Nobody forgets the cities, nobody forgets the standing position. Agriculture too is visible. But the spiritual revolution is invisible. And so people have forgotten it. I have done zazen for forty years; I have concentrated only on zazen, and so I understand: humanity has forgotten. Humanity is not interested in mind, but only interested in looking outside.

Even here there are some who only look outside. Like that man walking on the bridge in his black *kolomo*.

During the *sesshin*, please, follow the order, follow the rules. Go against them and you are like a cancerous cell. The cell must be operated on, expulsed, removed. Contrarily, a person who concentrates for just one hour, for just half-an-hour, he will have an influence in the four directions. Concentrate in *shikantaza* and he will influence all the cosmos, all existence. If you do zazen, if you have a good posture, if you have *hishiryo* consciousness—this will influence the cosmos for all eternity.

■

AUG. 24 / 8.30 P.M.

THE CONTRADICTION:
Halberd or shield?

What is true happiness? Is it to satisfy sexual desires?

Yesterday, during zazen, a man and a woman were together in a room. The *kyosakuman* found them. They were on the bed—doing.... They had thought that surely during zazen they could find a free room and not be disturbed. So they waited until it was time for zazen. They should receive the *rensaku*. But I will wait until it happens again. One time I permit. I know their names. They live in room number....

I have said from the beginning that this is not the Club Méditerranée. Surely a bad karma will now appear.

To satisfy sex and appetite—these are important for the happiness of man. But in modern times there is free sex and so it has become an important social problem.

Sex is difficult to satisfy. Two partners, a man and a woman are necessary.... Masturbation is easier. Kodo Sawaki used to say jokingly that masturbation is more convenient, because only one sex organ is needed. And this way it is not expensive, and it saves time. And afterwards it is not complicated.

This problem of sexual satisfaction afterwards becomes a problem of love.... Love has a spiritual value; without love it becomes complicated. Desire, love, and then no love. Some people want to change partners. They change and change and the bad karma piles up, and then the bad karma is realized.

Sexual morals are very important. Run after sex and bad karma will appear.

Perverted sex is no good. It influences the body and one's

health. There is a loss of social trust, respect, honor. People will no longer respect you and this will be an influence on the family, on the children and so karma arises.

To pursue a long love a healthy family is necessary. But in modern times families are not healthy and they do not last long. Most people are not satisfied. They want to desire and to love but they don't realize it. So contradictions arise and this becomes suffering. From the satisfaction of sexual desire comes suffering. Happiness becomes unhappiness.

So, to satisfy desires is not the object of true happiness. What should be done?

It is very important to control, to dominate. In traditional religions, sex was forbidden, it was denied. This way it became asceticism, which is not an authentic practice and therefore contradictions arose.

■

How do we resolve contradictions? This is the problem of modern civilization. Everything is in contradiction: happiness, desire, politics (the left and the right are in complete contradiction); spirituality with materialism, science with technology. So how can we resolve them? Religion cannot do it, nor can morality, and obviously politics cannot resolve it; nor can the universities, nor the parents.

This is a big problem, it is a problem of human consciousness, of man's mentality. And for the psychoanalysts too, this is a big problem. Modern psychoanalysts only complicate the matter even more. "What did you dream of last night?" They ask these sorts of questions. This kind of thing makes people even sicker. It makes them mad. It drives them to suicide.

In the ancient religions God managed everything. But then human beings developed the ability to look directly at nature, and so the natural sciences developed and this produced rationalism, materialism, technology and so on, and religion became what is called the opium of the people. In modern times religion and morality have fallen down to earth, while contrarily, rationalism, materialism and science have become the opium of the people. (The human brain itself is not rational. It has a big contradiction which includes the frontal intellectual brain, and the primitive animal brain.) So true religion without opium, and peaceful science without opium must become harmonized in this future civilization.

Ever since I arrived in Europe my *kusens* have dealt with this problem of contradictions, and of how to resolve them.

We cannot resolve, we cannot change human consciousness, human karma. The doctors cannot do it, nor can the psychoanalysts. And modern education, with its emphasis on the sciences only create dualities and categories.

Mujun means contradiction. *Mu* means halberd and *jun* means shield.... In ancient times in China, weapons merchants presented the emperor with a new halberd. It was a very strong halberd and it could pierce through any kind of shield. So the emperor ordered many of these halberds. Then the weapons merchants arrived with strong iron shields, so strong that no halberd could pierce them. So the emperor, who was intelligent, said to them: "You bring me both sorts. I want to use them both."

It was at this time that the ideogram *mujun* came into being— and from then on the contradiction arose. The modern crisis is just like this. Ideologies, always ideologies.

Professors, doctors, politicians, religious leaders are always teaching on one side or on the other. Either as the halberd or as the shield.

How do we solve this problem?

Perfect wisdom in Buddhism is *Hannya*. I am now writing a book on *Maka Hannya Haramitsu*. Dogen too: the first conference he made on his return from China was on *Maka Hannya Haramitsu*. Anyway, now I am writing a commentary of five hundred pages on this book.[12]

Wisdom is complicated. But the conclusion is very easy, very simple. We must understand both the shield and the halberd. In the right hand we must hold the halberd, in the left we must seize the shield. We must have both. We must not use these weapons, but we must have them—so they can solve the contradictions. And so it becomes wisdom. With which we can create even greater wisdom.

We can resolve all contradictions. Do not be complicated. Be always free. This is *hishiryo* consciousness. *Hishiryo* creates infinite wisdom.

AUG. 25 / 7.30 A.M.

HAPPINESS

and the American Declaration of Independence

When you begin zazen it is necessary that you swing seven or eight times to left and the right, in smaller and smaller movements. This way you will be fixed in zazen and you will not need to move. If you forget to do this, zazen will become difficult. Also, before you get up from zazen you must swing back and forth with bigger and bigger movements. This way the nerves coming out of the fifth lombar vertebra become strong. And so too with the nerves in the *kikai tanden*.

■

4th session

One of my oldest disciples, Stéphane, is sitting in zazen with his mouth wide open, yawning. He must put a hand before his mouth.

■

Why is modern civilization the way it is? Why is it that they have developed this great material civilization? Why this great technological development?

Two hundred years ago the United States of America declared their independence, and in the declaration it was written that every human being has the right to seek after his own happiness. Thirteen years later came the French revolution. And human rights, an enlightened philosophy, developed.

All the world sought after happiness. And for most people this happiness was (to be had through) the satisfaction of desires. If man had good food, a good house and good sex, and if he possessed money and material, then he would surely be happy.

When we read American history, we see that they sought after the material. At first, right after their separation with Britain, they rapidly expanded in the field of agriculture. At first they had a strong faith in Puritanism. They were strong for work. They were not lazy, they made an effort. For one hundred years after their independence—up until the Civil War—their currency did not change, and what's more the price of goods dropped by half. This was not inflation. America was very rich, it had great resources in food, and its pioneer spirit was strong. They succeeded in building the strongest economic power in the world. At first Americans worked with effort to create the material base of human life. And so they became the richest country on earth—leaving all the world to follow behind them in the economic field. Today, on the other side are the Communists, the Socialists; they have become the opposite and so they too have grown very strong.

But meanwhile the world's resources have become limited,

and this is a problem. Like petrol. This is how it is with progress: the world's resources are limited, and so we have more and more crises. Led by their desires, people seek for material satisfaction: their desires are realized and in so doing they have lost the root of happiness.

Material riches, practical conveniences, nourishment and so on are important, but they are not the end of happiness. The rise of the hippie in America is an example.

NEW PHENOMENON
The seeking for psychological happiness

Throughout the world in modern times people are seeking for another happiness, a psychological happiness. For people cannot become truly happy without satisfying their own minds and the bottoms of their own hearts.

Man has succeeded economically and materially to the furthest limit. And so the traditional morals, the morals of living, have changed. Free sex, pornographic movies.

Since my arrival in Europe the number of people who come here to these summer camps has increased, and without much publicity (on the part of the Association Zen to bring them). If we had a big dojo hall and if we did propaganda five thousand people would come. People are seeking psychological happiness; it is another phenomenon.

If you seek material happiness, you go to Club Méditerranée. Mr. Blitz, the head of the Club Méditerranée, says that every year the number of people who seek for the material, for food and for sex, decreases. Now they want to do Yoga, the martial arts, zazen. It is changing. So this is why Mr. Blitz is now organizing spiritual vacations.[13]

This is not easy to do; because each person is different. To organize food and sex is easier. But the spiritual problem is more difficult to organize because each person's karma is different. So each one must resolve his own problem himself, through the practice of meditation.

We must look at ourselves, at our own minds.

There are many type of meditation; but posture and breathing and the way we think during meditation is most important. So we have zazen.

Do zazen and you can find true happiness. Your karma changes; your bad karma decreases, and you can find the true happiness in the bottom of your heart.

In the beginning zazen hurts. Those who have not experienced zazen cannot understand. The ultimate happiness, the end of suffering, is through the posture and peace of mind. It is the end of contradictions. *Hishiryo* consciousness solves all contradictions.

8.30 P.M.

MAN'S PRIMITIVE BRAIN

The hypothalamus

Without muddiness
In the water of the mind
Clear is the moon.
Even the waves break upon it
And are changed into light.[14]

The clear moon is the posture of zazen. The waves are *bonnos*, illusions. *Bonnos* break (upon it) and at this moment (there is) illumination, light. At this moment: the light is *bodhi*, satori, nirvana.... Even waves, even *bonnos*, become nirvana.

Our desires, the illusions of daily life, are like the waves. The waves are only form, only phenomena. Their substance is only water. They disappear quickly, like bubbles. Waves have no substance. They are always changing, like water in a stream, always flowing. Impermanent. Sound, too, has no substance. What is its sound? Stones and rocks hit against each other and sound arises.

■

(Everyone is now walking one behind the other in *kinhin*. The master passes between the lines, looking at the people:) Tension is important; but not too much. After tension on the exhalation, there is relaxation on the inhalation. But a crisp face is not right. A little joyfulness is necessary, a little smile. Some here are completely crisp. The form of the face influences the mind. Some people who continue zazen become completely angry. It is not necessary to take on Bodhidharma's face. Bodhidharma sometimes smiled.[15]

■

(Zazen:) Dogen wrote in *Shobogenzo* that if one person does zazen, even for a short while, it influences all the cosmos and all existences. It influences even the mountains, trees and flowers. During the *sesshin*, the **sangha** becomes quiet, and all of Val d'Isère, all of its people, become quiet. Even the animals. Even the very mad. The mad understand. Their hypothalamus' understand. The hypothalamus of man and of animal is very pure.[16]

Just now a butterfly entered the dojo and I watched it to see where it would fly. She stopped on top of my head. The but-

terfly understands: this master is very quiet, he is not dangerous.... This afternoon Doctor Evelyne had come to my room
to do acupuncture; she was very surprised because a sparrow
entered the window. She was a little sick and she entered my
bed. "Sensei, Sensei, a bird, a bird!" It was very funny.... The
day before yesterday a black cat visited me while I was at my
desk. The cat completely disturbed me. She sat right down on
top of my work and would not leave.... I often experience this
during *sesshins*. Cats and dogs and other animals enter the dojo.
They want to sleep in the dojo during *sesshins*. Bilou[17] always
waits in front of the dojo, and in the mornings he leads the
procession.[18] But the moment there is the noise of a car, Bilou
barks. The moment there is noise, he makes noise. The hypothalamus understands.

When a mad person goes mad it is in the frontal brain that
it happens. The hypothalamus never gets sick, never gets mad.
If it did, the person would die immediately.... Mad people know
exactly where calmness is found, where danger does not reside.
They know by intuition. Their instincts want to come here,
want to do the *sesshin*.... But mad people make disturbances.

Zazen is very painful, very difficult to do, yet those who have
experienced it for a long time understand. They want to practice zazen, their hypothalamus wants to. It is the final happiness, the final peace, the final tranquil life. This is zazen.

Chukai!

AUG. 26 / 7.30 A.M.

THE FOUR ELEMENTS OF THE BRAIN:
Ju so gyo shiki

Last night I said *bonnos*, illusions, are like waves. Waves, which are water, have no substance. *Bonnos* too: no substance. They are only phenomenon, only *shiki*. So what is water? It is activity, it is *ki*.[19] What is activity?

In ancient Indian Buddhism, and in Hinduism too, they used the words *go un*. *Go un kai ku*....[21] What is *go un*? It is *shiki ju so gyo shiki*.[22]

Go un, what is this? We think it means body and mind. But in ancient India, and in ancient China, and also in Japanese Buddhism, it does not mean body and mind. It means *go un*.[23]

The first *shiki* of *"shiki ju so gyo shiki"* means the body—that is, its five sense organs. The other four (elements) have to do with consciousness, with mind, with that which is invisible, metaphysical.

HINDU THOUGHT

The ancient Hindus thought that the body was only composed of five elements of earth (i.e., bones), water (i.e., blood), fire (i.e., fever), air (i.e., gas), and mind.[24]

During meditation Hindus are always thinking: "What is the ego?" They observe themselves during meditation: "How is my body today? Today it's not so good. My body is indisposed. My bones are not so strong."

Bones are the earth. Blood (and urine, acids and other liquids) is water. "My water—my blood—is not so good." Or: "Today my body has too much fire. I have a fever." Or: "My body is too cold." (When we catch a cold we say, in Chinese and Japanese ideograms: *Kaze*. *Kaze* means that the wind enters the body. That cold air has entered through the skin or into the lungs.)

The Hindus thought that the body was connected to the cosmos, outside. The bones were the earth, the liquids were the water....

Anyway, in Japanese Buddhism the four elements which represent the mind are *ju so gyo shiki*. What is *ju? Ju* is the four elements of the mind. *Ju* means the accepted feelings or sensations coming from the six sense organs: *gen ni bi ze shin i*. *Gen* is eye, *ni* is ear, *bi* is nose, *ze* is tongue, *shin* is body, and *i* is consciousness.

Through *ju* (through the five sense organs), we accept things, we receive things, we feel things. We look through our eyes. And *so* (from *ju "so" gyo shiki*) is the image, the imagined: "Ah, this is a beautiful flower."

But if we look without image, without imagining anything, then nothing arises.[26] Then there is nothing. If we see a lovely woman but then do not create an image for her, then there is nothing.

"This is a beautiful flower—I must cut it." This is *gyo*. Karma arises. "She is a lovely mademoiselle. I must bring her to my room. 'Hello, how are you? Do you want some coffee?' "

This is *gyo*. *Gyo* means action. It is the will to act. It is to practice. Mind is in movement: *so gyo shiki*.

The last *shiki* (of *shiki ju so gyo shiki*) is not the same ideogram as the first *shiki*. This *shiki* means consciousness, all types of consciousness, the understanding which manages, which controls mind.

There are many kinds of consciousness: consciousness coming from the eyes, ears, nose, touch, or tongue. So this last *shiki* represents all consciousness coming from the five senses, and this includes memory. We feel, then we create the image, and next we act voluntarily, and so exactly we have memory. That which is imprinted in the neurons—the seeds—become memory. We quickly forget (i.e., what we have felt and imagined), but still it becomes seeds in the brain, and afterwards it will arise.... *So gyo shiki* are the three consciousnesses.

These seeds in the neurons arise later, like in dreams.

When we think during zazen, this is the subconscious arising.... Those who have done zazen for a long time do not think such bad things. They think of the sound of the river, they think of Sensei's *kusens*. "These conferences of Sensei's are not so bad; they are better than my thinking."

So this is mind. *Ju so gyo shiki.* This is water. From which arise waves, *bonnos.* This is the substance of waves, of water, of *bonnos. Shiki so gyo shiki.* The waves arise, and so bad karma is created; and sometimes good karma.

During zazen *shiki so gyo shiki* becomes calm. Were it to become strong, then karma would arise, bad karma would arise. Activity.... When activity is strong, when *shiki so gyo shiki* begins to move, bad karma arises.

Chukai!

8.30 P.M.

HOW BRAIN FUNCTIONS

Socrates said: *"Gnoti seauton;"* "Know thyself."

But how? How do we look into our mind? On this point Socrates was not very clear.[27] Occidental philosophy likes to analyze, but when it comes to mind, they do not analyze very much. Montaigne, which I have read many times, writes in his book *Essays* that "most people look to the outside, but I look to the inside." He repeats this thought three times in his *Essays*, yet he never tells us what is mind.[28]

How do we reflect upon mind? How do we observe mind? On this point Zen is very deep; it is more scientific, more logical than is occidental philosophy. Zen looks in on mind from many points of view, from many fields of vision. From *hishiryo*, from infinite consciousness.

■

Last year in Val d'Isère I spoke of concentration, of *samadhi*. Of the observation of our inside minds. When we look at a film on a movie screen, we are in complete concentration; we are marked, impressed. This is concentration. When the film is over an impressioned mind arises, and we admire or we criticize. This is observation.

So we have *ju so gyo shiki*. *Ju* are the senses, the sensations. *So* is the image: "This is a flower." *Gyo* is what comes after the image: what do we want? "Ah, this is a beautiful flower—I want to cut it." *Gyo* is the will to act.

If there is just *ju* and *so* and not *gyo*—if *gyo* is not realized—then karma does not manifest itself. If we only look: "That is a beautiful mountain," and then allow for another thought to come (i.e., another thought concerning, say, another matter), karma does not arise. When we pass in front of the Santa Lucia (the local bar), and only *ju* appears in our minds, and *so* and *gyo* do not manifest themselves, karma does not arise.

Bring ourselves to the level of consciousness, and this thinking will influence the neurons in our brains. The seeds of thinking (thus planted in the brain) become memory. Become a reminiscence, a souvenir. Then from *shiki*, from consciousness, the image arises.

■

The action of the human mind (the brain) is explained very realistically in Mahayana Buddhism. Its method of analysis is not at all hypothetical. Its method is a true fact of recognition.... Yet, on this subject (of method), occidental philosophy and psychology give no (such) explanations.

The body is a construction, but the mind is a systematized mechanism. We have factual knowledge of the state of moving mind. And so we can look objectively at our mind.

■

Tonight Bernard (the *tenzo*) and Mademoiselle asked me to marry them. Even during *sesshin* they think of making love, so surely with this ceremony their bad karma will finish. So I accepted to do the marriage ceremony.

Tonight I also received news that there is a new Pope. So I will do a *kito* for him. Pope John Paul the First.[29]

Kaijo!

(After performing the *kito* for the new Pope, the master performed the marriage ceremony, at the altar before the Buddha. When this was done he told the couple that it was "not necessary to go with other people now." And to the *tenzo* he said: "You must concentrate on madame." Then the three of them drank wine out of the same glass, and the master finished by saying: "I hope your marriage is a great success," and he kissed them both.)

AUG. 27 / 7.30 A.M.

CONTROLLING THE SENSES
AND OBSERVING THE MIND

(The open door at the back of the dojo, the cool morning breeze, the smell of earth and pine, the sounds of the river, of the *kyosaku*....)

Hear but not hear. It is possible.

Ju so gyo shiki. Ju is to hear the sound of the *kyosaku*. *So* is the image (of it). But if *ju so gyo shiki* does not arise, then we do not hear it.

Most people though, with the sound of the *kyosaku*, say:"Ah, that's the sound of the *kyosaku*," and next the image of the *kyosakuman* arises in their minds. Ju so gyo. *Gyo* is desire: "I want to receive the *kyosaku*." And *shiki* is judgment.

But if we do not imagine, if we do not desire, if we make no judgment, then there is nothing. This is thinking but not thinking, not thinking but thinking.

When we do not accept, do not look, do not hear, then ju does not arise. Only then do we have *so gyo shiki*. *So gyo shiki* arises—like a blind person who does not look, but looks. So then we can have *so gyo shiki* (without *ju*). This (too) is possible. It is then the opposite. It is imagination.

∎

Go un kai ku (i.e., the five **skandhas** or elements become emptiness). This is *hishiryo*. *Go un* are the five aggregates. They have no substance.

These *go un* become bonno, illusion, and karma arises.

When we hear sounds, smell odors, or when we look, if there is no image and (therefore) no desire, no judgment, then they have no influence; there is nothing.

There are no *bonnos*, so sometimes *go un* are *bonnos*, sometimes they are *bodhai*.[30] *Go un* (i.e., the five elements) is the source of *samadhi*.[31]

During zazen let (it) pass and it becomes *ku* (emptiness). So there will then be no *ju so gyo shiki*, no *bonnos*. Just *hishiryo*. *Go un* becomes *hishiryo* (i.e., from illusion comes satori).

∎

So there is no thinking. But during a dance, a waltz, a tango or an embrace, love arises and *so gyo shiki* becomes very strong (active). This is how it is: *Gen ni bi ze shin i* (i.e., the six body "organs").

Sometimes *go un*, sometimes *go un kai ku*. All is *ku*. *Go un kai ku*. These are important words. All becomes *ku*, emptiness, because there is no substance.

Control these *go un* (i.e., five senses) and we can recognize, we can observe inside mind. And we can recognize, we can observe outside.

These are the six roots, the six consciousnesses, the six objects. They are the sense organs.

∎

What is the sixth consciousness? It is intuition. (In modern psychology consciousness is not considered an organ, but it is in Buddhism. So in Buddhism the sixth organ is the root of consciousness, and this becomes intuition.)

The object of the eye is color. The object of the ear is sound. The object of the nose is smell; of the tongue is taste, of the body is touch, of consciousness is intuition. The object of the body is the mental.

So the six roots (organs, senses) receive, accept, feel the six objects. So at this time mental reaction arises, *ju so gyo shiki*. The four elements, the four mental reactions arise.

■

This is complicated, but still it is very systematic. If you understand this you can observe with exactitude the structure of your mind.

I am explaining the method for creating, for obtaining a true deep wisdom. So if you understand this you can get satori. But if you do zazen then you can realize this—*genjo*—automatically, naturally and unsconciouly (i.e., without going through the above analytic proceedure). Yet if you analyze this then of course it becomes clearer.

Don't move. Patience.

Kaijo!

AUG. 29 / 7 A.M.

CONSCIOUSNESS
or the hindering of wisdom

As of today we begin the last *sesshin*. Only today and tomorrow and half of the next. So concentrate. Especially the permanents who have been here since the beginning: concentrate here and now and the time will pass quickly. When we notice time passing by like an arrow, this is satori. Satori is not a special consciousness, not imagined enlightenment. Satori means to return to the normal original condition of the brain.

The forty days here pass by very quickly. At this time we understand that our life is impermanent. And that other things are not very important. That time passes by, only this is important. We are quickly approaching the coffin.

People wish to forget this, but if they do—if they escape this problem—then life is vain.

Understand this and life becomes strong. At this moment life becomes saintly.

So later, when you return to your home, try to remember this summer camp....

(*Kinhin* is over and everyone is returning, one behind the other, to his place.) You must not walk with arms dangling. Your hands must be crossed at the level of the navel.... Do not yawn. You have not enough tension, and this is why you are tired and you yawn. When you yawn you realize tiredness. It is not so bad, but then you must place your hand over your mouth.

(Zazen:) From the beginning of zazen to the end of zazen,

time is very long. So time is very short. Afterwards, when you remember, it is very short. Zazen is very long, very short.

■

When the inside subjective looks at the outside objective, and with the six roots of the brain feeling the six objects, then at this time a mental reaction appears.

Gyo: desire. Consciousness continues. The imagination.

If you do not imagine, if you do not think, then even if you look, you do not look; even if you hear, you do not hear. Contrarily, if you do not look, the imagination looks; if you do not hear, the imagination hears.

During zazen we must let (matters) pass. If we do (indulge in) imagination, it will expand. Foolish expansion.... The imagination becomes, makes, mistakes. It makes categories, and it becomes dogmatic. Mistaken thinking.

■

I am explaining to you how one creates true wisdom.

Look from the inside mind to the outside mind; look objectively, and the eye is just like a camera.

The image enters the eye through the lens (pupil) to rest on the retina. The optic nerve signals the brain. These signals are received in a buffer zone.... Ah, you must ask Doctor Durix. He can explain it all to you. He is an eye doctor....

So consciousness arises within the center of the sense of sight. This is *gen shiki,* sight consciousness.

So consciousness is created in the center of the sense of sight. *Gen ni bi ze shin i.*

But if this sight consciousness does not arise, consciousness is not created. If we do not think, if we do not create consciousness—within any of the senses—then consciousness does not arise. Then we do not look, we do not hear.

■

Some people say that Sensei never hears: "Even when I talk to him, he does not hear." This is sometimes true. Muriel, my old secretary, talked too much. She made too much noise.... Many people come to my room. They speak in French and I don't understand. They sound like birds.

Even if we do not hear, if we do not accept, and even if *ju* does not arise, if *so gyo* is not created and not entertained, then there will be no *shiki*, no consciousness (i.e., to hinder the appearance of true wisdom).

No one has yet taught what I am now teaching. It is the point of *hishiryo*. It is Dogen's Zen. What is thinking of non-thinking? It is *hishiryo*. And at this moment wisdom arises.

■

Even if we see, not see, there is no tiredness. With modern people though, it is the opposite. They don't look, but they imagine. This image becomes a desire, and now they can think of nothing else—they cannot create wisdom—and so they become neurotic and in the end crazy.

Chin in, chin in. Don't move. Posture and patience are very important.

10.30 A.M.

OBSERVATION OF MIND
The opening horizon

Ju so gyo shiki: even if *ju* does not manifest itself, memory still arises. And this is especially so during zazen. So if you continue zazen without hearing my *kusens*, then the subconscious arises. This is not *ju*, but it is *so*.

When the six roots of the brain feel the six objects, then at this time a mental notion appears: imagination. So, even if you look or hear, you do not look or hear. But you can also have the opposite: even if you do not look and you do not hear, you look and you hear. The image, *so* has appeared.

When we hear we do not hear. And when we do not hear, imagination hears. So if we do not imagine, then: nothing.

■

A brain is like a computer, only a computer has no life of its own. It is just a machine.... In ancient times people did not know of computers and of machines. The patriarchs did not know the function of the brain. But today, because we can make this comparison between a brain and a computer, we can see very clearly what is observation of mind.

■

The *kyosaku* must be strong. This one has a sleepy sound. (The *kyosaku* is now being administered.) Speed is necessary when giving the *kyosaku*. A strong speed, in the correct direction. Not on the bones, not on the face. If a mosquito land on your face, you must aim accurately and hit quickly. If you go slowly, it will fly away. It's the same with the *kyosaku*. If the *kyuosaku-man* does not concentrate, he will hit the bones, the face.... André is not at all effective. Only formalism. He knows very well how to make *kyosakus*, but... (he does not know how to administer one).[32]

◼

I am explaining to you how we create wisdom. And in the end it is *hishiryo*, this is wisdom.

A computer cannot create wisdom, but a computer receives, as does *ju*. Like a punch-card machine. The signal enters the computer's memory discs. This is *ju*. Feeling.

On the other side (and this is the same as root-consciousness or *manas*-consciousness), there is the program, the memory data, a logical register. It accounts logically. This is the sixth consciousness. *Manas*. But the result is the same: imagination.

So, by comparing the brain with a computer, you can clearly understand this method for observing mind.

◼

Our thinking is objective and subjective at the same time. But most people only think subjectively—they think egotistically, egocentrically—by their own proper preferences. This is the habit of our daily lives.

But during zazen we are looking objectively and subjectively at the same time. *Hishiryo* consciousness is subjective observation and objective observation. During zazen all this arises at the same time.

Our thinking is not the same during zazen as it is during daily life.

It is not necessary, nor is it effective, to think during zazen that, "I must think like a computer." If you think on your posture, then you do this unconsciously. By this means you can create and develop wisdom.

■

In modern times people cannot understand why zazen is effective. Even doctors of philosophy, even Professor Chauchard,[34] cannot understand this. Because he has never experienced zazen and he cannot explain it scientifically. Nor can the psychologists understand it. Jung too; Jung even studied zazen yet he never spoke of this (method for observing mind).

■

There is the body, the individual body, and the outside. We imagine that we think within our own bodies, within our own skin. This is ego. Outside the body is the rest. So we limit.[35] This is egocentric consciousness. There is always self-preference, self-protection, self-preservation, self-satisfaction, self-advertisement. We are always wanting to satisfy our egoistic desires. We are always wanting to escape from what we do not like, from anxiety, from fear, or from whatever we dislike.

But for those who continue zazen, it is another thinking which you practice. I can certify this. The thinking is not the same.

We are practicing objective observation—the same as do other existences. We can observe this sameness of other existences with the ego. So we can open up a large horizon. This is *Hannya Haramita*. The eye of wisdom, the observation of wisdom. This is the observation of Kanji-zai (the Bodhisattva Avalokitesvara). Our ego at this time is not the same as the common ego.

Heaven, earth and the ego have the same root. All existences and the ego are in unity; they are one body. There is no negation of the ego; this is not nihilism. All becomes ego. The entire cosmos becomes ego. This is interdependence. The ego has no substance, it has no noumenon. We are attached to nothing.

At this time we can wake up to the Dharma of immortality,

to beyond life and death. This is *hishiryo* consciousness. From here, from this consciousness, infinite wisdom comes, infinite wisdom is created and developed.

■

Chin in, chin in.

When people think, their chins drop forward. Their frontal brains are heavy and their heads fall. You must always stretch the neck, stretch the waist. From posture, create wisdom. The hypothalamus is the source and the energy of wisdom.

During zazen the hypothalamus and the thalamus[36] become strong with activity. This is the usefulness of zazen.

But it is not necessary to think, "I must create a strong hypothalamus."*Mushotoku*—without goal—this is what is necessary. *Mushotoku*: automatically, naturally, unconsciously.

MONDO

Analysis vs. repetition

QUESTION: During zazen what we practice then, is self-analysis?

Master: No, don't analyze, don't analyze! During zazen it is not necessary to analyze your mind. If you concentrate on your posture, you can be like this. (Sensei takes up the zazen posture), unconsciously, naturally and automatically. I have explained this. You don't understand? (The questioner shakes his head, no.) Zazen is not the same as when you read books. Practice is very important. Repeat: *Dokan*. This is very difficult to understand. Do you understand? (Silence). Sure, you cannot understand. You are trying to understand with your head. You observe with your frontal brain. Another question?

In the toilet

QUESTION: Why must one remove his *rakusu* before going to the toilet?

Master: So that your *rakusu* will not become dirty. If you let it fall into the toilet, it will come out dirty and smelly. The *rakusu* is better clean. Respect it.

It is also a bit of a custom (to remove one's *rakusu* or *kesa* before entering the toilet). Modern toilets are very clean; and in the old days the toilets were clean too, but they smelled. And to go to the toilet in a Japanese temple is a very complicated matter. To remove your *kolomo* and your *chukin*,[37] and to do so exactly, and to put them in order is quite difficult. And the pee-pee posture, which is not the same as the western style, is also complicated—in a Japanese temple it is necessary to sit down like a woman. Then you must do *gassho*. The preparation alone takes five minutes.

So it becomes a habit, a posture; it becomes deep. It is not the same as with dogs. For dogs it is very convenient; they can do pee-pee anywhere.

Very important, manners. Important! Another question?

■

QUESTION: To do zazen should one not be politically engaged?

Master: As you like. You must decide for yourself. I do not oblige or order…. Why, do you want to follow some political party?
Answer: Not a party, but a direction.
Master: People who receive my ordination, people who become

my disciples, them I can educate on this. But not others. It is as you like, you must decide: if you want to become a government deputy, or even a minister, it is possible. You can become that.... What do you like?
Answer: Ecology.
Master: Ecology is good. But to become too attached to it is not good. I like ecology. And I have read Konrad Lorenz. He is very interesting.

The anger of a true educator

Stéphane: Sometimes Sensei is very kind with his disciples and we like him very much, but other times he is very hard on us and we are not so happy.
Master: So?
Stéphane: So sometimes we don't like you. Does this matter?
Master: If you make a mistake it is necessary that I become angry. When one is always testing his parents, or the master, if the master does not become angry then he is a little crazy. A true educator must become angry.

In modern times parents are very protective and much too kind. So afterwards the parents become afraid of their children.... Democratic education is not always so good. The educators make mistakes, they rarely become angry, and when they do, even a little bit, people escape.

In my ten years here in Europe, many people have escaped. I do like this and like that (Sensei gestures with his hand for the presumed disciple to come closer, then he makes a grabbing gesture), and then *paf!* So they escape.... It is very difficult to educate. Another question?

4th session

QUESTION: Professor Dürckheim[38] sometimes has his followers practice meditation while in the posture of zazen. For example, he has them meditate on the symbol of the cup, the bowl, the tree, the symbol of the onion....

Master: Professor Dürckheim could not understand my Zen, and he left. He is basically a psychoanalyst, but he is not a Zen master and he does not at all understand Zen. Anyway, the method you speak of is professor Dürckheim's method, and if you want to follow it, it is possible; you can use everything. But this is not Zen. Another question?

Kito

QUESTION: What is *kito?*

Master: You looked, you saw it being performed didn't you?
Answer: Yes.
Master: So you can understand. It is like that.

QUESTION: Yes, but how can *kito* cut karma?

Master: This is a psychological and a metaphysical problem. Something arrives during *kito*. But if I explain it, it becomes a category, (it develops) a meaning.... *Kito* is a very delicate matter. For people who believe in it, *kito* changes karma. But for me, this is not so.

QUESTION: And for you, can the *kito* be effective?

Master: Other people doing a *kito* for me? I am beyond a *kito*.
But for believers, for people who believe in me, *kito* is very effective. For others, though, it is not at all effective.... During the ceremony the disciples sing the *Hannya Shingyo* and the

master chants the *kito* and so there is a special atmosphere, and a strong mental influence is created.

∎

QUESTION: I want to thank you very much for having opened up my karma and my ego, for having helped me to abandon my little ego.

Master: Sure!

QUESTION: But I am sometimes pessimistic. How can one change the karma of others? How can I change universal karma?

Master: You have not to manage the whole world.
Answer: Yes, but we are sitting on an atom bomb!
Master: True.... This Madame attends all the different religious congresses. Whenever there is a religious congress, she is there.
Madame: And at the political congresses as well. (Laughter.)
Master: Are they effective?
Madame: Not so effective.
Master: So what's your conclusion?
Madame: I am pessimistic.
Master: It is not necessary to be pessimistic. Just continue zazen. Like me. It is better. The middle way.
Madame: But we are not alone! For other people, other people, other people!
Master: Other people, other people.... During this camp more than one thousand people have come. It is spreading, and my disciples are becoming stronger, and they influence all of Europe, all the world.... To seek the way, this is important. What is the way? The way is under our feet.

4 P.M.

HEARING THE SUTRA
or cutting the mind which sticks

How obtain perfect wisdom? This is explained in *Hannya Shingyo*. All is *ku*, all is *mu*,[39] all is negated. (Sensei recites the Sutra *Hannya Shingyo*.) At this time perfect and complete wisdom arises.

■

Occidental philosophy is the world of epistemology, while Buddhist philosophy is the world of experience. We can make the immediate experience during zazen. We experience objective observation and objective certification of the ego. Because (sometimes) we are not looking, not hearing, not tasting, not touching. All this time there is no perception from the five organs of sense.

But imagination, coming from memory, rises up like a dream. This is the subconscious which we create. This is "meditation."

This is meditation in other religions. In other religions they imagine (create images) with their own consciousness. But zazen is not to continue imagination, not to continue *so*.... It is to be not attached to anything. Do not run after anything, do not escape from anything.

■

Eno, the famous 6th Patriarch: his father died when he was a boy, and he had no brothers or sisters, just a mother. So he cut wood and carried it off on his shoulders to sell in town.

One day while he was walking on the path it began to rain, so he took shelter in the doorway of a house. From where he was standing he could hear the beautiful chanting of a sutra. He did not understand its meaning, but still he was impressed.... (Even if you cannot understand its meaning, a good sutra will mark you, impress you. It's the same as when we chant them here. It is not like singing songs.)

(During the following twenty minutes, the master chants the *Diamond Sutra* in old Kanbun.)

"What is this sutra?" Eno asked the monk after he had finished chanting.

"The *Diamond Prajna Paramita Sutra*"[40] replied the monk.

When we do not stay on anything, at this time true mind arises....[41] True mind means the true nature of Buddha. Here true perfect wisdom arises.

So at this moment when he heard this phrase, Eno got satori. From this phrase of eight ideograms.

There are many famous short statements in the sutras. Like this one: (Sensei chants.) When a great master chants, one single phrase can change a person.... Satori—there are many stories of this in Zen.

If we are not attached, if our consciousness does not stay (on something), then we can have perfect satori, perfect wisdom. But most people always stay; most are always attached to the foolish ego. They cannot abandon the ego.

In modern civilization in particular, people have a strong ego. Selfish: they are always thinking of self-preservation; and they make their own publicity to give themselves more value.

So you must escape, separate, cut yourself from this mind which sticks! Then you can obtain true wisdom.

4th session

NÔ THEATER

Ze-ami, very well known in Japanese Nô theater, wrote books on the attitude of mind of Nô actors. It is looking-of-the-non-looking. (What is this? It is thinking-non-thinking. It is *hishiryo*.) Ze-ami was influenced by Dogen's Zen, and so it became Nô. Ze-ami wrote this himself.[42]

The actor's mask leaves only little slits for the eyes. So when he acts he is like a blind man. He looks through little holes and he cannot see everything. Yet when he acts he must look over the entire stage; and off it too. He must look at the spectators; not just at their faces but at their minds as well. He must see all, but he can't—not through the little holes.... This is similar to Zen. Nô actors must understand Zen.... Looking-not-looking. The actor cannot look subjectively, yet in order to play we must look at everything. This way *so gyo shiki* is developed. The actor acts through *so gyo shiki*.

So, if we are not attached to one detail, we can look at everything. And when we look at everything, we must not lose sight of the details. This is the relationship betwen art and Zen.

(Sensei recites a passage from *Shodoka* in Kanbun which finishes with: "...remember that Buddhism must cut the root and not the branches and the leaves.").... Cut the leaves and study the branches—I do not like this. What I like is to get to the root and not be anxious about the extremities.

Your postures here are not good. I have talked for a long time and everyone's chins have fallen out. (Everyone except for the ten-year-old American girl; she has not moved at all.)

Concentrate. Two more minutes. Then we will stop, for a *mondo*.

When times are difficult, zazen is most effective. Then you cannot stay. You stay only on pain.

MONDO

The beggars sang shomyo

QUESTION: I would like to know about the origins of *shomyo*. And I would also like to know about *daihishin-darani*.

Master: The Japanese language has become *shomyo! Shomyo* is a special singing. It is a special tone, a special modulation. (Sensei chants in *shomyo*.) This is Zen *shomyo*. But there are many other kinds of *shomyo;* there is Tendai *shomyo*, Shingon *shomyo*.[43] And then there is *daihishin-darani*. This is general, common singing (Sensei sings in *daihishin-darani*).[44]

Dahishin-darani is not the same in the Eihiji and the Sojiji temples. At Eiheiji it sounds like this: (he sings). While at Sojiji it is like this: (he sings again, this time more slowly). This singing is very slow; this is *shomyo*.

(As it is impossible, here, to transcribe Sensei's words in proper grammatical syntax, I have summed them up in my own words: Shomyo developed at the Soto temples of Sojiji and Daijozenji-noto. The master of Daijozenji-noto, and once a disciple of the great Soto patriarch Keizan, had to walk thirty or forty kilometers from home every day in order to be with his disciples at Daijozenji-noto for the early morning zazen. So as not to become tired and also to keep himself moving along at a regular pace over the mountain early every morning, he invented this singing technique that came to be called *"shomyo"*—a technique which consists basically in singing the sutras more slowly than was the standard custom.... This method became popular, and especially so during the Tokugawa period, when beggars chanted the sutras in *shomyo*. They sang these simple melodies ever so slowly (much more slowly than even the monks in the temples) and the people cried and gave them money. Anyway, it was primarily because of these beggars that *shomyo*, in its more mournful aspects, spread throughout Japan.)

(Sensei sings in *shomyo;* then he imitates a beggar's soliloquy:) "I cannot walk, I have no legs, and I am blind. Very pitiful am I, so please, have pity and give me money.... " They sang slowly, slowly. It sounded very pitiful, so people gave them money.... And then every night, when it grew dark, the (seemingly legless) beggars stood up and walked back home.

The beggars changed the sutras. Even though they could not understand them.

Shomyo is interesting. If I sang *shomyo* to a Japanese madame, she would surely cry.... Sometimes I sing this way at Japanese ceremonies for the dead. Exactly you can feel **mujo,** impermanence.

■

QUESTION: Sometimes you write poems or you sing songs or you paint calligraphies. At these times do you feel yourself more as an artist than as a Zen monk?

Master: Not at all. I don't reflect. When I write I am not conscious of it, I am not thinking, "Now I am an artist." And when I do zazen, I am not thinking about Zen or about Buddhism.

This is an objective problem. Subjectively I do not think at all. But since you want to understand this objectively: when I write I am a Zen monk writing. This is a name. But subjectively there is nothing.

Karma continues

QUESTION: What is karma?

Master: *Oh là-là!* This is the question which people ask the most. In the ten years that I have been doing *mondos* here I have had this question asked me more than one hundred times. I am always answering this question. This is why last year I gave *kusens* on karma. For forty days I talked only on karma. Philippe wrote it down in *The Voice of the Valley*. (Sensei turns to his secretary:) And in French?

Secretary: Yes, we have twelve *kusens* published in French on karma (Laughter).

Master (to questioner): If I again explain karma, you will have to pay for another ten days.

Anyway, for an outline on karma: karma means action. There are three kinds: body, mouth and mind. Concerning body karma: steal or kill and this action will completely influence the future. Action of mouth too, influences the future. You lie, you criticize and time will pass, but afterwards this karma, this action, returns exactly.... With action of mind it is the same: you say that you love, but in your consciouness you are always thinking hate. Well, this karma arrives in the future.

In traditional Hinduism there is the Atman, the soul.[45] At death, the body dies but the soul continues. In Buddhism this is not so. Still, karma continues. Even after death; for eternity.[46] So how do we cut karma? A religious man must cut karma. Another question?

■

QUESTION: When zazen is almost over and you say: "We must suffer for two more minutes," at this time I hate you. What I want to know is what is happening in my mind when I think like this.

Master: You think this way during zazen? Why? Why, during zazen?.... The American girl here is ten years old and she is more developed than you. You are childish. The little girl is the opposite of you: she does not at all move.
Answer: Sometimes, when I suffer, I think that you are Hitler.
Master (frowning): I am not Hitler. I have no mustache, and I am Japanese, not German. (Sensei turns to his secretary and asks her how many people have left the *sesshin*.)
Secretary: Four people left today.
Master: My education is very soft. But a little strength is sometimes necessary.

Western people have become completely foolish. Their egos grow stronger and stronger. They are only individuals. Ten people have escaped since the beginning of the *sesshin*. They are completely foolish. Surely they thought that a *sesshin* in Val d'Isère is the same as a holiday at the Mediterranean Club. So they ran away. Until death they will not become clever.

8.30 P.M.

ZEN AND BUDO

The Rinzai master, Takuan, taught Yaku Tajima no Kami, a *Kendo*[48] master and sage, the essence of kendo. (*Takuan* in Japanese means cucumber.) So master Cucumber taught him the essence. He gave Tajimanokami the *Fudo Shinmyo Chi Roku,* or the *Record of the Non-Moving Excellent Wisdom.*[47]

(Herein) is the essence of kendo: looking without looking. During a kendo tournament it is either to kill or to be killed. It is not like a baseball game. There is no waiting. In western sports there is always waiting time. In the martial arts there is none. Kill or be killed.

So it is necessary to look at the adversary's entire body, and not at just one part of it. You must attack the top of the head, but if you look only at the top of the head, this is a mistake. This is subjective, egoistic looking.... The adversary moves quickly, suddenly.... Does the hand move? The foot move? The eyes move?.... So looking without looking, this is very important.

The first look is objective looking. The second look—without looking—is subjective looking. So it is looking objectively without looking subjectively.... So it is, too, during zazen: think without thinking, think from the bottom of non-thinking.

■

In ancient *budo*, there are many different schools.[49] There is *Mu Gen Ryu*, the school of the blind.[50] There is *Mu Nen Ryu*, the school of non-thinking.[51] This school is completely Zen.

The school of *Otanashino Kamae*, which was founded by the blind samurai, Sukuae, means the school of attitude without sound.[52]

The two most famous samurai sages of kendo were Miyamoto **Musashi** and Sukuae. Sukuae was blind but, like Miyamoto Musashi, he killed during tournaments.[53]

To be blind is more convenient. If the techniques of the two adversaries are equal, then the blind man has the advantage. The blind man's intuition is strong, and if the techniques are the same, then it is mind vs. mind.... In the beginning the combat is in the visible world, but in the end it is in the invisible one. And the blind man has had much practice in the invisible world.

(The bell for *kinhin* has been struck and everyone stands up:)

The posture of *kinhin* is the basic posture found at the root of all the martial arts. *Kinhin* is not the same as walking. Tension, no tension. Look on one point, see everything. If you develop the habit of *kinhin,* your regular walking will have dignity.

(Zazen:) The metaphysical world is the world of the invisible, while the physical world is the world of the visible. And Zen is the visible of the invisible. Zen is the metaphysical world of the physical one, it is the physical of the metaphysical.

I too experienced Japanese martial arts. I am a 5th *dan* in judo (and also a 5th *dan* in kendo). This is by the ancient *dan* rating. A 5th *dan* in those days is an 8th *dan* today. (My grandfather was a 10th *dan* in yawara.[54] He educated the samurais during the Meiji Revolution.) I know the essence of judo, but I have forgotten the *wasa* (i.e., technique).

Kyushin Ryu[55] of judo—the ancient school of yawara—is the school of managing (of directing) mind. In daily life mind, the ego, the subjective mind, controls the body; but in *Kyushin* objective mind controls mind (i.e., the mind which looks at itself).

This is Zen. We must not follow mind, egoistic mind—we must control it.

◾

Kyosaku! (The *kyosaku* is now being administered.)

◾

There are infinite examples which show the influence of Zen on the martial arts…. And on Japanese art too.

Alan **Watts** liked Zen; he understood it superficially. Western intellectuals like Zen because of its relationship with art. They only understand the surface.[56]

Concentrate. Patience. I am not Hitler![57]

Kaijo!

AUG. 30 / 7 A.M.

HIS SECRETARY WAS HIS SHADOW

(The master enters the dojo and as usual, without losing any time, he walks quickly along the lines of those sitting in zazen, inspecting everyone and everything. Behind him follows the shusso. Gaining his seat to the right of the entrance and directly opposite the big bay window, the master does *gassho* and sits down. The first ray of sunlight, just then cutting through a cleft between two mountains, falls full on his face as he takes up the lotus posture. Meanwhile, the *shusso*, having stopped along the way (to correct someone's posture or something), regains his own seat (to the left of the entrance) some moments later. The master says:)

The *shusso* must look at everyone, at all two hundred people assembled here. It is not necessary for him to concentrate on only one person.

■

Some people have not come to zazen. I have asked the *kyosakuman* to check the rooms. He has now been away for half-and-hour.

(After a while the *kyosakuman* shows up. He re-enters the dojo, leans over and whispers into the master's ear.)

This *kyosakuman* caught one person, a sick person. Half-an-hour to catch someone who is sick. The *kyosakuman* must find by intuition, rapidly; he must not take half-an-hour.

During a *sesshin* you can concentrate only on zazen—on one thing. When the *sesshin* comes life is simple. But even then it is not so simple. Those who hold responsibilities here must not concentrate only on their responsibilities. Look not look.

To concentrate on one thing is very easy. Though some here

cannot even do that. Like crazy people, like children.

But in modern daily life to concentrate (on many things) is difficult to do. Before I became the secretary to my master Kodo Sawaki, I had been the personal secretary to the Japanese Minister of Finance, Matsunaga. Ministers arrived every day and it was very complicated: telephones, letters, dictations, questions, rendezvous. Wisdom was necessary. Looking not looking. Had I concentrated on one thing, I would have forgotten other things.

Those who become secretaries to important people become clever. They cannot solve the problems only by knowledge, so they must create. They create wisdom.

If you look only at the part, you cannot concentrate on the whole. Look only at the leaves and you cannot see the root. Look only at the root, and you cannot see the leaves. Do this and contradictions arise.

■

Eka was Bodhidharma's secretary for nine years—right up to his master's death. And Eka received the *shiho* just before Bodhidharma died.

Ejo became Dogen's secretary, even though he was older than Dogen. Still, right up until Dogen's death Ejo continued as his secretary. He was just like the shadow of Dogen.[58]

And so Dogen became famous. Ejo completely helped him. Dogen did not write *Shobogenzo* by himself, not at all. Ejo did most of it. He put it in order, he edited it. Ejo had a deep wisdom.

In Japanese temples the masters have five *gojisha* (secretaries), and they are very important. In Soto Zen the secretaries receive a strong education. The secretaries must take care of the *shoko* box (incense) and carry the ceremonies. They must receive the visitors, the dignitaries and other important officials. They must write letters, take phone calls, take dictations, take notes during the teaching. They must see that the master has clean shirts, *kolomos*. And they must take care of his food. For a Japanese master this is complicated: miso soup, soba, tamari.

FROM THE SIMPLE COME THE COMPLICATED

When I first arrived in France, life was not at all difficult. I lived in a little room in the back of a warehouse. I slept on the concrete, with only a *zafu*, and for a desk I used a barrel. I only ate *genmai* which I cooked myself. I rarely went out; once I did go out and I got lost. It was a simple life. Just zazen and a little writing.

Later people asked me to give conferences; so I gave them. Then the dojo arose. They arose in the provinces too, in Switzerland, in Milan, Brussels, London. And so it became more complicated. Editors asked me for books. Films, television. And now summer camps. These camps are now forty days long.

■

As much as possible I want to concentrate only on zazen. But to spread zazen, organization is necessary. So wisdom is necessary.

Sewing *kesas*, like Jeanne; it is very simple to sew *kesas* from morning until night. She is very happy.... But in daily life it is not so simple. Wisdom is necessary.

We must not look at one part; we must look at everything. *Shiki soku ze ku, ku soku ze shiki.* (Form is emptiness, emptiness is form.) *Ku* (emptiness) is zero; only one. This is very simple. But then *shiki* (phenomena) arises.... The source is very simple, very pure: only *ku*. But from this source arise many phenomena. And so it becomes *shiki*.

How do we solve these contradictions?

■

We must catch the root. It is not necessary to pay attention to the leaves. But naturally, unconsciously, automatically we can do both.

He who takes care only of the leaves, forgets the root, so he takes care of the little things, leaves, leaves... with his personal consciousness.

But he can catch the root, and from this wisdom arises.

AUG. 30 / 10.30 A.M.

WHEN MIND RESTS ON NOTHING
or why pilots do zazen

Shiki ju so gyo shiki. If you continue zazen for a long time, you do not feel *shiki* (the body). The same with *ju:* there is no act of looking, of hearing. *So* and *gyo* are finished too. There are no more images, no more desire. *Shiki* (consciousness) alone remains. There is only unconsciousness, subconsciousness, natural consciousness. This looking non-looking, non-hearing but hearing, thinking non-thinking and non-thinking thinking. *Manas* consciousness has finished and only *Alaya* consciousness remains.[59]

If we concentrate only on our hands, our thumbs, then we cannot concentrate on our breathing—someone asked this during the *mondo*. But with the habit of concentration in zazen, then we can concentrate on stretching the waist, stretching the neck, pulling in the chin, pushing the sky with the head and the ground with the knees: then we can concentrate on the entire posture all at the same time. Through repetition we can concentrate on everything.

■

In modern civilization life is complicated, and sometimes we must concentrate in many directions at the same time.

This is why Guy (who is a jumbo jet pilot for Air France) comes to zazen.... I am often asked questions by officials of the Japanese airlines. Zen instruction for pilots is very important. *Hishiryo*.... The pilot of a jumbo jet, while he is in the process of landing, must always maintain communication with the control tower. He must hear the information, and he must await orders and instructions. He must look outside and at the same time he must look inside—at the instruments. He must use his hands and his feet. He must talk with the flight steward and he must deal with the Red Army (i.e., sky-jackers). And at the same time he must realize an accurate landing, with the exact speed. So the pilot trains deeply. Only repetition: and so habit develops. He does not use his own personal consciousness, but only the unconscious. (What is necessary are three heads and six hands, like the Hindu God Shiva.)

The pilot is completely in zazen. There is no *ju so gyo* at this moment. It's like when in a tournament: to kill or not to be killed. Face to face with a sword: in one moment all is decided.

Some sleep in zazen. Zazen is not so dangerous. Some move and think of other things. But concentrate only on your posture and it is like with a jumbo pilot or like in the martial arts.

A DIFFERENT BREED OF MAN

If mind rests on nothing, true mind arises. Stagnate on one thing and this is a mistake. But if you concentrate on the posture of zazen, every day for one hour, two hours, and develop the habit of this posture, then you become different than other people.

■

Imagination, images, are created by our own mind, by our consciousness. Our mind makes *naraka* (hell); it makes suffering. Each person is living in a world which he creates by his own proper consciousness.

So, what is the ego?.... Each one of us think: "I am me," I am like this or like that; and we understand this through *go un*, the five aggregates (sensation, perception, thought, activity, and consciousness). This is *gyo* and *shiki*—egoistic *gyo* and egoistic *shiki*.

But to understand unconsciously, objectively—this is *hishiryo* consciousness. And so at this moment our egoistic desires can be sublimated to a higher level. This is the teaching of Zen. It is the highest wisdom for daily living.

So repeat zazen. One *sesshin* is effective; but continue zazen and it will become a habit, it will become deeper.

For beginners this is difficult to do; because they must use their willpower. But this is not so for those who continue zazen. Willpower is not necessary, for body and mind follow the cosmic order. Mind has developed the habit of following the cosmic order.

MONDO

The importance of self-certification

QUESTION: I have many questions to ask, questions which I write down in a notebook when I am alone. But when I do zazen my questions seem suddenly meaningless and useless, and I forget them all.

Master: This is because you progress, you progress in satori. When doubtfulness finishes: this is satori. So it is when you resolve your questions by yourself, when you understand them by yourself. If it is through my answers that you understand, then this is not true satori. Understand, by yourself, and at this time it is self-certification. Self-certification is very important, not only from the brain, but from the bottom of mind. Satori is not only one time.

■

QUESTION: What do you mean by cosmic order?

Master: The revolution of the planets, wind, storms. Science calls this the cosmic order. The movement of the stars; morning comes and the sun rises and in the evening it sets.
Answer: Therefore it is imposible not to follow the cosmic order.
Master: We must follow it, but some don't. When the sun rises, they go to sleep. All this is very simple, but still some people do the opposite.

During zazen we follow the cosmic order. Professor Chauchard wrote that when we are in deep meditation, we are following the cosmic order.

But in modern civilization the frontal brain goes against this, and so your autonomous system becomes tired; you become tired, neurotic, and in the end you go crazy and finish in the hospital. You, Doctor, you have studied the hypothalamus. You must teach others.

■

The truth?

QUESTION: Is Zen the true truth?

Master: Bien sûr! What is truth? (No reply.) If you don't know Zen and you don't know truth, then your question is empty. (Everyone in the assembly laughs.) Your question is funny.

What is truth? Everybody uses this word, but what is it? What is truth, what is the way? This is a big koan. Another question?

■

QUESTION: Is truth relative?

Master: Relative and not relative. True truth is beyond everything, it is universal. Relative truth is the truth for some and not for others; so it is not the truth. True truth is also objective. But the Madame who is asking this question is always making her own proper categories, and so her thinking becomes narrow.... Everybody makes their own proper categories. Everybody looks through his own colored spectacles. Another question?

The scientist is a searcher

QUESTION: You say that science certifies that the mind, during zazen, follows the cosmic order. And yet you also say that science is narrow, and that it, too, looks through spectacles.

Master: Yes, within the world of science: truth (i.e., inside the world of science itself, science certifies).Concerning the material and physical world, science is very convenient. But when it comes to metaphysical questions, science cannot certify them. Science cannot certify religion, it cannot certify mind. Nor can psychology. Objectively psychology can do so, but subjectively it is not possible. Because each person looks through his own colored spectacles.

Science is not complete. This is why scientists are always searching, searching. They have understood that science is not complete; so they are always thinking. They are always searching for more and more truth.

Isn't this so, Doctor? (Sensei looks at Doctor Durix). Science is not complete (nor is modern medicine), so you are searching, seeking to progress.

■

The brain bid

Doctor (nodding): This is why many of us practice zazen.
Master (laughs): Yes, like yourself. Please, Doctor, give us a conference.
Doctor (momentarily taken aback): Well, how much time is left?
Master (looking at his big silver wristwatch): Ten minutes.... Doctor Durix will now give us a conference.

(Durix, a disciple of the master, and also a foremost medical authority on the hypothalamus, gives an impromptu talk on the function of the brain as explained through the lastest discoveries made in the sciences. He talks for about half-an-hour.)

Master: Exactly. Posture is important. Breathing. I have studied this very deeply. And now so is the Doctor. Doctor Durix is very strong on the study of the hypothalamus.... But we (i.e., scientists and others) must continue to progress with relationship to zazen.

Many years ago scientists at the University of Tokyo made an examination of my body and my mind. And so now, whenever I return to Japan the doctors at the University want to re-examine me. And one day in Paris, Etienne and I were examined at the hospital of Sainte-Anne. For one full day we underwent electroencephalograph tests. (He shakes his hand to indicate that it was very exhausting.)

Tokyo University has many many recorded electroencephalographs of my brain. Three interns became doctors by doing their theses on my brain. (Laughter.) This is completely true! And Doctor Hirai—the thesis he wrote on my brain made him famous! And then Professor Chauchard of the Sorbonne later read Hirai's study and he was very surprised, very impressed by it. Doctor Hirai is younger than me. He became a doctor in his young days. Now he practices zazen.

Doctor: It would be greatly edifying were we to have you brain to study.

Master: Afterwards this can be made possible. But not now: I do not want to die yet.,... My master Kodo Sawaki gave his body to the University of Tokyo. (Sensei looks at the Doctor:) Ah, but Tokyo University has already asked for it, for my brain. Hirai wants it.

"*D'accord, d'accord,*" I had said to him.

AUG. 30 / 4 P.M.

THE SPLENDID BOOK

Philippe wrote *The Voice of the Valley* and today one hundred books arrived. The voice of the valley, its sound is marvelous. It is the sound of Kanzeon. *Bonnon kai kyo on. Bonnon* is the sound of complete purity. *Kai kyo on* is the sound of the ocean flux. This is beyond the sound of the sentient world.

Philippe made a deep *kan,* a deep vow, to write this book and to publish it in America. And even now he continues to write, without pay, without anything. "I am very poor, I have no money, Sensei."

But his daughter completely surprised me: she presented me a bottle of whiskey. Ah, I was very surprised. "Thank you very much, mademoiselle." I wanted to give her some money but she quickly escaped, saying: "No, no. I have money. I am richer than papa."

She is a very good daughter. I was completely impressed.

I am very happy. I received *The Voice of the Valley* written in absolutely beautiful, splendid English. It is a beautiful book. Philippe exactly wrote my English. He corrected it, wrote it in good English, in splendid English. (Some laughter—due perhaps to the humor in Sensei's voice when he says this.) But he follows my Zen-glish. He follows it exactly; he does not make mistakes. It is completely beautiful, *The Voice of the Valley*—an historical book.

AUG. 30 / 8.30 P.M.

In western education they teach that during conversation one must look each other in the eyes. In Chinese traditional rules and manners, they teach that one must look at the other's breast, at his heart, during conversation. Both are necessary.

Conversation is not only with words. One speaks with the eyes too.

Japanese people are completely.... (Sensei pulls in his shoulders, depicting someone who lives in a small space.) While Americans like Philippe, need space. They need a large scale. And when they dance too, they need space. The French are like monkeys when they dance, but when Philippe dances he is like a gorilla.

Birthplace and education and genetics are very different, and so sometimes it is good to imitate the opposite posture, and so wisdom can evolve.... Use both, one side and the other, and wisdom will arise, infinitely.

In *Shobogenzo Genjo Koan* it is written that the ego joins the cosmic order. This is *mayoi*, illusion. Then we have the opposite: the cosmic order certifies, makes shine the ego. This is satori.[60]

In the *Agama* sutra, it is written that *shiki*, consciousness, arises before everything. That everything consists of thinking. Thinking manages everything. So if we talk or act with evil thinking, it is like someone who runs after the tracks of a car. And so surely suffering comes.[61]

But if we talk, if we act with pure thinking, then at this time joyfulness, happiness, comes. The shadow follows the form.

AUG. 31 / 7 A.M.

THE 180-DEGREE CHANGE

This is the last day of this forty-day *sesshin*. Everybody is happy.... Those who have come here for the ten-day *sesshin*— you must change your mind. You must make contact with your true deep mind. This is *sesshin*. *Ses* means to touch, and *shin* means true mind.

And those who received the ordination yesterday, they too must change. They must stop taking drugs and return to original mind. Drugs are of no use. Drugs are special mind.... For those who took drugs and who have completely stopped taking them, this is satori.

■

I began the *kusens* of this camp by comparing Soto and Rinzai Zen. Dogen criticized Rinzai Zen, calling it *zusan*, negligent....

Both Soto and Rinzai are, I think, continuing to be practiced in Continental China. Dogen, however, brought Soto Zen to Japan, to an island, and a more delicate mind developed.

(Master Deshimaru again recounts the story of Rinzai and Obaku. Rinzai asked Obaku what was the essence of Buddhism, and Obaku gave Rinzai thirty blows; so Rinzai left the Obaku dojo to join master Taigu. The same incident was repeated with Rinzai and Taigu, the same question and the same reply—and Taigu hit Rinzai in the same fashion; but this time Rinzai got satori.)

The essence of Buddhism is very simple. And Rinzai understood what was satori.... But Rinzai made a little mistake. His Zen is a little *zusan*, a little negligent; so it is not so simple.

(Deshimaru, who is presently comparing the crucial moments, the respective awakenings, of Rinzai and Dogen, goes on to recount the story of Dogen and Nyojo. As recorded earlier in this text, Nyojo became angry with a monk sleeping in zazen, and he hit the monk several times with his wooden shoe. Dogen, who was sitting beside the monk at the time, received a big shock.)

The characteristics of Rinzai and Dogen differ on this point. Dogen at the time was younger; he was more pure, more delicate than Rinzai. When Dogen received his shock he did not escape, nor did he become angry.

So, after hitting the sleeping monk, Nyojo said: "I stop zazen today, I stop the education, I stop the *sesshin*," and he returned very angry to his room.

Dogen followed the master to his room and did *sampai*. Dogen was completely impressed. "*Shin jin datsu raku,*" he said. "Today, master I received a big shock. My body and mind have completely changed. It has changed by 180 degrees."

Master Nyojo's inside mind was completely satisfied. "My education has reached the mind of a disciple." He smiled, just a little smile, and said: *"Datsu raku shin jin."* He was telling Dogen to continue to throw down body and mind. Nyojo was a great master.

■

Rinzai people claim that Dogen got satori at this moment. But Dogen, himself, never said this. Dogen only wrote that he was impressed, shocked. Nyojo never said: "I give you the *shiho*, you got satori."[62] Nyojo only smiled. *Shin jin datsu raku, datsu raku shin jin.* More, more, *encore* more, until death. The way is not finished. This is Soto Zen.

■

289

What is *mayoi*, what is illusion? *Mayoi* is a strong self-consciousness, a strong personal consciousness. So the ego is transported (i.e., by one's own proper consciousness) to the side of *manpo*, to the side of all existence, the cosmic order. And the cosmic order causes the ego to progress—it changes the ego. *Mayoi* is the ego which turns the *Dharma*.

BE LIKE A DONKEY

The *Shobogenzo* is the text for Soto Zen.

However, it is not necessary to speak of "Soto" or to speak of "Zen." The essence of Buddhism is only one. Without zazen there is no essence. *Shikantaza*, this is Dogen's conclusion. With zazen, *hannya haramitsu*, wisdom, arises. Automatically, naturally, unconsciously. This is Dogen's opinion.

Practice, the hidden practice. This is not show, not demonstration, not decoration. It is only practice hidden inside, hidden inside mind. The secret practice.

Soto Zen is not very demonstrative. It is like the big fool, like the donkey. You must practice like the fool, so it is written at the end of the *Hokyo Zan Mai*. This means that you must practice sincerely, honestly. Do not show your cleverness, your intelligence. Hide them.

Be like a lion and people will be scared. So it is better to be like a donkey (not a real donkey) and people will not be frightened. Too beautiful a flower: people will immediately cut it. A big ugly tree with many knots: nobody will cut it down (except maybe, in the end, for wood).

This is the wisdom of life. Too intelligent, too beautiful—later this becomes dangerous. You must hide it. Be like the donkey, the fool. A great and intelligent person is like the Great Fool....

Kaijo.

AUG. 31 / 10.30 A.M.

ALL CIVILIZATIONS,
ALL RELIGIONS PASS ON

This is the last zazen. Concentrate.

In Zen Buddhism compassion and wisdom are very important. *Hannya haramita,* the perfect wisdom, Buddha's wisdom—this and compassion are like the two wings of a bird. With them you can arrive at the true truth. In Buddhism the true truth is itself these two wings.

■

Humanity today is in complete crisis. Communism cannot solve it or cure it—for they only try to resolve the problem through economics and through materialism. Socialism cannot solve it, nor can nationalism, science, ecology. They are in duality.

So each of us must find peace in his own mind. One must sublimate one's desires. Running after the material, running after money…. Decrease egoism, this is necessary.

Therefore all religions are important. The religious person must practice, not imagine.

I think that this forty-day meeting, which has assembled over a thousand people in the practice of zazen, is a great historic event…. Your existence is utterly necessary for the future of civilization…. Relative to world population the people assembled here are very few. In Christ's time, too, very few people assembled around him, but it spread.

■

The so-called exchanging of civilizations has been occurring since the First World War. The intellectuals, the intelligentsia, say that this East-West exchange is essential and indispensible to world peace.[63]

Christianity and the European civilization came to Japan during the Tokugawa period,[64] about three-hundred years ago. It was accepted by the Japanese, and so it developed and its influence spread. And after the Meiji Revolution[65] even the emperor changed his clothes: from a *kolomo* to a western suit.

Before then everyone, even the men, wore their hair long. Now they cut it. And today all Japanese people receive a western education. If a Japanese does not learn English while in secondary school, he does not receive a diploma…. The whole of Japanese life has changed. One hundred years ago the Japanese did not know milk, butter, cheese or bread. They did not even know what an apple was. And so too with knives, forks and houses. Houses are now built in the western style…. China also has changed. Mao changed it—Marx and Lenin: the Russian style.

Since my arrival in Europe, I have noticed that Europeans do not much accept Asiatic culture. Very few speak Chinese or Japanese. At the Sorbonne, some study orientalism—but I looked into the matter: they think of orientalism as an antiquity.[66]

Some westerners think that Japanese art is important. As with the Nô theater. But not at all. Japanese art is antiquity. Western art has completely developed and its art is better than that in Japan.

So zazen is the complete essence of Asiatic culture. Traveling from India, to China, to Japan, zazen has become today the essence of Japanese culture. What is left of Japanese culture is but western culture.

■

Everyone has a good posture. Please don't forget this posture when you leave here.

There will be no *mondo* today. It is not necessary to ask any more questions.

Three children will be receiving the ordination after zazen. This has a deep meaning.

■

The emperor changed his style of dress, and so did the military. They have changed to the French style. The hat and the uniform and even the sword has changed. The sword they use is no longer Japanese. This is very funny.

And now you, here, have changed to the black *kolomo*—and to the *kesa*! The highest!

The Japanese have forgotten the black *kolomo* and the *kesa*. And the Japanese monks, they have forgotten the true *kesa*. Japanese monks, in modern times, only wear the *kesa* for ceremony and for funeral services. They wear the *kesa* only while in the temple. When traveling, and while in daily life, one does not see many *kesas*. So it is in Japan and so it is, too, in Europe. This is why everyone who sees me, dressed in the true *kesa* of the transmission, are surprised.... But now this *kesa* is spreading in the West.

Socrates too wore one. All the great philosophers in that time in Greece word the *kesa*. Imitation *kesas*. At that time, Asia was an influence on Greece, and Greece on Asia. There was an exchange of cultures.

Nagarjuna wrote that to understand true Buddhism, true religion, the *kesa* is most important. The *kesa*, he wrote, is the essence of Buddhism.... You must study the true *kesa*. Nagarjuna, near the end of his life, studied only the *kesa;* he abandoned all his books to this study. And Dogen wrote that all the great patriarchs did likewise.[67]

If you practice zazen, and if you wear the *kesa*, it will influence all the West. And so, too, it will once again influence the Japanese.

Those who were ordained yesterday are the treasures of this East-West exchange; they are historical treasures. Since two or three thousand years, right up until today, the transmission of the *kesa* has continued.

◼

All civilizations change, and so too do the religions; they pass on like water in a stream. *Mujo.* Like bubbles on the water. But zazen and the true *kesa* have continued until today, from patriarch to patriarch; from China and Japan, and now to Europe. Zazen and the *kesa* have again become fresh.

◼

I thank you for your good postures, and for the good *sesshin....*

glossary

glossary

BASO (Ma-tsu 709-788). Great *chan* master of the Tang dynasty. Disciple of Nangaku and master of Hyakujo. Certified 139 disciples in all, many of whom became celebrated masters in their own right: Hyakujo, Nansen, Daibai Hojo and Layman P'ang. Baso was the first to use the rough-method technique of shouts and blows *(zusan)* to awaken his disciples. However, he was also known for his never-ending *gyoji*, his strong *samu*, and for his unremitting zazen which he practiced on a large stone. Baso set up his dojo at Kosei, west of the river Yangtse. At the same time Sekito set up his, south of the lake Toung-Ting, and the disciples often traveled between the two dojos. So you have the expression, "west of the river, south of the lake. " Here perhaps are the true origins of the two schools (later named Rinzai and Soto respectively), Baso and Sekito being their actual forefathers. "From the river to the lake," goes a line in an ancient poem dedicated to both of them, "how many times have they gone, how many times have they stayed?"

BODAI-SHIN (*Bodhi-citta* in Sanskrit). The mind which aspires to the way, which aspires to the highest Buddhahood. The mind which observes *mujo*, the impermanence of the world, which observes birth and death.

BODHI or **BODHIDHARMA** (Sanskrit). First Zen Patriarch and 28th in the line from the Buddha. Indian monk from Ceylon, disciple of Hannyatara and master to Eka. Spent the last decade of his life in China, where he died at the age of one-hundred fifty. After arriving in China, and after a brief and discordant, though celebrated, *mondo* with the emperor, Bodhidharma headed north to the Yellow River. Traveling thousands of miles by foot, he arrived in the northern mountains where he occupied a cave, later called Shorinji temple on Mount Su-zan (*Sho-lin* on Mount *Sung* in Chinese). Known in his own time simply as the Brahmin-who-faces-a-wall, he sat in this cave, facing a wall, for nine years.

BODHISATTVA (Sanskrit). Either a human or a celestial being. His basic characteristics are compassion and perseverence. He who dedicates his life to helping others by participating in the social reality. Nothing distinguishes him from others, yet his mind is Buddha. In fact a Bodhisattva is a living Buddha. His essence is *bodhi,* that is, the wisdom resulting from direct perception of truth. With the advent of Mahayana, the Bodhisattva ideal came to replace the older *arahat* ideal of Hinayana, and thereby brought in a whole new scope, a new goal, to Buddhism; for while the *arahat* aims at self-enlightenment alone, the Bodhisattva aims at leading all people to enlightenment. Like a house on fire, the Bodhisattva stays on until the last man is out of the flames before he himself steps out.

BONNO (*Klesa* in Sankrit). For lack of a better word, *bonno* can be translated as "illusion. " It is existence in obscurity, confusion and suffering. (*Bon* means trouble some, and *no* means suffering.) *Bonnos* are created when a person thinks with his personal, subjective mind. The basic *bonnos* from which stem all other *bonnos* are: ignorance, anger, pride, doubt, grasping and wrong views.

BONNO SOKU BODAI. *Bonno* becomes satori.

BUDDHA. A Sanskrit word containing many meanings:

1. as the legendary Buddhas of the past, present and future
2. an enlightened person
3. simply enlightenment or awakening
4. The fundamental cosmic power and/or the true nature of the universe
5. and more commonly the Buddha Shakyamuni, the man who was born in Kapilavatthu in 536 B.C. and who died in Kuchinagara in 483 B.C.

Shakyamuni was known in his youth as the Prince Siddhartha Gautama, being that he was the son of the king of the Shakya, a small kingdom in the Himalayan foothills of present-day Nepal; and later in his life-time he was known as the Buddha or the Awakened One; or more simply as Shakyamuni, which means the Silent Sage of the Shakya Clan. The life of the Buddha was very simple. He left home at the age of twenty-nine, had his satori under the Bodhi-tree at Bodh-Gaya at the age of thirty-five, and spent the rest of his life teaching his disciples. He died in the woods near the river Kushinagara, at the age of eighty.

Shakyamuni Buddha is regarded neither as a god, nor as a savior, but rather as a fully awakened, fully perfected human being. Again, on another dimension, he is regarded as no different than the five human Buddhas before him, or to the Buddha Maitreya to follow. In the latter case, Shakyamuni Buddha is regarded as one of the links in a chain of Buddhas which extends from the remotest past into the immeasurable future.

BUDDHISM. The name given to the teachings of the Buddha Shakyamuni (563-483 B.C.). It is the teaching of *ku* or *sunyata* which means emptiness. Buddhism is sometimes called the Middle Way, that is, a middle without extremes, which is *ku* or existence without noumenon (substance).

Buddhism is grouped under two main branches, *Hinayana* and *Mahayana,* and together they make up the dominant religion of the world numbering over three hundred million followers. Hinayana, or *Theravada* as it is more accurately called, arose in southern India and spread to Ceylon, Burma, Thailand, Cambodia and Vietnam. Mahayana meanwhile spread from northern India to Tibet, Mongolia, China, Korea, Japan and also Vietnam where both branches are firmly implanted.

Buddhism is above creed, color, dogma, ideology and racial barriers, discord, religious fundamentalism and fanaticism. On the contrary, it preaches compassion, selfless service, incessant good and happiness to one and all. Buddhism teaches man to free himself from the three root causes of suffering (greed, hatred and delusion), and it offers solutions to the timeless problems of human existence and personal growth. "Buddhism," says Kodo Sawaki, "is the question of how to live this life for the highest good, to live it with meaning." (see Mahayana and Hinayana).

BUDO (*bu:* war and *do:* the way). The way of the samurai, the way of combat. The martial arts. And *bushido* (*bushi:* warrior) is the warrior's code of honor.

BUSSHO KAPILA. The mealtime sutra chanted before breakfast and lunch; but not before supper, the reason being that the Buddha did not eat after mid-day. The sutra begins with a brief history of the life of the Buddha:

Bussho Kapila (Buddha was born in Kapila)

Jodo Makada (he got his satori in Makada)
Seppo Harana (he taught in Harana)
Nyumetsu Kuchira (he entered nirvana in Kuchira)

In the next verse are mentioned the names of the Buddhas and the Bodhisattvas, and a small wooden clapper is struck after each name. In one of the closing verses it is said that when eating the first spoonful we cut all the bad karma, with the second spoonful we create all the good karma, and with the third we save humanity.

CHAN (Chinese for Zen, *dhyana* in Sanskrit). Established in China by the Indian monk Bodhidharma in the sixth century, Chan (or Zen) is the teaching of Buddhism in its most naked, bare, unclad, pure sense. The Buddha's teaching transmitted from master to disciple.

After the death of Eno the 6th and last official Patriarch (713), Chan spread rapidly, breaking up into two major branches, the Northern and the Southern. In the succeeding centuries a variety of schools developed (Unmon, Honen, Igyo, Rinzai and Soto, or the Five Schools of Chan), but by the twelfth century all five schools became pretty much reabsorbed into two major teachings, that of Rinzai and Soto.

CHUKAI! Expression used by the master and directed to the *kyosakumen*. It means to stop the *kyosaku* (the stick). When the master says *"chukai,"* the *kyosakumen* replace the *kyosakus* on the altar below the statue of the Buddha.

DAICHI (1290-1366). Disciple of Soto masters Meiho-Sotetsu and Keizan. Traveled in China for eleven years and spent one year in Korea. Daichi had no disciples, and he died alone in his temple in Kyushu (later burned to the ground by the Jesuits). Famous for his numerous and original poems on zazen.

DAISHI (see *Genkaku*).

DAIE SOKO (*Ta-Hui* in Chinese, 1089-1163). Chinese rinzai master, and great champion of the koan method. He perfected this method with the explicit vow to save Chan from the "Soto blockheads who only sit upright with their eyes closed, neglecting enlightenment altogether. " Hailed by his disciples as the reincarnation of master Rinzai, and four hundred years later Rinzai master Hakuin writes, of Daie's teaching method, that it "was the supreme upward-striving Zen. "

DESHIMARU (Taisen, 1914-82). Disciple of Kodo Sawaki and great Japanese soto master who spent the last fifteen years of his life teaching in Europe. Received the monastic ordination, along with the robe, bowl and spiritual transmission from Kodo Sawaki in the year 1965. In 1975, while teaching at his dojo in Paris, Deshimaru received the official *shiho* from Yamada Zenji, Head Abbot of Eiheiji. And in 1985 was given the posthumous title of "Zenji" by Niwa Zenji, Abbot of Eiheiji. Established over one hundred affiliated dojos throughout western Europe, North Africa and Canada, and founded the Gendronnière temple in the Loire Valley. According to the temple register, he ordained over five hundred monks; and the number of people who practiced with him, at one time or another, ran to over twenty thousand. There was nothing special in Deshimaru's teaching, no programmed study of koans, no breath-counting, no sutra reciting, no *dokusan*, no *sanzen*, no particular quest for satori. What he taught was straight zazen, that which was practiced by Bodhidharma, Eno and Dogen, neither adding to it nor subtracting; he simply taught the seated posture without any personal modifications, the long deep breathing, and the mind of samadhi, the self beyond category, or what he called *hishiryo* consciousness.

DHARMA. Basically three different meanings:

1. the universal truth proclaimed by Shakyamuni Buddha; the teaching of the Buddha, the Buddhist doctrine.
2. simply, the truth. Ultimate reality. The cosmic order. The universal law. The word *Dharma* is, in this sense, ontologically anterior to Shakyamuni Buddha and, for that matter, to all the Buddhas of the past. (Buddhas come and go in the course of history, but the Dharma goes on forever).
3. dharma—with a small "d"—means a phenomenon. i.e., as in the phrase: "However numerous are the dharmas, I vow to acquire them all."

DO (*Tao* in Chinese). The way. Practice in harmony with the cosmic order. Do can mean the way of the warrior, like in *bushido* (see *budo*), and it can also mean the way of Buddha.

DOGEN (1200-53). Great Soto master of Japan, disciple of the Chinese master Nyojo, and himself master of Ejo. Founder of Soto Zen in Japan, and founder of Eiheiji, a small temple in the northern mountains of Japan (and today a kind of Vatican of Soto Zen). Dogen was born of noble birth; he lost his parents while a child, and left home at an early age, in search of Buddhism. He met the masters Eisai and Myozen, under whom he studied Rinzai Zen and the koan method for some years; then he left his country and crossed the sea to China, where he met Soto master Nyojo, on Mount Tendo in southern China; Dogen practiced under Nyojo for three years, then returned home to Japan. Dogen's teaching rests, fundamentally, on:

1. the practice without goal or object *(mushotoku)*
2. the dropping off of body-and-mind *(shin jin datsu raku)*
3. the excellent practice itself is true satori *(shusho ichinyo)*.

Dogen was also a great writer and most of his teachings are included in his voluminous work entitled *Shobogenzo*. His poetry, also of extraordinary depth and beauty, is included in the work entitled *San Sho Doei*.

DOJO (sometimes referred to in English as *zendo*). The place where one practices zazen, the place of the way. (*Do* means the way, and *jo* the place.) Originally the place where the Buddha had his satori (under the Bodhi tree) and thus a holy place. Dojos, as we know them today, first appeared with the patriarchs Konin and Eno, in seventh century China.

DOKAN. Ring of the way. The continual repetition of the acts of one's daily life. Repetition of posture, of body and mind attitude, as a continuous practice. (See *gyoji*.)

DOKUSAN. Private though formal interview with the master, in his quarters, at a given time. Usually structured around koan study, and as such is particularly used in the Rinzai school.

glossary

DOSHU. How one expresses the way. Expression of the way by body, mouth and consciousness. Expression of oneself, of one's satori. Utterance of the Dharma.

EIHEIJI. Principle temple of the Soto school in Japan. Founded by master Dogen in the thirteenth century and situated in the Fukui prefecture in the northwestern part of the country. Dogen, who greatly respected the sutras, named his temple "Eihe" (i.e., "67 A.D." according to the Chinese calender) because "Eihe" was the year that the Indian monk Matto arrived in China, riding a white horse and carrying with him forty-two sutras of the Buddha.

Today, Eiheiji is the headquarters of fifteen thousand Soto temples in Japan and elsewhere.

EISAI (or *Yosai*, 1141-1215). Japanese Rinzai master, and founder of Rinzai Zen in Japan. Established monasteries at Kyoto and Kamakura with the aid of the emperor, and became abbot of Kenninji, the first Zen monastery in Japan. Though Eisai was the first Japanese ever certified by a Chinese Zen master, and also the founder of Rinzai in his own country, he continued his functions, not only as a Rinzai monk, but also as a Tendai monk, a Shingon monk and a *kito* monk.

Eisai was no Rinzai, no Dogen; nevertheless, the eulogies delivered for Eisai in *Zuimonki* show Dogen's respect and indebtedness to him.

EJO (1198-1280). First disciple and secretary to master Dogen. Noted for faithfulness to his master, for helping Dogen to create his sangha and to build the first real Zen monastery in Japan, and also for his historical work as the transcriber and compiler of Dogen's *Shobogenzo*.

Born of a noble family in Kyoto, he met Dogen at Koshoji temple in 1234, and becoming his disciple, Ejo remained by his side until the latter's death twenth years later, in 1253. Ejo was thereupon installed as the second abbot of Eiheiji. Abbot that he now was, Ejo remained Dogen's disciple until the end—for the remaining twenty-seven years of his life, Ejo lived near his master's grave; and every morning after zazen he would visit his late master's room, to offer incense; finally, Ejo left instructions to have his ashes buried beside Dogen's, in the spot reserved for the secretary. (See *Shobogenzo.*)

EKA (*Hui-ke* in Chinese, 487-593). Disciple of Bodhidharma and 2nd Zen Patriarch. Reportedly cut off his arm and placed it before Bodhidharma as an expression of his desire to be accepted as a disciple.

Stayed with his master for nine years, practicing only *shikantaza*. After receiving the transmission, Eka went to live in town where he sometimes worked as a street-sweeper, and where he also began to spread the Dharma. Died at the age of 107, the victim of an assassination plot conducted by the local police chief.

ENO (Hui-neng, the 6th Patriarch, 688-713). Disciple of the 5th Patriarch Konin, and the master of such outstanding monks as Seigen, Nangaku, and Genkaku. It is said that Eno taught thirty-two enlightened successors who appeared in the world, and ten great hidden ones; and also innumerable others of all kinds.

Eno was a major catalyst in the spreading of Zen in China, and in the course of time his disciples established the Five Schools (including Rinzai and Soto) during the Tang and Sung Dynasties, extending from the eighth to the twelfth centuries.

Eno sold firewood; he was illiterate; he was awakened when hearing a monk recite the *Diamond Sutra*, he pounded rice at Konin's dojo on Mount Hobai; he received the *shiho*, barely escaped alive with it, spent fifteen years in seclusion with the fishermen, was recognized as the long-lost 6th Patriarch while passing through the marketplace in a local town, installed himself on Mount Sokai and instructed his many disciples in the practice of the way.

FIVE GO-I OF SOTO ZEN (five degrees, stages or steps). Formulated by masters Tozan and Sozan, the two founders of Soto in China, and considered as the basis of the Soto teaching. The five degrees are: *hen chu sho, sho chu hen, sho chu rai, hen chu rai,* and *ken chu toh. Ken chu toh*, the fifth degree has been added to Four Principles of Rinzai, and here form and emptiness (*shiki* and *ku*) mutually penetrate to such a degree that there is no longer any consciousness of either, and whereby ideas of satori and delusion vanish. The stage of perfect inner wisdom.

When the Soto master gives the *shiho* to his disciple, he gives him the five *go-i*. (*Go* means five, and *i* means principle.)

FIVE SKANDHAS (see *skandhas*).

FOUR PRINCIPLES OF RINZAI ZEN (*Rinzai Shi-Ryoken* or Four Measures). Used by Rinzai masters to measure the degree of attainment of their disciples. Put together the physical and the metaphysical, says Master Deshimaru, and you come up with four possible categories: life—non-death, death—non-life, non-death—non-life, life—death. The first *Rinzai Ryoken*, Deshimaru goes on to say, states that there is no one and that only the object exists; this is thinking with our will, *shiki*. The second: that in this world there is only ego and nothing else exists; this is non-thinking without our will, *ku*. The third: that in this world there is nothing; this is thinking of non-thinking, *shiki* and *ku*. The fourth: that the person and the object both exist; this is thinking beyond thinking and non-thinking—*shiki soku ze ku, ku soku ze shiki*, which is *hishiryo* thinking.

FUKANZAZENGI. Short text by master Dogen and not included in his *Shobogenzo.. Fukan* means to popularize, to spread; *gi* means the practical rules. Spreading the practical rules. Or in other words, to render popular for everyone. *Zazengi*: the ABC of zazen.

Its importance, beauty, brevity and easy accessibility make the *Fukanzazengi* the most widely used text in Dogen Zen.

FUKE (*P'u-hua*, dates unknown). Little is known of Fuke other than that he was a good friend of master Rinzai (d. 867). "Fuke was not a monk," says master Deshimaru, "though not quite a layman either. "

FUKE SECT. Founded in 18th century Japan, around one thousand years after the time of the "monk" Fuke, who died back during the Tang dynasty. While Fuke was known for walking the streets ringing a little handbell, the monks of this sect played the *shakuhachi* as they walked, as a kind of walking meditation. Very powerful before the Meiji revolution. Worked for the government, often in the capacity of spies. Today this sect is outlawed.

FUSE (*dana* in Sanskrit). A gift made without aim, without objective. Not based on profit. *Mushotoku.* The giving of spiritual guidance or material goods.

FUYO DOKAI (1043-1118). Great *chan* master of the Soto lineage. Stern though not *zusan* (rough in the Rinzai style). In fact Fuyo Dokai was a strong critic of this rough way of teaching very much in vogue in the Rinzai temples of the times. "Why do you sound the wooden clappers," says he of the Rinzai monks, "and wave about the *hossu* (stick and insignia) of the master? Why do you shout towards the East in such a loud voice? And why do you hit towards the West with the *kyosaku?* Why do you frown and your eyes glare with anger? Have you become a paralytic? Why do you shout and hit the *joza* (fellow monk)? Not only do you shout and hit the *joza*, but also you make fun of the patriarchs and mock them."

Fuyo Dokai holds a special place in the Soto transmission; master Dogen said of him:

He is a wellspring of Soto Zen
Its roots, spine, bones and marrow.
He had the Buddha mind, and true Zen
Grew and flourished thanks to him.

GAITAN. Entrance area to the dojo. Reserved for those who work in the kitchen and must leave during zazen. Also, for those who have problems, either with their health or with their postures, who cough and sneeze and move about crossing and uncrossing legs, etc.

GASSHO. A gesture of reverence in which the hands are joined, palm to palm, about ten centimeters in front of the face; the tips of the fingers almost at the level of the nose, with the forearms horizontal.

The left hand symbolizes the spiritual or holy world, the right the material or phenomenal world. The hands thus joined symbolize the unity of spiritual and material, of sacred and profane, of man and the cosmos. The hands thus joined make up the one mind.

GENJO. Immediate manifestation of things as they are. Accomplished in the present. The materialization of phenomena. The actualization of satori in our daily lives. Phenomena, reality, the truth which comes.

GENJO KOAN. Title of first chapter of Dogen's *Shobogenzo.*, composed in 1233. All chapters of the *Shobogenzo.* are a further development of *Genjo Koan.* This text, which was written originally as a letter to one of Dogen's disciples, is considered to be the skin, flesh, bones and marrow of his teaching.

Genjo means immediate manifestation of things as they are, and *Koan,* in this context, means real phenomena is-itself-truth. The truth of our daily lives, that which is active and which exists here and now.

GENKAKU (*Yoka Daishi,* 665-713). Disciple of Eno the 6th Patriarch. Called the-monk-who-spent-one-night because he spent one night with the 6th Patriarch, and in one night he was awakened. Known today primarily for his *Shodoka,* or *Song of the Immediate Satori,* one of the four oldest Zen texts in existence.

GEN NO BI CHOKU. Eyes horizontal, nose vertical. *Gen* means eyes; *no*—horizontal; *bi*—nose; *choku*—straight, vertical.

On Dogen's return to Japan, he was asked what he brought back with him from his master Nyojo in China. He replied, to everyone's surprise: *"Gen no bi choku"*—my eyes are set horizontally and my nose vertically, this is all." So, after three years study of Buddhism in China, what had Dogen brought back with him? Just the normal condition.

GENSHA (835-908). Great Soto master of the late Tang. Disciple of Seppo and master of Rakan. Gensha, whose childhood name was Sharo, had a desire to become a Buddhist monk and follow the way. But the professional transmission from father to son was an inviable rule, anchored deep in the mores, and Sharo, being the son of a fisherman, had to resign himself to his fate. So, every evening Sharo would accompany his father to their boat. One evening, while the father and son were out fishing on the river Nandai, his father fell overboard. Sharo extended his hand to help, and his father grabbed hold. But just then Sharo's overriding desire to follow the way and become a monk came back to him, and he pulled back his hand and his father drowned.

Sharo was no ordinary youth and in one second he cut his ties with society. He cut his karma. Anyway, he was ordained by Seppo at the age of thirty and eventually became his Dharma heir. So, though he may not have saved his own father from drowning, he nevertheless saved the lives of countless others.

GENSHI. Root, source. The fundamental source which fills the cosmos, like the moon on the lake, in a puddle, in every town, every village everywhere. *Gen* means deep or bottom, and *shi* means principle. So you have "deep principle," "true way. "

GODO. In the Zen hierarchy, he's number one after the master. Master-*godo-shusso*. While the *shusso* functions in conjunction with the master, a function limited to the dojo proper, the *godo* gives the teaching in the master's absence, both inside the dojo and out. (See *shusso*.)

GENMAI. Traditional rice soup eaten after the morning zazen. This soup as we know it today began with master Fuyo Dokai who died in 1118 (see Fuyo Dokai).

Consists of one portion of brown rice to one sixth leeks, celery, branch, carrots, turnips and onions. A simple nourishment for people who practice zazen and lead simple lives.

GYOJI. The continuous practice. Continual repetition of the acts of one's daily life, with emphasis on *samu* (holy work in the sangha). *Gyo* means to practice; *ji* means to continue, to perpetuate, and to protect. *Gyoji* is work without beginning or end, without profit or goal.

HAKUIN (1686-1769). Japanese Rinzai master, stayed at temple of Shorinji, in Suruga (today's Shizuoka prefecture) near Mount Fuji. "There are two things in Suruga which excel," went a saying during his time, "the one is Mount Fuji and the other is Hakuin of Hara." Also, one of the most important figures in the history of Zen painting, calligraphy and writing. Hakuin—unlike Dogen—was a staunch upholder of the koan method for obtaining satori.

Also, a staunch upholder of rigorous, marathon-like zazen sessions. He recounts how once, during his youth, he and his friend Jukaku went into the countryside and sat upright like telephone poles—for seven days straight. "We agreed that if either one saw the other's eyelids drop, even for a split second, he would grab the slat and crack him with it between the eyes. We sat ramrod straight, teeth clenched tightly. We continued that way in total silence for seven days. Between us, not so much as an eyelash quivered." (Hakuin, *Wild Ivy*, translation by Norman Waddell, quoted in "The Eastern Buddhist," vol. xvi, no. 1, Spring 1983, p. 110.)

A strong critic of false teachers and their teachings, and very outspoken when it came to his contemporary, master Bankei and his "Unborn Zen sect" for their easy, informal zazen practice. And again, quite impertinently of the Soto school for their "sitting-doing-nothing" method. "These counterfeit teachers get their hooks into peoples' fine, stalwart youngsters, and they turn them into a pack of blind and hairless dunces." (Hakuin, *Wild Ivy*, translation by Norman Waddell, quoted in "The Eastern Buddhist," vol. xv, no. 1, Spring 1983, p. 77.)

HANNYA SHINGYO. Short for *Makahannya Haramita Shingyo.* (*Maka Prajna Paramita* in Sanskrit.) Also called the *Heart Sutra.* Literally, it means the Great Sutra of the Profound Essential Absolute Wisdom and Beyond. *Hannya* means the highest wisdom (*prajna* in Sanskrit); *shin* means essential faith, the essence; and *gyo* (or *kyo*) means sutra. Represents the essence of an ensemble of six hundred books and sutras, and sets forth the "essence" or "heart" of the entire *Prajna Paramita* teachings. *Prajna Paramita* is the name given to a body of work (including for instance the *Diamond Sutra*) grouped together around the doctrine of *Ku* or *Sunyata.* The *Hannya Shingyo* is the "essence" of this teaching, and it is condensed into a very short sutra, running to less than a page long. It is chanted in all Zen temples after zazen.

SIT

HARA (see *ki kai tanden*).

HEKIGAN ROKU, or **BLUE ROCK RECORD.** Collection of one hundred koans compiled in 1125. Many of these koans were taken from the *Shin Jin Mei,* a long poem composed by master Sosan (d. 606). The *Blue Rock Record* derived its name from a scroll containing the Chinese characters for "blue" and "rock" which happened to be hanging in the temple hall where the collection was being compiled.

Interestingly enough, this collection of koans (*Hekigan Roku*) is widely used in Soto Zen; in Rinzai Zen they use the *Mumonkan,* another koan collection.

HINAYANA, or Theravada. The so-called Lesser Vehicle of Buddhism, as opposed to Mahayana, or the so-called Greater Vehicle. The way of the *arhat.* The way of *sravada* and *pratyeka* Buddhas. Largely based on the ideal of purity, on a code of morality, on the extinction of passions. This form of Buddhism is practiced primarily in the southernmost countries such as Ceylon, Burma, Thailand and Cambodia. The word Hinayana, when used to describe a limited practice lacking both in wisdom and in compassion, refers merely to an *attitude of mind,* and not to Theravada Buddhism per se. "The highest merit," master Deshimaru once said, "is not different in Hinayana and in Mahayana."

HISHIRYO, beyond thinking. *Hi* means beyond, *shiryo* means thinking. *Hishiryo* is the secret of Zen, and it means thinking not-thinking thinking. Thinking without thinking. Thinking from the bottom of non-thinking. Thinking not thinking, hearing not hearing, looking not looking, smelling not smelling, etc.

To stop the thinking process which occurs in the frontal brain (as opposed to the central or primitive brain, the hypothalamus) and to think instead with the body.

Hishiryo-consciousness occurs when one's personal consciousness follows cosmic consciousness. *Hishiryo*-consciousness is mind in complete harmony, complete unity, with the cosmic order.

First used by Master Sosan (d. 606) in his *Shin Jin Mei,* and later taken up by Master Yakusan (d. 834). One day, while Yakusan was sitting in zazen, a monk came up to him and said: "Master, what do you think when you sit?" "I think not-thinking," Yakusan replied. "How do you think not-thinking?" "*Hishiryo*," Yakusan replied.

HOKYO ZAN MAI. Literally, the *Samadhi of the Precious Mirror.* Poem composed by Soto master Tozan (d. 869) and one of the four oldest Zen writings. Considered by all masters to be the textual embodiment of the essence of Zen. Recited in Zen monasteries in Japan.

HOSSU. A short staff used primarily by the master during the ordination ceremony, and not to be confused with *kotsu*, the curve-topped staff the master carries with him in the dojo, at the table and elsewhere. About a foot long, with a tuft of horse or yak hair knotted at one end.

HYAKUJO (*Huai-hai* in Chinese, 720-814). Disciple of Baso and master of Obaku. A kind and gentle man *(men mitsu)* and rather different in temperament to his own master, Baso, who was more prone to the roughhouse methods *(zusan)*, later to characterize the Rinzai school. In fact, one day Baso shouted so loudly in his ear, that Hyakujo remained deaf for three days. Known today for, among other things, his celebrated *Shingi*, the Holy Rules of the dojo. "*Chan* schools all over the land," goes one account, "followed this example like grass bending in the wind." In fact, he had established the basic rules as they are still practiced today in all Zen dojos and temples, in both Rinzai and Soto alike. One of the most outstanding *chan* masters of the Golden Tang dynasty, he taught the Buddhist Dharma for forty years, had one thousand disciples, thirty of whom received his transmission, including Issan and Obaku.

HYPOTHALAMUS. The instinctive, primitive, central brain as opposed to the rational, intellectual, frontal brain. Located approximately in the lower rear of the head, somewhat below the thalamus and directly above the spinal column. The hypothalamus is the connecting point of body and mind, for it directs the senses, and controls homeostasis (i.e., the tendency for the internal environment of the body to remain constant in spite of varying external conditions). The brain center which opens during zazen. (See thalamus.)

IMMO. *Tathata*, suchness, "that," "it. " That which is. The body and mind of the eternal present. *Immo* (truth) is sometimes called "that" or "it" because if any name or label is given at all, "it" is already missed. *Immo* is the symbol of the authentic Buddhist way. *Immo nin:* the man of satori.

INKIN. Small, delicately shaped bell-with-handle. Carried in the hand and struck with a tiny bronze rod attached to the *inkin* by a string. When the bell is held upright, a silk cloth falls about the handle covering the hand. Struck with measured cadence by the *inkin*-ringer, when accompanying the master to the dojo, after the beginning of zazen. Its resonance, when struck, is faint and pure.

I SHIN DEN SHIN. (*I* means with; *shin* means mind; *den* means to transmit). Thus from mind to mind, from master's mind to disciple's mind. Kodo Sawaki once identified this expression with "heart-mind to heart-mind. " In fact, *I shin den shin* is the key factor in the teachings of both Kodo Sawaki and Taisen Deshimaru.

First used by the 6th patriarch, Eno.

IWAZU, "I won't say." One day the monk Zangen pointed to a coffin containing the body of a man recently deceased, and addressing his master, he said: "In this coffin: is there life or death?"

Master Dogo replied: *"Iwazu! Iwazu!"*
The *Iwazu* koan is often used in the Soto school.

JOSHU (Chao-chou, 778-897). Disciple of Nansen, and one of the great Chinese Rinzai masters. Much admired by Soto masters Dogen, Kodo Sawaki and Deshimaru.

Joshu met Nansen when he was sixty-one years old, followed him for more than twenty years, and establishing himself as his own master at the age of eighty, he set about "instructing men and gods for the next forty years. " He died in 897 at the ripe old age of one hundred twenty.

Joshu's teaching was somewhat uncharacteristic of his own Rinzai school, indeed it was *men mitsu*, very soft and gentle and Soto-like. Joshu was mild-mannered and he did not use the stick-and-fist to teach his disciples, nor was he ever known to shout, *"KWAT!"* Joshu was beloved by all, and greatly admired by Rinzai and Soto masters, even today. "Joshu received the Dharma from his master," writes Dogen, "and correctly transmitted it to others. Everyone called him an ancient Buddha."

KAI (*Sila,* in Sanskrit). The precepts, morality. The three most important *kai* are: avoid doing the bad, practice doing the good, and help others. In Theravada Buddhism the monks follow two hundred fifty *kai* and the nuns five hundred (forty-eight of which they both share together). In Mahayana Buddhism, and particularly in Zen, the monks follow only ten kai, which they take at ordination time (don't kill, don't steal, don't be sexually abusive, don't talk triviality, swear or lie, don't take drugs which trouble the mind, don't praise yourself and/or revile others, don't be vain, don't indulge in wordly amusements, don't get angry, and don't blaspheme the Three Treasures, the Buddha, Dharma and Sangha).

These *kai* or precepts are not taken upon oneself as "commands" coming from without, but rather as "aspirations" or "vows" coming from within. In Zen, the *kai* are considered as "natural" morality, not as "prescribed. "

The *kai* are of use only for those who need them, for the killer who kills, for the thief who steals, for the blasphemer who blasphemes. Only the killer need know the precept "not to kill," the thief "not to steal," the blasphemer "not to blaspheme. " One must *live* the precepts to know them, and this means: one can only know a precept once one has *stopped breaking it.*

Indeed, when you sit in the manner of the masters and the patriarchs, what precept are you not oberving, what merit are you not actualizing?

KAIJO. *Kai* means open, free; *jo* means zazen. *Kaijo* is the moment the drum is struck to indicate the end of zazen; and to indicate the hour of the day. When the master says: *"Kaijo!,"* a monk strikes the drum, and depending upon the given hour of the day—be it 9 A.M. or 10 P.M.—the drum is struck nine or ten times to correspond to that hour.

KAN. A great vow. All the Buddhas and Bodhisattvas make them. A solemn promise or pledge. *Kan* usually comes from within one-self. The vow to live according to one's own true ideal, this is *kan*.

KANNA-ZEN. Another name for Rinzai or koan Zen. *"Kanna"* means: observing the spoken word—so you have "Kanna-Zen" or "Spoken-Zen. " Also refers to discussion, "debate" and "Dharma-combat" Zen. First promulgated by Rinzai master Daie in twelfth century China. (See also *Mokusho*-Zen.)

KARMA, action. The totality of all one's acts, plus the consequences. Karma is created through the action of body, mouth and mind; and when created, it is forever, for what has happened has happened and cannot be undone. Karma is the law of cause and effect, and from karma we have transmigration and *samsara*—the chain of existences, or rebirths, resulting from one's past actions.

And yet karma is beyond causality, beyond destiny (it includes both). It has nothing to do with destiny, predeterminism, fatalism, or nihilism, for though karma cannot be done away with (i.e., erased), it can indeed be *changed.* "All great religious leaders transform the bad karma of mankind," said master Deshimaru.

KATSU or *kwatz*, and again *"Kwaat!"* when shouted. An exclamation which has no particular meaning. Used primarily by Rinzai masters to shock the mind out of its "dualistic ego-centered thoughts."

The *kwatz* is a cry which, when uttered on the exhalation, says Master Deshimaru (in his *Zen and the Martial Arts*), can paralyze one's opponent. Conversely, it is the cry of universal energy ("pure energy without cause and effect," says Deshimaru), and can bring back to life someone who has just died.

Also a technique for re-awakening the *ki.*

Most often associated with master Rinzai. First used, however, one hundred years before him, by master Baso.

KEIZAN (1268-1325). Great Japanese Soto master, practiced under both Ejo and Gikai (two of Master Dogen's closest disciples), founder of Sojiji (one of the two head Soto temples), author of the intuitive and almost mystical *Dendoroku,* and responsible for the initial and widespread promulgation of the Soto teachings throughout Japan.

KENSHO. A technical Rinzai term which means to look at your true nature, or to find the Buddha nature in your own mind (*Ken:* seeing into, and *sho:* one's own nature), and sometimes described as a "small" or "preparatory" satori—and quite unlike anything you might find in Soto Zen.

KENTAN. Inspection at the beginning of zazen. (*Ken:* to examine, to inspect, and *tan:* the raised zazen platform.) The master passes through the dojo, observing those who are present. He examines the seated postures and looks to see if anyone is sick.

KESA (*Kasaya* in Sanskrit). Monk's robe usually received during the monk ordination. It is worn over the left shoulder and symbolic of the first robe worn by the Buddha (directly after his great satori) and made by him from old rags he picked up in a cemetery. Actually the *kesa* is more a sacred garment than a "robe" per say, as it is worn over the *kolomo* and only covers one shoulder and has no sleeves.

The *kesa* means faith, the essential force in Zen; also monks prostrate themselves *(sampai)* before the *kesa* as they would before the master or the Buddha—for nothing is so highly venerated in Zen as this *kesa;* on the other hand, those who practice zazen for long years, while never once wearing the *kesa* itself, let alone receiving it, their practice remains only a training method for obtaining good mental and physical health, like Yoga.

The *kesa* is symbolic of eternal life and all masters of the transmission believe this. The *kesa* brings you nourishment in time of need (it is designed with vertical and horizontal lines depicting the patterns in a rice field), it protects you from accidents, can cut off sickness of the mind, can cut off bad karma, and can bring infinite good merit in the three worlds. To use Yoka Daishi's expression: "The *kesa* is the mist, dew, rain and fog which clothe the body." (See *rakusu.*)

KETSUMYAKU. Certificate of lineage, of geneology, transmitted from Buddha and the patriarchs to the disciple. Given by the master when the disciple receives the monk ordination.

KI. Body energy, activity, vitality, force. Located not simply in the mind, nor in the *kikai tanden* (*hara*), but in all the nerves, fibers and cells of the entire body.

In Buddhism, *ki* is a technical term signifying the mind capable of responding to the spiritual impulsion. Comfort and the material life dull man's *ki*; *ki* is the source of life—it is manifested by means of the breathing and if you lose *ki*, you lose life.

KIKAI TANDEN. *Ki* means activity, energy; *kai* means ocean (so *kikai* means ocean of energy); *tan* means essence; and *den* means field. *Kikai tanden* is the essential source or center of energy, and it is located approximately two inches below the navel.

KINHIN. Zazen in motion. Practiced between periods of sitting. One steps forward about half a foot, presses down on the ground, particularly at that point where the big toe begins, and stretches the knee. The backbone is straight, chin in, neck taut, and eyes lowered. The thumb of the left hand is enclosed in its fist (which is held within the palm of the right hand), and together the hands are pressed against the solar plexis, just below the breastbone. The back of the hands are facing upward, the lower arms horizontal to the ground, and the elbows out. The exhalation of air begins with the first step, and at this moment the body is in tension. The inhalation then occurs with a relaxation of tension. *Kinhin* is practiced in a line, one person behind the other, and it lasts for five or so minutes.

KITO CEREMONY. Ceremony of ancient origins which the master or abbot sometimes performs upon request. *Kito* means grace, and to ask for a *kito* is, in a way, to ask the grace of the gods; it is to make a special petition to heaven.

Kito has to do with metaphysics and psychology and is considered in Mahayana to be of low dimension. Also being that the *kito* ceremony is directed, not to Buddha but to man, for his personal needs, and has to do not with wisdom but with phenomena, *kito* is not considered to be the embodiment of the essence of Buddhism. Nevertheless, when a believer asks the master for a *kito* (say, for a relative who is sick) then, with the master's consent, a photo of the relative is placed on the altar and the service is performed.

For those who believe in this sutra, and who have faith in this ceremony, the *kito* can be very effective.

KOAN. A statement, a saying, an act or gesture that can bring one to an understanding of the truth. An absolute, eternal truth transmitted by the master. Also, a tool used to educate a disciple.

Koans are generally construed from earlier *mondos* which occurred between ancient chan masters and their disciples, and which are used today, particularly in the Rinzai tradition, as a means of study and/or as a way to obtain satori. In Soto, both the use of koans and the interpretation of satori are quite different. Koans are used in Soto, but in a very free and open fashion and not at all like in Rinzai whereby the koan-solving procedure is carried out in a much more formalized fashion, along with private meetings with the master, and so on.

KONTIN. When the mind, during zazen, falls into obscurity, doubt, delusion, melancholia, or into just plain dullness. (*Kon* means darkness, *tin* means to sink.) Characterized by fatigue both mental and physical. During zazen the chin falls, the thumbs drop, the backbone slumps. The cutting off of all thoughts; *kontin* resembles a state of mind similar to sleep. (See *sanran* for the opposite.)

KOTSU. Curve-topped staff the master carries with him in the dojo, the dining room and elsewhere. Less than two feet in length and curved in a form that resembles the human spinal column. Not to be confused with *hossu*, a yak-haired staff used during certain ceremonies.

KU (*Sunyata* in Sanskrit). Emptiness. Not, however, in the sense of "nothing" as opposed to "something. " Indeed, *ku* is something, for it includes all things, all phenomena, even the phenomena of mind. All things come from *ku*. It is the pure source, the essence. Literally, *ku* means sky.

While most Buddhist schools primarily teach the doctrine of karma, Zen teaches *ku*.

KUSEN. The oral teaching given by the master in the dojo, during zazen. (*Ku* means mouth, *sen* means teaching.) The teaching transmitted to the master by his own master. The long line of the oral transmission of the Buddha's teaching.

The *kusen* is not a *teisho*, a lecture or a conference.

KU SOKU ZE SHIKI. Emptiness becomes phenomena, form. *Shiki soku ze ku:* phenomena, or form, becomes emptiness. Said differently, the object is in the subject, the subject in the object. *Ku* (emptiness) and *shiki* (phenomena) are inseparable.

KWATZ, see *katsu.*

KYO GE BETSUDEN. The special teaching outside the scriptures. (*Kyo* means teaching, or scripture-teaching; *ge* means outside; *betsuden* means another transmission, or a special transmission.) This expression is often used in the Rinzai school, and it underscores one of the fundamental differences between Rinzai and Soto. It is said that in Rinzai, as opposed to Soto, the sutras and other ancient texts are not so much studied and respected.

KYOSAKU. The wake-up stick. (*Kyo* means attention, *saku* means stick.) Stick with which the master or **KYOSAKUMAN** strikes the disciple on each shoulder near the neck, on points corresponding to two principle acupuncture meridians. A long, tapered stick flattened at one end, and usually made of oak. Calligraphied on one side with the name of the temple, the master's signature, stamp and date; on the other with a poem. (On Kodo Sawaki's *kyosaku* was the calligraphy: "Yesterday my body was a stinking sack of flesh and bones; today, on the mountain of *bonnos,* I attack the clouds and the thunder.") Administered when the monk falls into either *sanran* or *kontin,* and regarded as the stick which promotes satori. Used both in Rinzai and Soto—though, traditionally the Rinzai *kyosaku* is much bigger and heavier than the Soto *kyosaku.*

MAHAKASYAPA. Dates uncertain; however, he lived during the time of the Buddha, in the fourth century B.C. Came from a rich and comfortable background (he was born to a Brahmin family from Magadha), left his home and entered the mountains of northern India where he practiced yoga asceticism and mortification.

He then met the Buddha Shakyamuni, practiced with him the
Middle Way, and became one of the Buddha's ten great disciples.
Also, he is considered the 1st Indian Patriarch in the Zen tradition.
After the Buddha's death, Mahakasyapa continued the teaching,
bringing about him an immense number of disciples. Convened
the First Buddhist Council in 483 B.C., expressly "to preserve the
teaching." Passed on the transmision to Ananda.

MAHAYANA. The Greater Vehicle of Buddhism. (*Maha* means great,
yana means salvation.) One of the two major branches of
Buddhism—Hinayana or the Lesser Vehicle being the other. Also
known as the Northern School, for unlike Hinayana, it originated
in Northern India from where it spread to Tibet, Mongolia, China,
Vietnam, Korea and Japan. In India the two principle schools of
Mahayana were the Madyamikas and the Yogacaras. While in
China, Tibet and Japan, the principle schools were, respectively,
Tendai, Vajrayana, Pureland, Shingon and Zen. Noted for the
emphasis it places on wisdom *plus* compassion, and also for the
bodhisattva ideal (i.e., the renunciation of nirvana until all beings
have been led to enlightenment themselves: *Shu jo muhen seigan
do*, Beings, however many they be, I vow to save them all).
Sometimes refered to as the "Middle Way" (i.e., without the
extremes found in all pairs). The great spokesmen and Bodhisattvas
of early Mahayana were Nagarjuna, Asanga, Vasubandu and
Santideva.

MEN MITSU. Delicate, careful and/or attentive. (*Men* means cotton,
mitsu means soft, thick, intimate, honey.)

Men mitsu is associated with the Soto teaching in as much as *zusan*
(i.e., rough) is associated with the Rinzai teaching.

MOKUGYO. A hollowed-out wooden drum, carved in the shape of
a fish. Struck by a padded mallet during the chanting of the *Hannya
Shingyo*, and for certain *dharanis*, in order to maintain rhythm.

MOKUSHO ZEN. Silent shining Zen. (*Moku:* silence, *sho:* to shine
or illuminate.) Chinese Rinzai master Daie (d. 1163), wishing to
criticize the Soto teaching, invented the expression "*mokusho* Zen"
during his longstanding controversy wit h Soto, to imply a Zen

which does nothing but sit in silence. "Soto people," he said, " practice an evil Zen of silent illumination." Interestingly, Soto master Wanshi (d. 1157) promulgated the Rinzai *"mokusho"* declaration in its literal sense (silently shining), calling *"mokusho"* the true symbol of Soto. By merely turning on the meaning of the word, Wanshi clarified the essence of Soto. (See *Kanna*-Zen.)

MONDO. Question-and-answer period between master and disciples, it occurs directly after zazen. In the broader sense, however, a *"mondo"* can be a spontaneous exchange occurring between master and disciples, within the dojo or without, and in front of others or alone. Not to be confused with a "Dharma combat," or with any other form of competition, wit-wise or other. Then, too, there exists the historical *mondo*, the ancient exchanges which were put to writing by the disciples. These recordings, the *Rinzai Roku* included, make up the bulk of Zen literature today.

MU (*wu* in Chinese). *Mu* can either mean:

1. "no" as in the words *mushotoku* (no profit), *mushin* (no-mind), etc.
2. "nothing"—though not in the sense of "nothing" as opposed to "something. " That which is neither beyond existence nor not-beyond—that is non-existence.

When a monk asked Joshu if a dog had Buddha nature, Joshu did not reply "no"—he replied "mu. "

MUJO (*Anitya* in Sanskrit). Impermanence of all things. Eternal change. Fundamental principle of Buddhism, *"Mujo* never ceases to spy on you, not even for a moment," writes master Daichi, "and when he delivers his attack, it is with such speed and brutality that it strikes you down before you even realize it."

MUMMONKAN. *The Gateless Gate.* Book of forty-eight koans, compiled and commentated on by master Mummon (d. 1260) of the Rinzai lineage. The Mummonkan, along with the *Hekigan Roku*, are the two best known collections of koans composed in Chinese.

MUSASHI, Miyamoto (1584-1645). Famous Japanese samurai, great *sumi-e* painter and disciple of Rinzai master Takuan—from whom he received the Bodhisattva ordination. Near the end of his life and until his death, Musashi lived in a mountain cave, where he composed his treatise on the art of combat, *The Five Rings.* Musashi called himself *"doraku"* which means lover in two heavens (i.e., pleasure along the way).

MUSHIN. No-mind, non-mental, without consciousness. (*Mu:* no, *shin:* mind.) *Mushin* means there is no deluded foolish mind; it doesn't mean there is no mind to discern false from true.

The source of all forms of mind, says Dogen, undivided, beyond opposites, and containing no analysis.

MUSHOTOKU. Nothing to obtain. (*Mu* is the negative prefix; *shotoku* means to obtain, to profit.) So you have the practice without aim, purpose, profit, goal or object. Expresses the philosophical essence of Soto Zen—to be without hope of attaining satori or of becoming Buddha. The philosophy of non-profit.

MYOZEN (1184-1225). Great Rinzai monk and chief disciple of Eisai (the founder of the Rinzai school in Japan). Also the master of Dogen for over nine years. Travelled with Dogen to China. Died while on Mount T'ien-t'ung, in southeastern China, at the age of forty-two, of dysentery. A statue was erected at the place of his death. When Dogen returned to Japan some years later, he brought all Myozen's relics along with him.

NAGARJUNA (100-200). Great Indian Buddhist philosopher, founder of the Madyamika (or Middle Way) school of Buddhism, and 14th Patriarch in the line from the Buddha. Spent most of his life in southern India where he was born, of a Brahmin family. The first to teach the Mahayana doctrine of *ku* (*sunyata* or emptiness), and for this was called "the father of Mahayana. " The *Madyamika sastra* was his greatest written work. Near the end of his life, Nagarjuna burned all his books and sutras and devoted himself entirely to the study of the *kesa.*

NANGAKU (*Nan-yeh* in Chinese, 677-744). Pre-Rinzai lineage. Disciple of the 6th patriarch, Eno, and himself master of Baso. Along with Seigen, he was Eno's most important disciple; also, Nangaku was the precursor of Rinzai Zen (much as Seigen was the precursor of Soto). Practiced under Eno for more than fifteen years, and when he received the transmission from him, "it was like water passing from one bowl to another. " (See Baso.)

NEMBUTSU. This word has two different meanings:

1. Generally speaking, when the word is written with a capital "N," it refers to a branch of Mahayana Buddhism which includes the Tendai and Jodo schools.
2. With a small "n," *nembutsu* refers to the invocation *"Namu-Amida-Butsu"* (I trust in Amida Buddha) which is practiced by this branch of Buddhism, in lieu of meditation.

NIRVANA

1. A blowing out, as in the extinguishing of a flame. Thus death.
2. The complete and final dying out, as in the word *"paranirvana,"* when there is complete freedom from the chain of births and deaths.
3. The deepest *samadhi,* as when the flame of delusion has blown out, and original enlightenment, true satori, reveals itself.

NOUMENON (*Svabhava* in Sanskrit). A thing in itself. Substance. Buddhism does not teach the doctrine of noumenon, it teaches the doctrine of non-noumenon. Nagarjuna writes: "Those who perceive self-existence and other-existence, and who perceive an existent thing and a non-existent thing, do not perceive the true nature of the Buddha's teaching" (i.e., all things are empty of own-being or noumenon).

NYOJO (*Ju-ching.* 1163-1228). Disciple of Stecho Chih and master of Dogen. Soto master during the Sung dynasty and abbot of Tendo monastery. Travelled from dojo to dojo, and in the course of his wanderings came into contact with all the different types of Zen existing in his time. Some schools blended zazen with the recitation of the *nembutsu,* with breath-counting, with Taoism and Confucianism, and others with koan study. Saddened by this state of affairs, Nyojo installed himself as abbot of Tendo monastery (in southeastern China), and taught only zazen. Strong critic of the amalgamation process then occurring on mainland China, and, more particularly of mixture-Zen, or what is today referred to as "spiritual pluralism." In other words, he felt you don't blend the One Teaching of Bodhidharma and the patriarchs by adding to it. He called those monks and teachers who advocated such practices "the debasers of the true teaching" (i.e., the teaching of Bodhidharma) and "the destroyers of the Buddha Dharma."

Nyojo was the last of the great Chinese Zen masters. However, thanks no doubt to Dogen, who carried Nyojo's teachings back with him to Japan in 1225, it still continues today.

OBAKU (*Huang-po* in Chinese, d. 850). Disciple of Hyakujo and master of Rinzai. One of the great masters of Tang China. His manner of teaching was often very *zusan* (rough) and widely imitated by his later successors in the Rinzai line. He is nevertheless held in the highest esteem by all masters, regardless of school or sect. Dogen writes in *Bukkyo* that, "Obaku's expression and knowledge surpass even that of his master Hyakujo. Obaku was an ancient Buddha beyond time, far superior to Hyakujo and much sharper than Baso; and Rinzai by comparison was small time. "

OBAKU SECT. Founded by Obaku's *shusso*, this sect no longer exists in China. Introduced into Japan by Ingen in 1654, Obaku Zen still exists in that country, along with Rinzai and Soto. The head temple, built in the Chinese style, is called *Mampuku-ji*, and is located in Uji, near Kyoto.

Curiously enough, Obaku Zen is not the Zen practiced by master Obaku (let alone by Rinzai or Dogen). In Obaku they chant the *nembutsu* during zazen; so here the word "Obaku" is simply used as a namesake.

PRAJNA (Sanskrit, *hannya* in Japanese). Transcendental wisdom, intuitive insight. One of the six *paramitas* (or perfections).

PRECEPTS (see *kai*).

RAKUSU. Small token *kesa* worn over the neck and breast, and given usually by the master to the disciple during ordination. Also can be worn by all Mahayana Buddhists (monks, nuns and lay disciples), for it symbolizes the original patched robe of the Buddha Shakyamuni. Rectangular in shape and approximately thirty-three centimeters long and twenty-three wide. (See *kesa*.)

RENSAKU. A series of blows given with the *kyosaku* on the muscles located between the neck and shoulders. Its purpose is to educate, not to punish.

RINZAI (*Lin-chi* in Chinese, d. 867). Disciple of Obaku and great master of the golden Tang. His method of teaching was very *zusan*, very fierce and direct, but also very effective; for though his teaching career covered a span of not more than ten years, he had many disciples and his line continues until today.

RINZAI'S FOUR PRINCIPLES (see Four Principles of Rinzai).

RINZAI ROKU (*Lin-chi Lu* in Chinese). The sayings of master Rinzai recorded and compiled into a small one-volume work by his disciple Enen. According to Rinzai master Shibayama, "The *Rinzai Roku* is valued as the foremost Zen book in the Rinzai school."

RINZAI ZEN. The most important and far-reaching school of Zen, after Soto. Founded upon the teachings of master Rinzai (d. 867), much of which can be found in the *Rinzai Roku*. Adheres to the formal use of the koan method, and to the quest for satori. Transmitted to Japan by Eisai in 1190.

ROSHI. A respectful title meaning "old master" (*Ro* means old, *Shi* means master). Title used when a Zen master is of advanced age (though today readily appropriated by teachers of all ages).

SAMADHI (*zanmai* in Japanese). Complete concentration of mind. Concentration not based on any one notion or any one thing. The pure working of no-mind (*mushin*). "The samadhi of the Buddhas and the patriarchs," says Dogen, "is frost and hail, wind and lightning. "

SAMPAI. Prostration—or more correctly "three prostrations. " In Buddhism one generally does three prostrations at a time, and so we have the expression: *san* (three) *pai* (prostration). *Sampai* is the highest salutation and it is done, more than not, before the Buddha or the master. The giving up of body and mind to all things. The feet, knees, hands, and forehead touch the ground. "The death of *sampai*," says master Deshimaru, "is the death of Buddha."

SAMU. Concentration on manual work, such as scrubbing floors, cleaning toilets, sweeping the walks, etc. Work, but not done for pay. Rather, *samu* is work done without object or goal, for nothing. It is said that if you do *samu* everyday, you will obtain great merit. Holy work.

glossary

SANDOKAI or **SAN DO KAI**. Poem composed by Master Sekito (700-790). One of the four oldest written works in Zen. Considered as the textual embodiment of the essence of Zen.

SANGHA (Sanskrit). Lit. "the assembly of the monks. " *The good holy company.* The gathering of three or more disciples around the master. The very heart of Buddhism and all the different schools come together in the *sangha.* Shortly after the Buddha had his great satori at Bodh-Gaya (Buddhagaya) in the sixth century B.C., his former companions, and those he met along the way, Ananda, Sariputra, Mahakasyapa, etc. came to him, and this gathering was called "the *sangha* of Shakyamuni Buddha." In fact, of all existing religious orders, the Buddhist *sangha* is the oldest. In Japanese the word *sorin* is sometimes used (*so* means group and *rin* means forest). A forest or place where various kinds of trees live together.

SANRAN. *San* means dispersed, *ran* means thought. A mind that is distracted, in nervous tension, overly active, excited, ecstatic. A state of being when one's mind is carried to the outside; and also, when one's body is in excessive tension, particularly in the shoulders. During zazen the eyes move, the head moves, and the hands and fingers move. (See *kontin* for the opposite.)

SAN SHO DOEI. Collection of thirty short poems composed by master Dogen in the thirteenth century. *Sansho* means parasol pines; and it is also the previous name of Mount Eihei in northwestern Japan; and *Do* means the way.

SATORI. Unsurpassed right awakening. Return to one's true nature, to original mind. Directed not by one's personal ego, but by the fundamental cosmic power. The realization of *mushotoku.* Contrary to what is generally believed, satori is not something special. Satori does not exist; it is something and it is nothing. It is neither good nor bad. It is the normal condition of mind, and beyond the realm of morals, beyond that which makes for good merit and rebirth in paradise. True satori is unconscious; conscious satori is not satori. In Soto, as opposed to Rinzai, there is no searching for satori. For zazen itself is satori.

SAWAKI, KODO (1880-1965). Great Soto master of twentieth century Japan and master of Taisen Deshimaru. Ordained by master Koho Shoryu in Kyushu at the age of eighteen, and later studied under master Shokoku Zenko. Spent most of his teaching career traveling around Japan, going to the universities, town halls and prisons, and he continued in this manner until the mid 1960s when he could no longer walk. He never had his own temple and was called "homeless Kodo." Kodo Sawaki taught only zazen, and he was a very revolutionary master. "Those who think they have to work to earn a salary," he once said, "are poor fellows; and those who study in order to earn money afterwards are hopeless. "

SEKITO (700-790). Disciple of Seigen and master of Yakusan. Leading Chinese master of the golden Tang. He always did zazen on a large stone—thus his name "Sekito," which means "stonehead. " Author of the poem *San Do Kai.*

SENSEI. A respectful title for "teacher" used widely in the social context. Not so limited as the word "master," which refers specifically to a master of Zen, a master of Judo, etc. or "roshi" which means "old master" and which has a more honorific connotation than *"sensei."*

SESSHIN. Period of time (be it two days, three, four, five, six or seven) given to concentrated zazen practice. *Ses* means to touch and *shin* means true mind. To touch, to make contact with our true mind, to look toward the inside. To make contact with the universal cosmic ego.

SHIHO. Traditionally, a secret ceremony that takes place at midnight between the master and one of his disciples, and during which the master passes on the transmission to the disciple. And, in this sense, it represents the most genuine, the most authentic and pure, the highest ordination existing in Zen. When the master certifies the disciple's satori. The true *shiho* is not a formal affair, but simply the act of giving and/or accepting the Dharma of a true master. In the colloquial sense, the *shiho* can also mean the actual "certificate" of transmission officializing the Zen monk in his functions and privileges. (See also footnote 21, Session 1.)

glossary

SHIKANTAZA, only sitting. Concentrated sitting in the posture of zazen. The act of dropping off body and mind while in the seated posture. Single-minded sitting. Sitting without purpose or goal, without supportive devices, without breath-counting, without koan study. If a person were to describe the Soto practice in one word, he would say "*Shikantaza.*" *Shi* (literally only) means state of concentration, *kan* means state of observation, *taza* means upright correct sitting.

SHIKI. Phenomenon, form, substance, noumenon.

SHIKI SOKU ZE KU. Phenomenon becomes emptiness. *Shiki* means phenomenon, and *ku* means emptiness. Reality becomes the ideal. (See *ku soku ze shiki* for the opposite.)

SHIN. Depending upon the *kanji* (ideogram), it can mean either: "sharp attention," "heart," "mind," and/or "faith." Faith without object.

SHIN JIN DATSU RAKU. *Shin* is mind, *jin* is body, *datsu raku* is to throw down, to throw away. Thus, literally, body and mind throw down (i.e., to abandon body and mind). The credo of Dogen and Deshimaru Zen.

SHIN JIN MEI. Literally, *Poems on the Faith of Mind.* The oldest of the ancient Zen poems, composed by master Sosan (d. 606), and in which the term "*hishiryo*" is used for the first time.

SHOBOGENZO. Title given to the monumental work by Dogen. Put into writing (i.e., recorded and compiled) by Ejo, Dogen's secretary; and so it is no doubt thanks to Ejo that this teaching has reached us so freshly and strongly, seven centuries later. *Shobo* means the absolute truth concerning the Dharma, *gen* means eye (thus to wake up to the truth), and *zo* means the storehouse, the treasury. So literally it means the "treasury-eye of the true teaching."

SHODOKA. Literally, *Song of the Immediate Satori.* The second oldest Zen composition, written in the form of a long poem, by master Yoka Daishi (665-713). Yoka Daishi was known as the-monk-who-spent-one-night because he spent one night with the 6th Patriarch Eno (Hui-neng), and in one night he was awakened.

SHUSSO. The *shusso*, in a dojo, is number one after the master (or the *godo*). He is responsible for everything that happens in the dojo proper—responsible for how everyone is seated, for the *kyosaku-men*, the columns, the ceremony, and for the atmosphere as a whole. He sits to the left of the entrance, and he is considered the master's first disciple. (See *godo*.)

SHUZEN. Stage by stage zazen practice which entails moving from one level of understanding to the next. Usually associated with the Rinzai school and their different levels of koan study.

SIX PARAMITAS. Six perfections:

1. giving or *dana*. 2. precepts or *sila*. 3. perseverance or observance, *kshanti*. 4. effort, *virya*. 5.meditation, *dhyana*. 6. wisdom, *prajna*. *Para* in the word *"paramita"* means "gone to the other shore. "

SKANDHAS or **FIVE SKANDHAS.** Five categories or aggregates of mental activity that make up our mind/body experience: form, sensation, perception, mental conceptions, consciousness. *Shiki, ju, so, gyo, shiki* in Japanese. That which is loosely termed as "the self. "

SOSAN (d. 606). Disciple of Eka and master of Doshin. Third Zen Patriarch. Author of the *Shin Jin Mei*, the very first true Zen text in existence.

SOTO's FIVE GO-I (see five *go-i*).

SOTO ZEN. *Ts'ao-tung* in Chinese. The oldest and most dominant of all the Zen schools (Rinzai and Obaku being the only other two Zen schools in existence). Though its line and tradition can be traced back through masters Seigen, Eno and Bodhidharma, the Soto school was formally established in ninth century China by masters Tozan and Sozan. Transmitted to Japan by Dogen in 1228. In Soto (as opposed to Rinzai), zazen is practiced facing a wall—without object, without goal. And though the koan system is used in Soto, it is used without formal and systematic application. (See Sozan.)

glossary

SOZAN (840-901). Close disciple of Tozan (the *"so"* and the *"to"* in their names were eventually put together to make up the word *"soto"*). Famous primarily for his development of the theory of the five *go-i*.

SUNYATA (see *ku*).

SUTRA (Sanskrit, *kyo* in Japanese). Literally "a thread on which jewels are strung. " Buddhist scriptures. The sermons of Shakyamuni Buddha. The Hinayana sutras were originally recorded in Pali, the Mahayana in Sanskrit. The Zen school, as opposed to all other Buddhist schools, does not depend on any particular sutra, but on all and on none alike.

SUZUKI, Professor D.T. (1870-1966). Buddhist scholar, translator and great promulgator of Zen in the East and West. An adherent to the koan method for obtaining satori. He wrote over one hundred books.

SUZUKI, Shunryu (1905-1971). Great American-based Soto master. Arrived in the United States at the age of fifty-three. Settled in San Francisco where he taught the practice of zazen until his death at sixty-six.

TENZO. Head cook. Also, one of the most important monks in the Zen hierarchy, in one of the most challenging positions in the temple or monastery.

THALAMUS. Region located in the center of the brain and above the hypothalamus. Region through which pass sensory impulses on their way out to the cerebral cortex. The thalamus regulates the circulation of energy and it works as a link or exchange-center between the primitive (instinctive) and the non-primitive (cerebral) brain hemispheres. For this reason, the term "thalamus" (much as the term "hypothalamus") is used to denote the instinctive or primitive brain. (See hypothalamus.)

TOKUSAN (782-865). Disciple of Ryutan and master of Seppo. Once a famous scholar of the *Diamond Sutra*, he burned his books and sutras to follow the way and practice zazen. Great Tang dynasty Chan master. Though of the Soto lineage, he was known, among other things, for his heavy use of the stick (*zusan*).

SIT

Zen Teachings of Master Taisen Deshimaru

TOZAN (*Tung-shan* in Chinese, 807-869). Great chan master of the late Tang dynasty. Disciple of Ungan and master of Ungo Doyo, and himself regarded as the founder of the Soto school. The "to" of Soto came from the *"To"* in "Tozan" and, according to some sources, the *"So"* of "Soto" refers to Mount Sokei, where Eno, the 6th Patriarch, lived. Author of the *Hokyo Zan Mai,* one of the basic Zen texts, and still recited in Zen monasteries in Japan. Also formulated the "five *go-i* theory of Soto Zen." Tozan's outstanding characteristic was his independence in regard to all religious dogma and all established, stereotyped teaching. Known for his gentleness *(men mitsu).*

WANSHI (*Hung-chih* in Chinese, 1091-1157). Wanshi and his brother Shingetsu (d. 1151) were both disciples of Tanka (d. 1119). Chinese Soto master of great repute and much admired by Dogen. Created the expression *"mokusho* Zen" (silent sitting Zen) in answer to the expression *"kanna* Zen" (koan-talking Zen). Compiled the *Shoyo Roku* (the sayings of previous Chan masters), and composed the first *Zazenshin* (later re-adapted by Dogen).

WASA. Technique. Term used in *Budo.* A sort of super-technique transmitted from master to disciple. The *budo-wasa* dates back to the historical epoch of the samurai. A power, or force, beyond individual strength.

WATTS, Alan (1915-1973). Born is England, died in France and lived in California. Famous for his popular writings on Zen.

YOKA DAISHI (see *Genkaku*).

ZAFU. Cushion on which one sits when in zazen. Packed with kapok. (The Buddha and his disciples used *zafus* packed with dried grass.)

ZAZEN (*Tso-chan* in Chinese). *Za* means to sit, and *zen* means the intellectual functioning or "the philosophy. " So it means to sit with legs crossed on a zafu, facing a wall, in a quiet place. To sit in zazen means to give one's entire body and mind to the present moment. The practice of being here now. To sit in complete concentration, without koans, *kensho,* chanting or praying; to sit without anything. Zazen is *Shikantaza* only.

ZEN (*Chan* in Chinese, *dhyana* in Sanskrit). Branch of Mahayana Buddhism. Introduced into Japan from mainland China by masters Eiai and Dogen, during the twelfth century. A religion whose teachings and practice come directly from the Buddha Shakyamuni in India, and from the 1st Patriarch, Bodhidharma, in China. Being a meditative religion, the word "Zen" is often used in the same sense as "zazen. " Includes two distinct schools, Rinzai and Soto. (See *Chan*.)

ZUSAN. Negligent, indelicate; wild, rough and inattentive. Word used by master Dogen to denote Rinzai Zen. (See *men-mitsu* for its opposite.)

endnotes

endnotes

INTRODUCTION

1. Okubo,Doshu. Paper delivered to a conference of Soto Zen educators, 1976. (Kosen Nishyyama and John Stevens, translators.) Professor Okubo was former president of Zen University of Sendai Fukushi.

2. Dumoulin, Heinrich. *Zen Buddhism: A History*. New York: Macmillan, 1988, p. 180.

3. cited in: Deshimaru, Roshi Taisen. *The Voice of the Valley, Zen Teachings, Roshi Taisen Deshimaru*. Philippe Coupey (editor). Old Tappan, N.J.: Bobbs-Merrill, CO, 1979.

4. Gensha (d. 908) let his father drown in the river. Freed thereby from the father-son tradition, he was finally able to follow the way. See Glossary.

5. Dogen came from an aristocratic background, while Kodo Sawaki and Gensha came from backgrounds of great poverty.

6. Finney, Henry, Ph.D. "American Zen's 'Japan Connection': A Critical Case Study of Zen Buddhism's Diffusion to the West," *Sociological Analysis*, 1991, 52:4, p. 395.

7. Sivarksa, S. A Talk at Bad Ball Academy, Germany, April 13, 1986 (printed in *Seeds of Peace*, a review published in Bangkok, Thailand).

SESSION 1

1. Known for its Spartan approach to education.

2. Professor Heinrich Dumoulin writes that "...this account of Rinzai's great experience belongs among the most famous cases of enlightenment in Zen history." (In *Zen Buddhism: A History*. New York: Macmillan, 1988.)

3. On his return from China, Dogen wrote about master Rinzai with admiration and respect; and twelve years later he wrote about him again, though this time more critically.

4. Master Deshimaru, in quoting from the *Rinzai Roku* and other texts written originally in Japanese or Chinese (as he does throughout this sesshin), often spontaneously adapted the translations to suit the needs of his listeners in the present situation. At other times he translated directly from these original texts, also rendering spontaneously. Unless otherwise stated, the reader is advised to consider the translations of the texts mentioned in the Master's teaching to be his own adaptations, not the verbatim versions of translators.

   According to Schloegl, I. (translator) *The Zen Teaching of Rinzai (The Record of Rinzai)*, Berkeley, CA: Shambhala, 1976, p. 13, these last three sentences read as follows: "Rather, is there some skillful general to deploy his troops and hoist his standards? Let him step forward and prove his skill before the assembly."

5. Freely adapted from Schloegl, #1d, p.14.

6. *Shobogenzo: Shobo* means the absolute truth concerning the Dharma (i. e. the truth concerning the truth); *gen* means eye (i.e., that which wakes up to the true truth); *zo* means storehouse or treasury (i.e., the place where the eye wakes up to the true truth).

7. See *mondo* concerning this matter: July 27, 10 A.M., *A dojo is a holy place, not a hospital.*

8. Tozan and Sozan were famous Chinese Zen masters of the ninth century. The *To* and the *So* in their names were eventually put together to make up the word "Soto." The well-known *Goi* method (or Five Steps), introduced by Tozan and further developed by Sozan, is a philosophical arrangement of the two basic Soto texts, *Sandokai* and *Hokyo Zan Mai.*

9. See *skandhas* in Glossary.

10. See *Four Principles of Rinzai* in Glossary.

11. Here, as elsewhere, the master is citing a Soto mondo by way of comparison with the above mentioned Rinzai mondo.

12. See Schloegl, #4b, c and #5a, b, p. 16.

13. Some people sit in the back during the ceremony and only watch.

14. On a list of the master's closer disciples, the best, or the "golden," are on top.

15. The master's only financial backer at this time.

endnotes

16. It is recounted that master Taigu, on hearing Rinzai's question ("What is the essence of Buddhism?"), hit Rinzai much as Rinzai then hit Obaku.

17. Slight adaptation from Schloegl, #10, p.19.

18. The master comments fully on *Genjo Koan* later; see Session 3, August 12, 8:30 P.M., *Genjo: The Highest Realization.*

19. See endnote #44, Session 3.

20. Here the master adapts Rinzai's Principles to the matter at hand.

21. There are basically two kinds of *shiho*, the one being the transmission from patriarch to patriarch, the transmission of mind, of the Dharma (Deshimaru's first response to the question, "What is shiho?"), and the other being the transmission from temple chief to temple chief (referred to in this section). These days, this latter *shiho* is usually given patrimonially, that is, from father to son.

22. Master Deshimaru first experienced Zen under a Rinzai master.

23. Dogen wrote thirty poems assembled together under the title *Sansho Doei,* and they deal with mind during zazen.

24. Certificate of lineage, of geneology, transmitted from Buddha and the patriarchs to the disciple. Given by the master when the disciple receives the monk ordination.

25. That is, which doctrine, which teaching, which practice is the truest and the best?

26. Deshimaru is freely adapting from the *Rinzai Roku* as translated by Schloegl (*The Zen Teaching of Rinzai,* #11a, pp. 19-20).

27. *Mu:* nothing. This exchange, which occurred during the latter Tang dynasty, and known as "Joshu's *mu,*" has become the most famous koan of all times (see Glossary).

28. Violet *kolomo:* also referred to as the purple robe or the variegated Dharma robe. Sometimes these robes are passed down from master to disciple, sometimes from the emperor, governor or other to the master. Masters of the Soto line rarely, if ever, wear their purple robes and sometimes they even refuse them outright as did Doshin, Fuyo Dokai, Nyojo, Dogen, etc. "He who takes delight in a beautiful robe is a lowly man," Nyojo once said to Dogen. "Any dusty rag conforms to the old monk tradition. Remember this."

Anyway, scholars and others often confuse the word "robe" with the word *"kesa,"* not understanding that the difference is to be found, not in the garment's shape or form, but in its essence. Unlike with the robe, the *kesa* is given by the master to his disciple, usually during the monk ordination. It is a question of who gives the garment—if it is the emperor who gives the garment, then it becomes a matter of shape, color, quality and value, and therefore it is called the "robe." But if it is a master, a patriarch or a Buddha who gives it, then whatever the shape, color or quality, it is called a *"kesa."*

SESSION 2

1. There are approximately one hundred fifty new arrivals. This, minus the number of people who have left the session, give us a count of about two hundred fifty.

2. D.T. Suzuki is universally celebrated for his great ability in promulgating Zen in the East and West. But as far as zazen, or sitting meditation is concerned, Suzuki is not known at all. For this reason, among others, he has a large intellectual following in the Zen world. "...apart from the koan exercise," writes Suzuki (in his *Introduction To Zen Buddhism*, New York: Grove Press, 1964, p. 101), " the practice of zazen is a secondary consideration."

3. Due to the large number of German people present, these *kusens* (oral teachings) are presently being translated into on-the-spot German.

4. "Rinzai's zen style has earned him the name General Rinzai," writes the contemporary master, Hisamatsu, of the Rinzai school. (In, *The Collected Works of Hisamatsu Shin'ichi*. Vol. vi, "Kyoroku-shu." Tokyo: Risosha, 1973.)

5. The last two days were *hosan*, holiday. Of the two hundred or more at the previous sesshin, only about fifty stayed on. During the "holiday" many of us helped out on the premises, getting the place ready for the next wave of arrivals, etc.; others meanwhile went hiking in the Alps or hung out at the local bar in Val d'Isère, the Santa Lucia.

6. i.e., look at yourselves.

7. Castaneda, Carlos. *The Teachings of Don Juan: A Yaqui Way of Knowledge*, Berkeley, CA: University of California Press, 1968.

endnotes

8. Short staff with a long tuft of horse or yak hair knotted at one end, and often carried by a Zen master. Good for chasing off flies, demons and other vermin.

9. *Kito:* A magic ceremony, a prayer, an invocation, of low dimension, but usually well renumerated. A person wishing longevity, good health, success in his affairs or whatever, requests the *kito* priest (normally an abbot or other temple chief) to make him a kind of petition to heaven in return for gifts and money. The bigger the gift the bigger the petition. Used by emperors, governors and the common people—for instance farmers will request a *kito* for rain during the dry season—and a priest of this caliber can make a very good living performing such ceremonies, especially today.

10. Narita Roshi: One of Deshimaru's co-disciples under master Kodo Sawaki.

11. Eisai (1141-1215): Founder of Rinzai Zen in Japan.

12. While Kukai (d. 835), a Japanese monk, went to China and brought back Chinese Tantric Buddhism, and while Denkyo (d. 822), also a Japanese monk went to China and brought back the Chinese Tendai teaching, Eisai, another Japanese monk, went to China and brought back the Zen teachings of Rinzai. So, now it was Dogen's turn, and in 1227 he came back with the Soto teaching of Nyojo.

    It should perhaps be added that these were no pleasure trips. The boats were flat-bottomed (keels were yet to be invented), and the monks embarked on the voyage to China at the risk of their lives. In fact, it is on record that more than half of them drowned at sea.

13. i.e., by not sinking into sleepy darkness, nor by rising into wakeful agitation, one makes room for cosmic consciousness.

14. She is not the same mad woman referred to in Session 1.

15. The master is here using an historic Soto *mondo* (i.e., the Dogen-*tenzo mondo*), in order to compare it with the preceeding Rinzai-type *mondos*.

16. Unmon (d. 949). Famous Chinese Soto master, known among other things for his one syllable Zen.

    "What is the Buddha?" asked a monk.
    "Shitstick," replied Unmon.
    "What is it that surpasses the Buddhas and the patriarchs?"
    "Buns," Unmon replied.

17. While "...the House of Rinzai made abundant use of dialectical formulas, the House of Soto is famous for the precision and care with which all things were done." Dumoulin, H. *Zen Buddhism: A History.* New York: Macmillan, 1988, p. 214.

18. For comparison with Deshimaru's rendition, see Schloegl, I.(translator) *The Zen Teaching of Rinzai (The Record of Rinzai),* Berkeley, CA: Shambhala, 1976, #20b, p.43.

19. When we sit about seven hours or more per day. During the preceeding days we sat about four hours or more per day.

20. Rinzai people still maintain the same attitude today. "Since long ago, the motto of Zen," writes contemporary Rinzai master Hisamatsu, "has been the expression: 'self-dependently transmitted, apart from the scriptures, not dependent on words or letters.' From the Zen perspective, scriptures are nothing but scraps of paper for wiping up filth." *The Collected Works of Hisamatsu Shin'ichi.* Vol. vi, "Kyoroku-shu." Tokyo: Risosha, 1973, p. 21.

21. Besides being the title to Dogen's monumental work, this word *shobogenzo* is also used as a common noun, and as such can be roughly translated as "the center of the true teaching."

22. "It is a sign of rawness and indigestion to disgorge our meat the moment we have swallowed it. The stomach has not performed its function if it has not changed the condition and character of what it was given to digest." (Montaigne)

23. The four oldest Zen classics and the textual embodiment of the essence of Zen.

24. The "permanents" are those who remain throughout the entire camp. All of them work, in the kitchen, in the administration office, on the temple maintenance, as sewers of *rakusus* and *kesas*, as secretaries of the master, as his writers, etc.

25. So, this situation continued throughout the twenty-eight patriarchates, from the Buddha to Bodhidharma (the one dying in 483 B.C., the other in 528 A.D.); that is, for approximately one thousand years.

26. He is here referring to a certain woman—another woman—who had been causing a disturbance in the dining hall by repeatedly sitting in the secretary's seat, next to the master, and then refusing to move.

27. "Professors and scholars who come to sit with me," writes Master Sokeian, "say they know all about meditation, and they sit with the monks, and fall asleep in five minutes." (from *Zen Notes*, Vol. XXXVII, No. 4, April 1990.)

28. Soto Zen temple and administrative center for the fifteen thousand Soto temples in Japan and elsewhere. It is like the Vatican for Soto Zen.

29. When this took place Sensei had no dojo. The few who gathered about him did so in a basement of the building where he worked as a masseur.

30. Tamura is presently teaching in France. He is an Aikido master and disciple of master Ueshiba.

31. Concerning the posture, the master has said elsewhere that a fallen chin indicates fatigue; a dropped head, thinking; a head tilted to the right or the left, madness, and so on.

32. *Kai* means open, free; jo means zazen. i.e., free of zazen. The *kyosakus* are returned to the altar and the big drum is struck —eleven times— for it is now 11 P.M.

33. August or not, we are high in the Alps, almost two thousand meters above sea level, and the snow is heavy on the mountains.

34. Again, the master is intent on comparing Soto and Rinzai *mondo/koans* for their respective meanings; this one here being, of course, a Soto *mondo*.

35. To avoid possible disturbances, the *kyosaku* is not given while the master speaks.

36. The *shakuhachi*, a flute made of bamboo, first came to Japan during the Kamakura period in the thirteenth century.

37. Freely adapted from: Scholegl, #44, pp.66-67.

38. Compare this Rinzai-type *mondo/koan* between Fuke and Rinzai with the Soto-type *mondo/koan* between Nyojo and Dogen (see, August 7, 4 P.M. The Chinese were dramatic.) for their respective meanings. Anyway, the point here is that master Rinzai makes no commentary, no observation, no further reference, apart from this—from Rinzai calling Fuke a "robber." See, Schloegl, #45, 46, pp. 67-68.

39. Nansen (748-834). Disciple of Baso, and master of Joshu.

One day Nansen's disciples were arguing over a cat. Nansen happened by, heard them arguing and said: "If you can say a word about Zen, I will spare the cat. If you cannot, I will cut it in two!" No one said anything, and Nansen cut the cat in two.

His disciple Joshu arrived on the scene shortly thereafter and Nansen told him the story. "Now, what would you have done?" he asked Joshu.

Joshu took off his sandal and put it on his head.

"If you had been there," observed the master, "I could have saved the cat."

40. Known as "Marco Polo" because he is always traveling. It was he who asked the previous question concerning the necessity of hearing *kusens*.

41. See, Schloegl, #49, p.69

42. See, Schloegl, #50, p.69.

43. Being that we (of Dogen school) have been inculcated with long and glorious stories of Soto *tenzos*, the brevity by which the Rinzai *tenzo* is dispatched seems, to us, quite funny. See, Schloegl, #50b, pp. 69-70.

44. See, Scholegl, #51b, p.70.

45. Hakuin (1685-1768) founded what is called the modern Rinzai School of Zen, to which the present-day Rinzai masters trace their line of transmission.

46. Master Hau Howo, *A Critic of Rinzai Zen*. Tokyo: Pacific Ocean Publishing Company.

47. This is nothing to what it later became. During the *sesshins* conducted in China at the turn of the century, "...the monks who found it impossible to make any mental breakthrough either because they were too 'stupid' or because they could not stop thinking about their parents, wives, children and other things they had left behind, would at first be unable to keep their minds on anything. Then they would begin to have hallucinations and 'talk nonsense.' At this point they were usually locked in a room and a Chinese doctor called to examine them. Some recovered, some died... Fatalities were most common during meditation weeks and the bodies were not burned immediately... They were wrapped in quilts and left to be disposed of when the meditation weeks were over." (Hoffman, Yoel *The Sound of One Hand Clapping*. Great Britain: Paladin, 1977, p. 18.)

This may not mean that koan-practice, per say, killed the poor fellows, but it does mean that too much zazen, too hard, did it.

48. "I trust in Amida Buddha." This repeated invocation is generally practiced in Pure Land Buddhism.

49. The great *kaijo* or drum.

SESSION 3

1. Everyone is walking one behind the other in *kinhin*, but instead of walking in straight lines, they are walking in zigzag.

2. In this passage, and in others to follow, the master first recites the sutra in *kanbun*.

3. Levi-Strauss, Claude; French anthropologist.

4. The rug which covers the concrete in this improvised dojo is thinner than a French pancake.

5. 420-500. Founded the Yogacara school of Mahayana Buddhism.

6. i.e., *Genjo* means, for instance, koan accomplished in the immediate moment.

7. Like the grace of God!

8. Those designated to sit facing out; they sit in the four corners of the dojo, motionless like columns or pillars. They are disciples of long standing and their exact postures influence those about them. Also, it is their job to look without looking and to indicate to the *kyosaku-man* if anything is amiss—if someone is sick, asleep or agitated, and if the *kyosaku* is necessary.

9. This French monk was the one who had given the American girl the bad haircut a few days before. See, August 13, 7:30 P.M., *Satori visits you.*

10. "All men live by truth and stand in need of expression. The man is only half himself, the other half is his expression." (Emerson)

11. i.e., Expression (*doshu*) is subjective realization; when this realization (*genjo*) is expressed objectively (i.e., beyond personal ego), then we have true expression, wisdom or *genjo*. True expression (as for instance the words of Buddha) is realization of the here and now.

12. This short sutra, also known as the Heart Sutra, is chanted by everyone after zazen.

13. After receiving his great satori under the Bodhi tree, Buddha considered with whom he should share it first, and remembering his five friends then residing in the Deer Park in Benares, he went in search of them. At first the friends refused to listen to him as he, Shakyamuni, had given up his fasting and practice of mortification to return to the free use of the necessities of life; nonetheless Buddha quickly succeeded in imparting and in sharing his realization with them (i.e., *genjo* expressed in the Four Noble Truths), and so began the teaching of Buddhism among companions. This gathering, called the *sangha* (the good, the holy company), is the oldest monastic order in existence.

14. Worlds on worlds are rolling ever
    From creation to decay,
    Like the bubbles on a river
    Sparkling, bursting, borne away. (Shelley)

15. Founder of Le Club Méditerranée, and good friend and supporter of master Deshimaru's. He received the Bodhisattva ordination from the master. Blitz's ashes are buried at the Gendronnière.

16. *Shuzen:* Stage by stage meditation practice, whereby the adept moves from one level of understanding to the next. "In Rinzai Zen we do it step-by-step," writes the professor and Rinzai adept, Wienpahl. "So it's often called ladder zen." (Wienphal, Paul. *Zen Diary.* N.Y.: Harper and Row, 1970, p. 187.)

17. The American girl is now on her second haircutting! This second haircutting incident occurred when another girl, in a fit of jealousy, caught the American by surprise and cut off more of her hair.

18. Prior to the first haircutting, the American girl had been planning on taking the nun's ordination. Ironically, this ordination, if done according to the tradition, entails shaving the head completely.

19. For a different translation of this Japanese tanka, see August 25, 8:30 P.M., *Man's primitive brain.*

20. *Kontin,* which is sleepiness, is the activity of the parasympathetic nervous system, and *sanran,* which is excitement and illusion, is the activity of the autosympathetic.

endnotes

21. Hugo Lasalle is a German Jesuit priest who teaches Rinzai Zen in Japan, where he lives.

22. A short, curvetopped staff the master carries with him in the dojo.

23. A record made by an electroencephalograph, an instrument recording small electrical impulses produced by the brain.

24. The normal condition: *Gen-no-bi-choko* (eyes horizontal, nose vertical). See August 15, 7:30 A.M., Eyes Horizontal, nose vertical.

25. Sensei is again reiterating points he had made earlier, for those who did not assist the previous session.

26. A monk asked: "How about when the lion growls?" Unmon said: "Never mind about when the lion growls, try it when it roars." The monk did so, but Unmon said: "That's an old rat squeaking."

27. The master reads these words, which, once translated into "on the spot" French, ring particularly preposterous. English version from: Schloegl, Irmgard, (translator). *The Zen Teachings of Rinzai (The Record of Rinzai)*. Berkeley, CA: Shambhala, 1976, #61, p. 74.

28. "Hey, Mr. Abbot, dirtiest monk in the world," says master Ikkyu, "give me a *kwat!*"

29. See, Schloegl, #62, p. 74.

30. i.e., Better to leave your home to teach; love (spiritual love) is necessary and harder come by back home.

31. See Glossary.

32. Sensei's note to *Shin Jin Mei:* "As our mind believes in our essential mind, *shin* and *jin* are same mind. Not two, only one. *Shin jin mei*— the mind which believes and essential mind which is believed—is not two, only one. The concluding phrase *'shinjin funi'* gives the full meaning of the entire poem. *Funi* means non-two, only one. So it means only one mind which is our believing mind and the object mind which is the essence of mind."

33. 1173-1264. Great Japanese Buddhist master and founder of the Jodo Shin sect.

34. Sengtsan in Chinese (d. 606). Author of *Shin Jin Mei*.

35. "Nothing much is known of Sosan, and this is as it should be," says Bhagwan Shree Rajneesh during his talks on Sosan's *Shin Jin Mei*. "Sosan's biography is not at all relevant—because whenever a man

becomes enlightened he has no biography." (Rajneesh, Bhagwan Shree. *Neither This Nor That: Talks on the Sutras of Sosan.* Poona, India: Rajneesh Foundation, 1974, p. 3.)

36. Sensei's note: "As *shin* is belief in our essential mind (in true Buddha, true God), we do not need another Buddha, another God—because we can find essential mind itself in zazen or in the *kesa.*"

37. Sensei's note: "In Japanese, mind is called *kokoro,* which means conscience, heart, spirit. *Kokoro* means *koro-koro* which means always changing.

38. *Fu* is the negative and *shiki* is consciousness.

39. And older than Dogen himself. Dogen 1200-1253, Ejo 1198-1280. See Glossary.

40. Imagine referring to God, as certain Zen masters do to Buddha, as a "shitstick." See footnote 16, Session 2.

41. Master Deshimaru had been invited the year prior to meet with the Pope in the Vatican but he did not go.

42. It should be remembered that this *mondo,* like the others, occurred in 1978.

43. Yasutani, who died in 1973, was the master of Kapleau, Maezumi, Yamada, Aitken, etc, and theirs is the predominent line of transmission now existing in the United States.

44. It didn't influence the Americans very much, finally. Distribution of *The Voice of the Valley* (in its original English version) was abruptly stopped one month after publication; and today it (the English version) cannot be found anywhere.

45. *Dokusan:* A private, formal, traditional interview with the master in his room. In Rinzai Zen, *dokusan* is taken very seriously. The disciple arrives at the given time, does *sampai* (prostrations) before the closed door, opens the door and does *sampai* before the master; and again, before departing, he does *sampai* all over again. Philip Kapleau Roshi, a Rinzai master writes that the "...zen koan practice reaches a crescendo of beatings and shouts just before the encounter with the roshi, culminating in the dokusan-rush, better called a stampede. In dokusan, the roshi has a stick, which he is not loathe to apply to the students' backs when they are bowing down before him." (Kraft, K. [editor]. *Zen, Tradition and Transition.* N.Y.: Grove Press, 1988, p. 282.) With

Sensei, however, it was another matter. No *sampais,* unless of course you wished to do them; no fixed time schedule—you called him up on the telephone and set a rendezvous. Here, *dokusan* was always free and natural.

46. Buddhist vegetarians claim, to the contrary, that Buddha died eating a mushroom. The mushroom was simply mistaken for pork by those who wrote about it in the sutras. Theravadan sources point out quite specifically the look-alike between an Indian mushroom and a piece of pork.

47. "If we could look back on our lives once in the coffin," says master Kodo Sawaki, "we'd probably think: 'it sure would have been nice not to have gotten so serious about things.' "

48. "Is there any creature on land or sea which does not find its greatest pleasure in other creatures of its own kind? If it were otherwise, why should not a bull take pleasure with a mare, or a stallion with a cow?" (Cicero)

49. Following this interplay of the wood and the metal, the *shusso* strikes the small bell, then the *kyosakuman* hits the big gong, and on the fourth stroke the entire assembly begins to chant *Hannya Shingyo.* The monotone of the chant is accompanied by two instruments, the big gong and the *mokugyo.* The gong, which is a thick metal-hammered bowl, is struck at the beginning, at the end and during the breaks with a muffled cloth-bound mallet. The *mokugyo,* which is made of wood and looks like a bloated fish with its mouth partly open, is also struck with a clothbound mallet. So, while the gong is an indicator or a signal of sorts, the *mokugyo,* with its measured beat, works as a controller to the pace and to the volume of the chant itself.

50. A *biwa,* a kind of Japanese guitar.

51. i.e., A *biwa* influences the mind of even the inelegant; a flute without holes even harmonizes with the strong man ("moves": influences; "sleeves": mind; "wooden": inelegant; "iron": strong).

52. Dogen Keizan Meiho Sotetsu Daichi (1290-1366).

53. Another name for a dojo is "the place of dry trees," while another name for zazen is "dry trees" *(koboku).*

SESSION 4

1. The master is here primarily addressing the new people who have come for this final ten day session.

2. Rinzai master. Also known as Yoken Kisei. His exact dates are not known.

3. Rinzai master. 991-1067.

4. Soto master. 942-1027.

5. Laurent and Guy are this dojo's two *tenzos*.

6. Only the master is allowed to wear socks in a dojo.

7. See, Session 2, August 4, 7:30 A.M., *The dojo became a battlefield.*

8. The *kanji "taigu"* means "great fool."

9. "You must not let everyday experience in its variety force you to permit the eye, which does not see, or the ear, which is full of noise, or the tongue, to rule your thought." (Parmenides, sixth century B.C.).

10. Looking through the window before him, Sensei sees someone dressed in a monk's robe walking along the river bank.

11. Like Pythagoras, the Greek philosopher of the sixth century B.C., who went to the East in search of knowledge, and then founded a brotherhood of disciples in Italy. He taught reincarnation and he gave oral teachings on a new way of life inspired by the love of wisdom without goal or purpose *(mushotoku)*.

12. Deshimaru, Maître Taisen. *Le Sutra De La Grande Sagesse.* Editions Retz, 1980. *Maka* means the highest, the greatest. *Hannya* is perfect wisdom. *Haramitsu* means to save all mankind. (The highest most perfect wisdom to save all mankind.)

> "When asked: 'What is your religion?,'
> I answer: 'The power of *Maka Hannya.*'
> Sometimes affirming things,
> sometimes denying them,
> it is beyond the wisdom of man.
> Sometimes with common sense,
> sometimes against it,
> heaven cannot make head or tail of it."
> (Yoka Daishi, d. 713)

endnotes

13. See endnote 15, Session 3.

14. Dogen's poem, *Zazen*. See, Session 3, August 18, 8:30 A.M., *The wave strikes and the wave breaks,* for a less polished rendition of the same poem.

15. Maybe, but going by his portrait—fierce scowl, eyes like burning coals under beetle brows—and by his words, you wouldn't know it.

16. Hypothalamus is the instinctive primitive brain as opposed to the frontal or intellectual brain, and it is located approximately in the center of the head. It is the connecting point of body and mind; it directs the senses, and it controls homeostasis—the tendency for the internal environment of the body to remain constant in spite of varying external conditions.

17. A dog belonging to the dojo.

18. Every morning after zazen and before breakfast Sensei leads a procession through the woods at the foot of the mountain behind the dojo.

19. See Glossary.

20. *Go un* are Japanese ideograms which, roughly translated, mean body and mind. *Go* literally means five (i.e., the five elements). *Un* means elements, aggregates, the visible, the material. It means a lump, a mass, a group.

21. *Go un* (also written as *go on*) makes up part of the phrase in the sutra *Hannya Shingyo* which goes: *Go on kai ku,* and this means "the body and the five *skandhas.*" *Go* is five, *on* or *un* are the elements, *kai* is all, and *ku* is emptiness. The five *skandhas* or aggregates are: sensation, perception, activity, thought, consciousness. The five elements become emptiness *(kai ku)*—and at this time we have the perfect wisdom through the *hishiryo* of zazen.

22. The first *"shiki"* in *shiki ju so gyo shiki* are the five sense organs: eyes, ears, nose, tongue, body and consciousness. *Ju:* that which is felt, or registered, through the five sense organs (i.e., "Ah, there is a flower"). *So:* the image, the imagined caused by the object (i.e., "This flower is beautiful"). *Gyo:* Action, the will to act. Practice (i.e., "I will pick this flower"). *Shiki:* Here *shiki* means intellectual consciousness. This *shiki* controls the mind. Judgment.

23. Sometimes it is unnecessary, let alone impossible, to translate certain words. Thus we have the Japanese ideograms (all the italicized words, including the book title) above.

24. Mind (i.e., consciousness, God).

25. In western thought, reportedly based on a medical viewpoint, there exist only five senses; while in eastern thought, reportedly based on selfknowledge, there exist six.

   Anyway, *mu gen ni bi ze shin i* is a famous line in *Hannya Shingyo* we chant every morning, and it means "no eye, ear, nose, tongue, body, mind." *Mu*, the "prefix," can mean many things but here it pretty much means "no"—"no eye, no ear,...."

26. These italics are my own. (P.C.)

27. And yet it is said of Socrates that he taught virtue (or knowledge) to be true only once it reaches the stage of expression (i.e., *doshu*. See August 15, 7:30 A.M. and 9 P.M.)

28. "The world always looks outward, I turn my gaze inward; there I fix it, and there I keep it busy. Everyone looks before him; I look within. I have no business but with myself. I unceasingly consider, examine, and analyze myself." (Montaigne)

29. This was the Pope who died shortly thereafter. Nonetheless, the *kito* is a very powerful incantation, and so surely it has helped him on his way to paradise, as the master would say.

30. Awakening.

31. The pure working of no-mind transcending both action and quietude. It denotes a state in which the mind is aborbed in intense, purposeless concentration.

32. André is the master's *kyosakumaker.*

33. *Manas*, not to be confused with *mana*. While the latter refers to the left hemisphere of the brain, the ego-center, *manas* here refers more specifically to rational subject-object consciousness. (In *Lankavatara Sutra* "mana" is defined as intellectual consciousness, as that which sorts out and judges the results of the five kinds of sense-consciousnesses. However, the same sutra also says of *manas* that it is one with universal mind by reason of its participation in transcendental intelligence, etc. Thus, the word *manas* has two different meanings, depending upon how it is used.)

endnotes

34. Paul Chauchard, French philosopher, well-known in Japan for his writings on mind. He is a friend of Deshimaru's, and they are co-authors of a book entitled, *Zen et Cerveau (Zen and Mind)*. (Paris: le Courrier du Livre, 1976.)

35. "This is like the vision of a man who observes the manifold forms and colors of a landscape and feels himself different from it (as 'I' and 'here')." (Lama Govinda)

36. See Glossary.

37. A long cord worn about the waist. The monks in the temples wear black-colored *chukins*, while he who has received the *shiho* wears a brown *chukin*. The master wears a violet one. Master Deshimaru, however, seldom wears a chukin.

38. Karlfried Graf von Dürckheim, German philosopher and psychotherapist, and author of *Hara: The Vital Center of Man*. (London: G. Allen and Unwin, 1962).

39. *Mu* (or *wu* in Chinese): means not or no—that which is beyond mere positive and negative. *Ku* (*sunyata* in Sanskrit): means emptiness—in the sense that all things come from *ku*.

40. Known as *Kongo Kyo* in Japanese, in Sanskrit as *Vajracchedika Prana Paramita Sutra* ("*The Perfection of Transcendental Wisdom which Cuts like a Diamond*") and in English as the *Diamond Sutra*.

41. A famous phrase from the *Diamond Sutra*.

42. Ze-ami (1363-1443) the founder of Nô; wrote a book entitled, *Kanedsho*. In this work he considered that in any form of activity it was essential to harmonize the *yo* (the positive, the light), with the *yin* (the negative, darkness). Ze-ami retired from the Nô acting tradition when he was sixty, became a Zen monk and devoted the rest of his life to the way.

43. *Sho* means chant and *myo* means light; a pentatonic plainsong similar to the Gregorian chant. Nowadays *shomyo* is primarily performed in the Tendai and the Shingon sects.

44. *Daihishin-darani:* a solo chant. A chant for the maintenance and the preservation of one's better attributes and/or qualities. *Daranis* are magic formulas that lay hold of the good so that it won't be lost, and the evil so that it won't arise.

45. *Atman:* the supreme self, the universal consciousness, the divine element in man.

46. After Buddha's death a deep philosophic conflict arose over this issue, and it still persists today. The Buddhist doctrine of vanishing phenomena tells us that all phenomena are illusion; therefore karma, being something, must also vanish. Contrarily, the Buddhist doctrine of karma tells us that non-manifest karma does not vanish, but rather that it continues, even unto eternity. Reality in Buddhism, however, is the reality of existence and of non-existence; it is the existence of each separate being, of affirmed existence as well as of negative non-existence. Therefore, what's the contradiction? I can't see it.

47. *Fudo* is non-movement; *shinmyo* means magic, excellence; *chi* is wisdom; *roku* is record.

48. Kendo: literally, the way of the sword.

49. *Budo*, the way of the samurai. It includes kendo, judo, aikido, etc.

50. *Mu gen* means no eyes; *ryu* is school.

51. *Mu* is no; *nen* is thinking.

52. *Oto* means sound; *nashi* means without; and *kamae* means attitude.

53. Miyamoto Musashi was one of Japan's great samurais, and he killed many people. Later in life he left off the sword and, like the blind samurai Sukae, he became a disciple of Zen master Takuan. In the last years of his life, Musashi lived in a cave in the mountains. He died in 1645, an ordained Bodhisattva.

54. Traditional judo. Known as the teaching of gentleness.

55. *Kyu* is to manage, direct, control. *Shin* is mind. *Ryu* is school.

56. Alan Watts himself noted that in some Zen practice there is no emphasis placed upon zazen, but rather a focus on the "...use of one's ordinary work as the means of meditation. This was certainly true of Bankei, and this principle underlies the common use of such arts as 'tea ceremony,' flute playing, brush drawing, archery, fencing and ju jutsu as ways of practising Zen." (Watts, Alan. *The Way of Zen*. New York: Vintage, 1957, p. 111).

57. This statement is in reference to a woman's question in the *mondo* earlier.

58. Ejo the secretary; see Glossary.

endnotes

59. *Alaya* consciousness is universal mind; the store-consciousness of the pure essence of Mind. Coomaraswamy says of Alaya consciousness that it is the cosmic, not impersonal, all-containing, ever-enduring Mind. Ernest Wood says that *Alaya* is the self-nature present in sentient beings and it is this which Buddha experienced at the time of his great satori under the Bodhi tree. And in the *Mahayana Sraddhotpada Sastra* it is said, of both *manas* and *alaya*, that, "...the mind *(manas)* has two doors from which issue its activities. One leads to a realization of the pure essence of mind *(alaya)*. The other leads to the differentiations of appearing and disappearing, of life and of death."

60. "Those who experience satori concerning *mayoi* are all Buddhas," writes Dogen. "Those who take the great *mayoi* for satori are called the mediocre and the common."

61. "We were mind-created spiritual beings, nourished by joy," goes a passage from one of the *Agama* sutras (a collection of ancient Buddhist scriptures). "We soared through space, self-luminous and in imperishable beauty....But when evil, immoral customs arose among us, the sweet-tasting earth disappeared, and when it had lost its pleasant taste, outcroppings appeared on the ground...."

62. Kapleau writes of this incident that Dogen had "...achieved full enlightenment through these words uttered by Nyojo." (Kapleau, Philip. The *Three Pillars of Zen*. Boston: Beacon Press, 1965, p.6.) While Sekida writes of the same incident that, upon hearing these words of Nyojo *(shin jin datsu raku)*, "Dogen had completed the Great Cause...Satori." (Sekida, Ketsuki. *Zen Training*. Tokyo: Weatherhill, 1975.)

63. "To live this synthesis of East and West is the most valuable kind of pioneer work I can imagine—never mind who approves or disapproves." (Christopher Isherwood)

64. The powerful House of Tokugawa ruled as shoguns, 1603-1867.

65. Period from 1868 to 1912, corresponding to the reign of the emperor Meiji.

66. The master has, on occasion, given conferences at the Sorbonne.

67. Nagarjuna (100-200). 14th Patriarch and founder of the Madhyamika School; he was the greatest philosopher and Bodhisattva in the history of Buddhism.

index

index

index

index

◼   ◼

index

index

index

Musashi (the samurai
Miyamoto), 274, 320-321,
352
mushin, 158, 320-321, 324
music (*see* sounds), 18, 125,
208, 221
mushotoku, xxii, 3, 44, 48, 56,
60, 107, 128-130, 144, 158,
165, 173, 262, 302, 306, 320-
321, 325, 348
Myozen (master), 81-83, 302,
321

■

Nagarjuna (patriarch), 49, 293,
319, 321-322, 353
Namu Amida Butsu, 144
Nansen (master), xxxiii, 134,
297, 312, 341-342
Narita (master), 83, 339
negligence (*see* zusan), 93, 100
Nembutsu, xx, 47, 123, 144,
322-323
neurons, 116, 135, 188, 250,
252
nirvana, 145, 161, 214, 216,
246, 300, 319, 322
normal condition (*see* also
satori), 4, 24, 75, 79-80, 83,
85, 150, 158, 169, 180, 185,
187-188, 215, 307, 325, 345
no object (*see* mushotoku), xxii,
3, 55-56, 60
Nô theater, 269
noumenon, 49, 261, 299, 322,
327

Nyojo (master), xxii, xxix,
xxxiv, 9, 29, 47, 77, 81-82,
92-93, 100-101, 103-105,
111-113, 121, 131, 133, 169,
289, 302, 307, 322-323, 337,
339, 353
Nyojo and Dogen, xxii, xxix, 66,
341
Nyojo Roku, 123-124
Nyojo Zen, 109

■

Obaku (master), xxi, xxxiii, 8-
13, 18, 35-36, 59, 125-126,
231-233, 288, 311, 323-324,
328, 337
Obaku sect, 9, 46-47, 76, 323
objective certification, 267
objective understanding, 105-
106
observation, 161-162, 164, 175,
231, 251, 259-261, 267, 327,
341
ordination, xxvii, xxx, 15, 57,
82, 90, 111, 171, 195, 198,
203, 218, 228, 263, 288, 293,
301, 311, 313, 315, 320, 323,
326, 337-338, 344
originality, 58, 157, 173-174,
189-190, 206, 219

■

pain, 61, 77, 84, 95, 120, 137,
151, 155, 181, 193, 217, 269
paramitas (*see* six paramitas),
69, 323, 328

index

index

319, 323, 328, 343, 348-349, 351-352
without object (*see also* mushotoku), xxiv, 48, 324, 327-328
Wood (Ernest), 353
word(s) (*see* doshu), 163-165, 170, 196, 350
world, invisible, 274

■

Yasutani (master), 212, 346
Yawara (*see* martial arts), xxv, 275
Yui Shiki, 231

■

Zangen (monk), 45, 52-53, 312
zazen, xx, xxiii-xxv, xxviii-xxx, 3-4, 6, 8-9, 13-14, 17, 22-23, 26, 28, 30-32, 36-37, 39, 42-44, 46-48, 51-52, 54-56, 58, 60-64, 66, 68-71, 75-77, 79-80, 82-87, 89, 91, 93, 95-100, 102, 104-121, 124-125, 130-131, 135-138, 143-145, 149-150, 152, 154-156, 158-161, 163, 166-169, 173, 175-180, 182-184, 187-191, 193, 195, 197, 200-201, 203-208, 211-213, 217-223, 227-232, 234, 236-239, 242-247, 250, 254-257, 259-263, 265-267, 269-276, 278-282, 284-285, 289-294, 297, 300-303, 305-306, 308-309, 311-313, 315-318, 320, 322-323, 325-331,

337-338, 341, 343-344, 346-347, 349, 352
zazen posture, xxiii-xxiv, 51, 75, 114, 150, 167, 180, 188, 204, 262
zazen in the West, 160
Ze-ami (master), 269, 351
Zen, xix-xxii, xxiv-xxx, xxxii-xxxv, 4, 6-14, 16, 18-22, 24-26, 28, 30-32, 34-36, 38-42, 44, 46-50, 52, 54, 56-60, 62-64, 66-68, 70, 72, 75-78, 80-84, 86, 88, 90-96, 98-104, 106-112, 114-116, 118-120, 122-124, 126-128, 130-132, 134-136, 138, 140-144, 146, 150, 152-154, 156-158, 160, 162, 164, 166, 168-170, 172, 174, 176, 178, 180, 182-186, 188, 190, 192, 194, 196-198, 200-202, 204, 206-208, 210-214, 216, 218, 220, 222, 224, 228, 230-234, 236, 238, 240, 242, 244, 246, 248, 250-252, 254, 256, 258, 260, 262, 264-266, 268-278, 280-284, 286, 288-292, 294, 297-298, 300-332, 335-342, 344-346, 348, 350-354
Zen, American, 153, 211-212, 335
Zen and art, 57
Zen, Chinese, xx, xxix, 8-9, 11, 303, 323, 336
Zen culture, 111
Zen, Japanese, 9
Zen and science, 282-283